Oxford Observed

Oxford Observed

Peter Snow

John Murray

© Peter Snow 1991

First published in 1991
by John Murray (Publishers) Ltd
50 Albemarle Street, London W1X 4BD

*British Library Cataloguing in
Publication Data*

Snow, Peter
Oxford observed.
I. Title
378.425

ISBN 0–7195–4707–5

Typeset in $11\frac{1}{2}$/13pt Times Monophoto
Printed and set in Great Britain by
Butler & Tanner
Frome and London

Contents

═══════════

Illustrations

═══════════

Acknowledgements

In writing this book I have been liberally assisted by many people and institutions – far too many, regrettably, to be individually acknowledged.

I owe an especial debt to my editors, Hugo Brunner and Grant McIntyre, and my agent, Arthur Goodhart, for their support and guidance; to Christina Hardyment who most valuably commented on draft chapters; and to Professor T. J. Reed who published versions of several in the *Oxford Magazine*.

The Fellows, staff and students of University College were invariably patient and open in the face of persistent badgering. In particular I must thank: George Cawkwell, Elizabeth Crawford, Paul Kiefer, Richard Primer, Rev. Bill Sykes, Ian Williamson; also Douglas Millin, Leslie Mitchell and Gwynne Ovenstone for allowing me to reproduce the extracts from the *University College Record* on pp. 112–14.

Among undergraduate informants to whom thanks are due are: Alex Bellos, Duncan Gray, Luke Harding, Ben Hopkins, Richard Jolley, Ian Katz, Marianne Macdonald, Felicity Spector and Stewart Wood.

It is a particular pleasure to recall the assistance and insights of: Brian Aldiss who opened up the odd world of 'the Hill'; Alison Denham, who contributed cognac and a welcome transatlantic accent on things; Colin Dexter for solving several Oxford mysteries; David Ellis for his birdwatcher's view of the city; the Foremans for providing a family passport to North Oxford; Olive Gibbs who drew generously on her long experience of the city; Roger Green, the 'bard of Wolvercote' for much information and for permission to quote his poem 'A borderline case' on p. 193; Desmond Morris for his invaluable knowledge of the local zoology; my neighbours who planted a seed; John Wain who not only granted me permission to quote the extract from *Sprightly Running* on p. 225 but also lent his interest and encouragement throughout; and Ann Whiteman, a long-time Oxford observer.

In addition, I am greatly indebted to the many others who opened doors to me, including: David Christie and the staff and pupils of St Edward's School; Dr Henry Drucker of the university's Development Office; Pat Goodwin of the Probation Day Care Centre; Edward Greene and the staff of Edward Greene's Tutorial Establishment; Mike Hall, staff and residents of the Simon House; Brian Harrison, Fellow of Corpus Christi College and General Editor of the *History of the University*; Ann Lonsdale and Georgina Ferry of the University Press Office; John McLeavy of the Elmore Community Support Team; John Mann and Sue Mason of the Oxford Academy of English; Paddy O'Hanlon, staff and residents of the Night Shelter; Mike O'Regan of Research Machines; the staff of Oxfam, in particular Joan McCartney and John McGrath; the staff of Oxford Polytechnic and especially Pauline Brown; Nina Nowakowska; Tom Parker of Rover plc; Martin Roberts and the staff and pupils of Cherwell School; Margaret Skarland and staff of St Clare's; A. J. Stapleton and staff of the John Radcliffe Hospital; Tris Torrance; the Venerable F. C. Weston, Archdeacon of Christ Church.

I must also acknowledge the following permissions: Toby Young for the quotation on p. 134 from *The Oxford Myth*, ed. Rachel Johnson (Weidenfeld & Nicolson, 1988); and Routledge & Kegan Paul for the quotation by Tom Richardson on pp. 43–4, taken from the Television History Workshop's *Making Cars: A history of car-making in Cowley by the people who make the cars*, 1985; also Christ Church for allowing Norman McBeath access to Tom Quad for the photograph reproduced in this book.

Finally I must thank the staff of the Oxford City Local History Collection; and Mrs Lydia Foreman who decoded not only my text but the folkways of Oxford.

Peter Snow
March 1991

Introduction

═══════════

In researching this book I must have interviewed several hundred people. Their usual reaction, when told of another book on Oxford, was either dismay or a sympathetically troubled 'Whatever for?' And, I have to admit, their feelings carry weight. The shelves of the city's bookshops practically bend with books on Oxford. It must be one of the most written-over patches on the globe, a literary market garden. After scanning the literature for some time I coined a term for it – 'Ox-lore'.

Ox-lore comes in all kinds of packages and granules: solid volumes of collegiate and university history, lavish coffee table tomes as big as the slabs in Bodley's courtyards, light technicolour brochures, ripe garnerings of reminiscence and charming snippets of anecdote and quotation. No cranny of Oxford seems uncharted – its buildings, gardens, ghosts, its characters, clubs and customs. At times Ox-lore seems to penetrate the very air of the place as snatches of it – history-bytes – shower down from the open-top touring buses that jam Oxford's streets each summer.

Generally speaking, Ox-lore falls into two camps: pro and anti – each in its contrasting way tending to set the teeth on edge. The pro camp speaks with all the smoothly winning accents of the insider, ripely nostalgic and mellowly pleased with its doings. This is the literature of 'Our Oxford', which assumes that its reader is an insider too or else would dearly love to be.

Speaking against it are shriller, thinner voices, hungry and resentful tones from without, those of the opposers and detractors attacking 'Their Oxford'. Then there are other writers, often junior litterateurs newly hatched from the university, casting about for a topic with which to make a name, who manage to pull off the difficult feat of simultaneously battering and buttressing the Oxford myth. In this they are wisely provident, taking care only lightly to bruise the Alma Mater goose that, generation after generation, goes on laying the golden publishing egg.

In addition, the habit of regretful retrospection is firmly ingrained amongst writers about Oxford. The city has always been a better place in the past. The stages of its development have been portrayed as a series of further falls from Eden. On average the nostalgia intervals are fifty or so years in length (suggestively the space in a single life between remembered youth and regretful old age). Today, as in Kingsley Amis's poem 'Oxford', they compare the horrors of the modern inner city development with the simpler town they knew as students. Yet writers on Oxford at that time were shuddering under the impact of Cowley and the car and complaining like Warden Fisher of New College that 'those who know only modern Oxford, with its thronged streets, its roaring motor traffic ... can hardly conceive of the stillness and charm of the place in the eighties of the last century'. In the eighties of the last century writers such as the Rev. William Tuckwell were recoiling from the arrival of the railway terminus and the then bitterly resented but now prized new suburbs of North Oxford and lauding the city of the 1830s – at which time no doubt they were mooning about the pre-canal Oxford of the 1780s. 'The wind which blows in Oxford,' said Emerson in *English Traits,* 'blows out of the past', and any writer on the city cannot escape its prevailing pressure.

Yet as someone who was first a student at the university, then lived for many years in various parts of the city, I found little in traditional Ox-lore that actually corresponded with the reality I experienced. Those coffee-table books, those solid slabs, were suspiciously bare of actual faces; in them, too, Gown all but obliterated Town. By turning their attention to the past or the glories of Oxford's architecture, they seemed to me to be overlooking the reality springing up now between its stones. And in subscribing to Oxford's specialness they ignored its broader connections with society. Between these twin fictions of nostalgia-conservation or demolition-detraction the real Oxford seemed to stalk, substantial but undetected. This book is an attempt to capture and record that Oxford.

Town

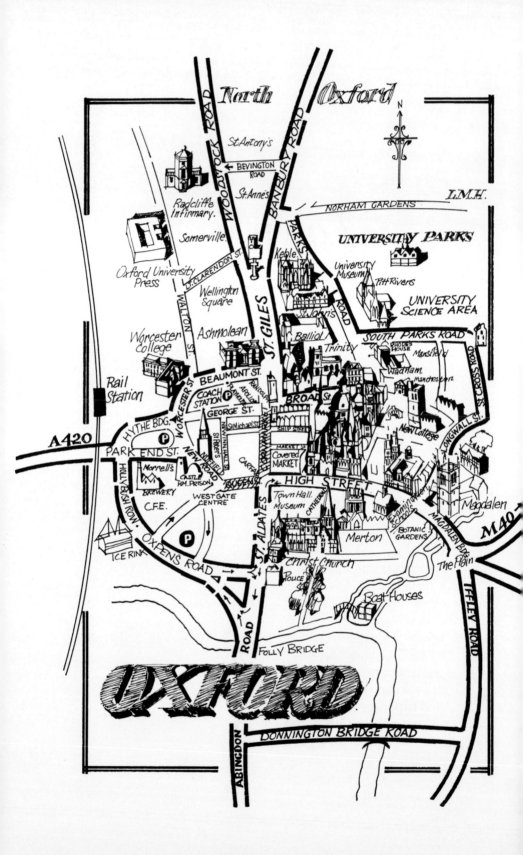

– 1 –

Split City

Each year up to half a million visitors come to Oxford, making it the third most popular venue in Britain after London and York. Most pause only a few hours before fast-forwarding on to the next stop on the tourist itinerary. All the same, directly and indirectly, they leave behind a tidy pile of money – over £300 million a year according to one estimate. But in return Oxford has traditionally done little for them. 'Welcoming while not encouraging', was one local councillor's exquisitely phrased formulation of policy. Under-hotelled, without clearly signposted routes and marshalling areas and lacking until recently a proper tourist centre, the city has a poor record in regulating the human tides that wash its streets each summer.

Just what impressions of Oxford do the visitors carry away with them? Various versions are on offer. There are guided walking tours of varying reliability (the official ones are good, the others often walking mines of misinformation, overheard snippets of which are prized by the more knowledgeable natives). The Madame Tussaud's-like tableaux of *The Oxford Story* present a mostly Gown version, a steady progress onward and upward, through scenes of violence and squalor to the academic excellence of today and with Town rarely getting a look in. Other visitors get a more open-topped experience from the tourist buses that trundle round the city. Many visitors, though, simply jam the streets, gazing blankly at the façades of colleges or trailing through Cornmarket's chain of eateries and retail outlets.

Probably they come expecting in the ancient cradle of colleges and quadrangles some sort of historic time capsule or Athenian city state of the mind complete with gowned and learned figures gravely discoursing in the cloisters. Certainly the spires and cloisters exist but they are interspersed – submerged even – among *all the other bits.* Those who go on the bus tours must have at times the dislocating sense, as the buses traverse the cluttered terrace-land of East Oxford, of being allowed to see round the *back of the set.*

Even a walk round the centre can be a bewildering, not to say distressing, experience. Above soar the stones of the spires but, lower down, reality jump-cuts before your eyes: four-square Saxon church; medieval college; postmodern office block; timbers and gables; pompous civic wedding cake of a public building. There are bits of Bath-style restoration, courts and closes teetering on the brink of tweeness, and there are shopping malls – the glitzy, blue-hooped vulgarity of the Clarendon Centre, and, then, the Westgate, barracks-like without, within a soft bubble bath of illuminated spheres, like the mad dream of a pawnbroker, with, to top it all off, an oriental pagoda plonked surreally in front.

Oxford is a place that seems to choke on its own rich contrasts, a jumble of impression fragments, on which competing visions of the city can be projected and superimposed. There is medieval Oxford, county market town Oxford, university Oxford, modern city centre Oxford, industrial Oxford, suburban residential Oxford ... None of the versions seem entirely to fit the face beneath. Indeed at times fiction overrides reality altogether: soon we shall have Oxford as Inspector Morse-land, a set of tourist trails as originally trodden by the super-sleuth, tripping the connections of a recollected episode on TV.

Somehow the city's new Gloucester Green development sums up the whole chaos of contrasts. Local opinion about it varies wildly – from vulgar monstrosity to wittily exuberant extravaganza – but to me it is the perfect symbol of the modern city, a postmodern barock n'roll, a restless ransacking of the wardrobe of the past, emitting its clash of scales and styles, with just the right Oxford hints of illusion and unreality.

What this pile of contrasting shards reflects is that Oxford is a deeply split city. In Oxford the divisions open and cross in all directions. The longest and sharpest is of course that between Town and Gown, stretching back to the twelfth century when the first wandering scholars settled in the city. As the gownsmen won their charters and powers, what had already been for five centuries a vigorous Saxon borough was reduced to a medieval equivalent of a company town, serving the Gown's wants and subject to its rules and regulations.

At first Town fought back in bloody uprisings and massacres of the scholars; later in a long train of complaints to the Crown or in pompous displays of civic self-assertion. Slowly the relationship settled down into a chronic, grumbling conflict, like that of an ill-matched man and wife tied despite their differences inextricably together. Today, the conflict still rumbles on in a distant, background kind of way. You catch it here and there – in the sly thieving of a college cook, the sullen rudeness of a trader, a random attack by local lads on a student. Perhaps most of all you see it in occasional squabbles between the city council and the university over a new lab or cycle track. So what started with mass knifings ends in minor planning niggles.

Earlier this century a third Oxford suddenly sprouted up, unsettling the old antagonistic factions of Town and Gown. This was the Oxford of William Morris's car factories, the smokestacks and thundering presses and assembly lines of Cowley – the Oxford called by John Betjeman 'Motopolis'. 'Motopolis' finally saw off the old county and cathedral town of Oxford, spreading its net of suburbs round the city and pouring streams of traffic into its streets.

Between 'Motopolis' and the colleges – Nuffield's later generous benefactions to the university notwithstanding – gaped a huge gulf. Those who lived on the new estates and worked on the line knew little and cared less about what went on in the cloisters and the quadrangles. Meanwhile, for its part, the university turned its back on its smoking and offensive new neighbours to the east, pursuing its largely arts-based studies, and continuing to fulfil its role of feeding the professions and matriculating the English middle classes – focusing in a single city the larger splits and snobberies of our society.

Now 'Motopolis' is itself in decline. From a peak of nearly 30,000 employees the car plant is down to little over 5,000 and still falling. Having already announced the closure of one of its factories, it has now unveiled plans to close the others, intending to replace them, it claims, with a new smaller factory on a nearby site. Yet as 'Motopolis' contracts, other Oxfords rush in to replace it – the Oxfords of high tech and biotech industries, of anonymous offices, business parks and residential developments. Despite the economic downturn of the early 1990s, the city is still proving a honeypot to developers.

At the centre of all these Oxfords, trying to reconcile them and hold them together, is the city council. Since the early 1970s it has been, one brief break apart, a socialist administration. It is a benign backwatery version of the provo-ish powers of places like Amsterdam and Camden. How boldly it bears aloft the green and red minority-chequered flag of its little republic. Clutching its concerns, hatching affirmative action kits and well-meaning, caring initiatives, it goes gaily on its way, planting its bulbs and sowing its cycle tracks.

But it would like, one suspects, to be something more. Although stripped of many of its powers in recent years along with other local authorities, the brave little borough loves to take a stand or tilt at a windmill. Currently it has got its teeth into one local resident who had the temerity to build a shark on his roof and, rather humourlessly, it will not let go. But what it really seeks is the big national or international issue. Fluttering the flags of CND and ANC from its town hall turrets and delighting in twinning with Nicaraguan Leon, it campaigns against acid rain from Didcot Power Station and the nuclear hazard from Harwell. Such concerns would be no more than mildly diverting, like those of Dickens' Mrs Jellaby, if they did not deflect attention from the planning problems of growth pressing at its own feet.

In Oxford the splits still open at every turn. Look at almost any area of the city, and you discover a rich mosaic of differences. In part this reflects the development of a diversity of individual excellence, in part deep and enduring social divisions. Its shoal of schools exemplify the splits and inequities between public and private systems of education. Similarly, underlying the array of specialisms of its hospitals is something of a social division. Of its two psychiatric hospitals, for instance, the Warneford is felt to be the institution catering for the middle class 'intelligent' patient while Littlemore doses the lower orders. Even in the sphere of the university the word 'gown' cloaks a contradictory, highly tentacular beast, composed of many competing constituents in its departments and colleges. At times Oxford seems like a great patchwork, similar to the chessboard in Lewis Carroll's *Alice* (based, it is said, on nearby Otmoor). But if it is a board it is one on which not just a single game is being played but several simultaneously.

In recent years the more ancient of Oxford's divisions have begun to be broken down and bridged. If the city was once a simple mixture of opposites, sometimes violently stirred, now it represents a much finer suspension. At the same time that the old manufacturing of 'Motopolis' is waning, the university is edging its way uncertainly towards industry. Many of the new high tech firms ringing the city are the brain children of university science departments. Oxford has even got – a generation after Cambridge – its first science park, developed by Magdalen College out at Littlemore. Borrowing a curricular leaf from the polytechnic, the university is gradually shedding its old snobberies towards practical and vocational subjects: by the end of the century its biggest graduate schools will be not in classics or medieval history but in business and management studies.

Residentially also, a new diversity is emerging in the city. Once the social pattern of Oxford neighbourhoods was clear-cut. There was, for the better-off, North Oxford or the nearer villages; and for the working classes the terraces of Jericho and East Oxford (or, if dislodged from there, the new housing estates of Barton and Blackbird Leys); and, for those in between, the semis of Botley and New Headington. Now, with academic incomes eroding in relative value, with more and more newcomers pressing into the city while at the same time any fresh development is sharply cinched in by the surrounding green belt, a great wave of gentrification has swept over the old working-class neighbourhoods, minor eddies of it even reaching out as far as estates like Barton. The days of the don as a member of a separate caste in his mock Gothic castle off the Banbury Road are long gone. Workers by brain and brawn are to be found on the same street, though how far this represents a real homogeneity of social differentiation is open to question.

* * *

In a curious way another unifying and homogenizing factor affecting Oxford in the 1980s was the impact of – to use that overworked phrase – the Enterprise Culture. Cutting across all Oxford's divisions, concentrating and reducing, it left its stamp on the city. In the course of researching this book it was borne in upon me that I was seeing, in a score of different contexts, the same process – a small, highly traditional society on the turn, where change was thrusting between the stones of the city and market forces exposing and threatening old certainties. In every direction the links and interconnections spread. What you saw one week in a hospital, the next week you would see reflected in school, polytechnic or university. Everywhere there was a stripping away, a sharpening and hardening, a brisk new sense of coldly commercial imperatives. It could be seen in the income-generating plans of a college bursar, the hard-eyed career ambitions of the new 'realistic student' or – at the bottom of the pile – in the anxieties of a social worker struggling to cope with the increasing numbers of homeless finding their way on to the streets of the city. Across a range of fields – education, health, industry or planning – it became clear Oxford was a sharply focused microcosm of larger national issues.

To see the city in this light, to view it as a screen on which to catch and plot the signals of social change seems at first sight highly idiosyncratic. It seems far too special a place, one too uniquely and eccentrically shaped by its history to be treated in any way as typical. Its colleges and churches and the streets on which its citizens tread are a permanent palimpsest of its past. Yet I would argue it is unusually equipped to serve as an index of change. Such is the variety created by Oxford's rich pattern of contrasts that it approaches the comprehensive and in a roundabout way achieves representativeness. An amazing range is crammed into it: town and country, ancient university and modern poly, decaying traditional industry and rising high tech replacements, ethnic communities (in East Oxford) and New Town-style problem estates, a major international organization (Oxfam) and even – at Harwell – a nuclear installation. Like some small imaginary kingdom it has one of everything.

Moreover, if you look closely at that past which so dominates the city it does not seem so odd to see Oxford as representative of larger trends. Its history has been dominated by a strange but characteristic dynamic, a continuous oscillation between being on the margins and intense involvement, between what might be termed – looking at its basic geography – the Fortress and the Ford. Originally a prosperous little Saxon borough going about its small business, Oxford became after the arrival of the scholars a source of trained talent to Church and State and a place of national and even international consequence. Sinking back into a period of decay and decline in both Town and Gown, it reassumed the centre stage during the religious battles of the Reformation and, later, in the actual battles of the Civil War, only to subside once more into the lazy somnolence of the eighteenth century. Bypassed by industrial and political revolutions, it once again swung back, this time in the university as a nursery of empire, and, in the town, after a long period of economic restriction, to explode into a major industrial centre.

This alternation between a dreamy backwatery aloofness and occupation of the historical centre stage is characteristic of the city. In so many of its aspects Oxford seems suspended between a series of polar opposites – centre and periphery, ancient and modern, fixity and mobility and between reality, on the one hand, and the fictional and fantastic, on the other. Behind the solid presence of its shops and banks and crowds and industries shimmers another Oxford – the Oxford of thought and imagination, the Oxford hung about with the fantasies and fictions of authors like Carroll, Lewis and Tolkien. Similarly, despite being so settled in the weight of its traditions, it is a highly ephemeral, mobile sort of place – a 'kinetic city' as Thomas Sharp called it in his book *Oxford Re-Planned*. It is full of the traffic of transients, not just the students that pass through its colleges and the summer clouds of tourists, but all the young and rootless spending a season in the bedsits of the city and all manner of latter day pilgrims, Scholar Gypsies and Judes the Obscure who come here seeking an answer.

These polarities, along with all the other splits and oppositions in the city create its particular atmosphere and charm. The tensions between them generate Oxford's peculiar charge of attraction. The very compactness of the city heightens its contrasts and fosters a love of whatever is contrary, individual and eccentric, adding a rich leavening of irony and humour. Oxford resolutely pits the particular, the exceptional and the personal against the general, the rule and the imposed; it delights in all manner of linguistic reversals and verbal subversions. It is a city based not just on words but also infinite nuances of tone and of voice. Despite its many divisions, it is not at all a bitterly fraught or antagonistic place. Rather it is tolerantly indulgent, patiently absorbing – qualities it now needs more than ever given the pressures of growth to which it is being subjected.

– 2 –

The Fortress and the Ford

Oxford lies in a patchwork of streets and meadows where the roads and rivers meet. Perched on a long finger of gravel pointing down to Radley, at a point where the Thames may easily be forded and the Cherwell safely bridged, it straddles a natural crossroads from North to South and East to West. But, bounded on nearly all sides by rivers and marsh it is also naturally defensible – a place therefore of double character, as much fort as ford.

Matching its geography the city grew up to be a split creature, at its most divided in the long antagonism between Town and Gown. In the course of that antagonism Town was to suffer centuries of subordination. But long before it became a university town Oxford led a thriving independent life. It began some time in the eighth century, founded as a royal *burgh,* a Saxon frontier fort, whose military rectilinear grid is still preserved in the city's central street plan of today. With royal lands nearby in Headington, and the King's hunting lodge in Woodstock, it soon grew in importance, becoming a centre of councils and coronations.

Long before the scholars came, Oxford was a place of some consequence. Its Freemen (those entitled to carry on business in the city) showed the sturdy civic enterprise to purchase the royal free farm, thus exempting themselves from taxes in return for an annual payment. By the city charter granted them by Henry II they, like the citizens of the capital, were freed of tolls elsewhere in the land and entitled, if embroiled in lawsuits, to claim trial in their native city. A further mark of their status was that, again like the citizens of London, they could send representatives to assist in coronations, with only their humbler reward – cups of ash, as opposed to London's gold ones – to distinguish them.

By the twelfth century Oxford's Ford had overtaken Fort. Its market and leather-working and weaving guilds were thriving. Had you entered one of its four gates at this time you would have been confronted with a scene of semi-rural smells and squalor but also of busy commercial activity. All along the High Street would have been stalls selling straw, wood, pigs, earthenware and ale. Advancing from the Southgate were the sellers of fish, hides and faggots and – as Cornmarket's name indicates – grain. Narrow frontages of workshops lined the streets, pierced by 'gunnels', long narrow passageways leading to courtyards, stables and sties.

On this vigorous borough the first scholars of the university descended. The transformation to a university town must have happened quite rapidly. The first fairly reliable reference to academic activities comes in the 1180s: twenty years later the university is regularly electing chancellors and laying on courses of lectures. If you had been an Oxford citizen born, say, in the 1160s, you would have witnessed a small market town of some 4,000 souls stretching itself to absorb 1,500 scholars and clerks. Some of these would have lodged in inns or private houses (as did 'hende Nicholas' in Chaucer's *Miller's Tale,* the first Oxford figure to appear in literature) but mostly they congregated in the so-called 'academic halls', sets of rooms run by 'principals' (who would either have been townsmen or, increasingly, older and more experienced scholars). A rough division sprang up in the city, with the 'latin quarter' – the majority of halls and lecture rooms concentrated to the north and east of the city, around the University Church and Catte Street – and the town area to the west – a distinction roughly perpetuated to this day.

Divisions of a more serious nature began to appear. The townsmen, while resenting the incomers, were not at all averse to exploiting them as a captive market needing accommodation and provisions. A regular stream of complaints started about overcharging and poor quality goods. Tensions rose, squabbles became frequent, often breaking out into violence and full-scale riots. 'There is probably not a single yard of ground in any part of the classic High Street that lies between St Martin's and St Mary's which has not, at one time or another, been stained with blood,' has written the historian, Dean Rashdale: 'There are historic battle-fields on which less has been spilt.' The first major riot took place in 1209 when townsmen seized and hanged a clerk on (probably mistaken) suspicion of murdering a local woman. In protest the scholars temporarily decamped to Cambridge (thereby in the process establishing Oxford's sister university). A whole string of further riots was to follow.

Indeed, violence became endemic. It is easy to imagine the impact of several hundred teenage boys periodically let loose in a town far from their homes. The early regulations of the university reveal a preoccupation with curbing indiscipline, particularly that of the 'chamber deacons', the students who lived largely ungoverned lives in private lodgings. But the violence was not limited to Town–Gown encounters. Often the clerks, organized factions or gangs called 'nations' reflecting the regions of their origin did battle amongst themselves on the city streets.

These tumults culminated on St Scholastica's day in 1354. The spark, as always, was small – 'several snappish words' (in the words of the Oxford antiquary, Anthony Wood) about bad wine in the Swyndelstock Tavern in Carfax. This led to a brawl, and the bells were sounded in St Martin's and St Mary's, the respective signals for the forces of Town and Gown to gather. After several skirmishes, the next day a mob of countrymen under 'a black dismal flag' marched in. 'Such Scholars as they found in the said Halls or Inns they killed or maimed, or grievously wounded. Their books and all their goods ... they spoiled, plundered and carried away. All their victuals, wine, and other drink they poured out; their bread, fish, etc. they trod under foot.' The incident ended, if Wood's account is to be believed, with disembowellings and ritual scalpings.

The pattern after these outbreaks was always the same. Town and Gown would both sue for justice to outside authority (usually the King), holding out self-serving stories of what had happened. The King, intent on the generally more violent part played by the townsmen rather than the resentments which gave rise to them and aware that the university was a valuable source of trained clerics for the royal administration, almost invariably found in favour of the university. In charter after charter its power steadily extended over the town, giving it a say in the Assize of Bread and Ale and jurisdiction in cases involving clerks, and finally total power over the Assize and any breaches of peace in the city. From 1246 an annual oath of loyalty was extracted from the Mayor and sixty elected Freemen. The aftermath of the St Scholastica's Day riot brought even heavier retribution – an annual penance and fine of 100 marks, a penalty not lifted for some 500 years. 'The Burghers', wrote the historian, J. R. Green, 'lived henceforth in their own town almost as the helots or subjects of a conquering people.' The 'Fort' had descended on Oxford with a vengeance.

'We conceive', stated a university submission to the Crown in the seventeenth century, 'that where two Corporations live together, there is necessity that one of them be subordinate to the other, for it cannot be expected that they should live together peacefully, if they be of equall power, and independent; as this very place hath found heretofore by bloody experience', adding that the 'Towne of Oxford lyes out of the road; and is no way usefull to the publique by any trade or manufacture. It serves only for the intertainment of Schollers, and the Townesmen have no other possible meanes of subsistence but by the Universitie . . .'.

Economically Oxford became an academic version of a 'company town'. The old prosperity of crafts and market withered and were replaced by an economy servicing the university, based on tailoring, shoemaking and supplying provisions. The city, even within itself, had always had its exclusive and fortress-like aspects. Although its earliest seal ('a fortified town, with a river in front, an ox within the town . . .') proclaimed it represented 'all the citizens of Oxford', authority was vested not in all the burgesses but in the Gild Merchant, the association of Freemen or licensed traders. On the defensive against the university, the Gild Merchant retreated deeper into the castle of its restrictions, excluding 'foreigners' ever more tightly from trading in the city. Indeed much of the resentment against the university was stirred by its high-handed habit of 'matriculating' into its service 'privileged persons' – useful tradesmen such as tailors and barbers and even, on one occasion, a dentist. The Freemen were irritated by being bypassed but, characteristically, often buttered their bread on both sides by getting matriculated themselves.

It is hard to escape the conclusion that Town was not only

subordinated to Gown but in the process diminished and corrupted. Chronically short of cash, the Council in one notorious instance in the eighteenth century tried to sell off its parliamentary representations in perpetuity in return for clearing its debts. Oxford elections became a byword for corruption ('I went down to Jericho', said Thackeray of one election in which he stood, 'and fell among thieves.'), reaching such a nadir in the 1880s that the city was formally disenfranchised for several years.

The Town for its part responded like any subject people with a mixture of outward deference and barely suppressed hostility and rivalry. In the spirit of keeping up with the Joneses the City Council became ever more conscious of the civic pomp of furs and scarlet and the elaborate detail of its offices and their regalia. Sometimes the rivalry reached an absurd pitch with Town and Gown tripping over one another in their attempts to define and defend their privileges. When the university licensed one of its carriers to set up a flying coach between Oxford and London in the seventeenth century, the Council reacted by immediately licensing one of its own – from whose services the university promptly disbarred its own members. Often the city bailiffs and the proctors would dog one another in their evening patrols, leading sometimes to the ludicrous situation where the city's own officers were arrested by the proctors for 'noctivagating' (being out unauthorized at night) and thrown into jail until the next morning.

Publicly, confrontation, rivalry or passive resistance were the norm between Town and Gown, but at a private level there was a dense rootwork of personal contact and informal cooperation. There the Ford could replace the Fort. There are records of landlords standing surety for students in law courts or, in wills, of bequests passing between Town and Gown. These ties would have included marriage – if nothing else the university would have provided the city with an ever re-stocked pool of eligible bachelors. University-educated clerics manned Oxford's churches. Local grammar schools, attached to the colleges or run by the university, opened the door of opportunity to Oxford boys, and many of the university's scholars were of city origin.

Indeed Town made a much greater contribution to Gown than by simply giving it board and lodging. Oxford scientists such as Boyle and Hooker made use of the facilities in local apothecaries' shops in pre-laboratory days. John Wilkins, Warden of Wadham, and chief scientific luminary in what later became the Royal Society, was the son of a local goldsmith. Oxford masons played a huge, unsung role in creating the university's magnificent buildings. Prominent amongst these was Thomas Wood, an untrained local builder who was the architect of the exquisite Old Ashmolean building built in 1683. For a long time posterity refused to acknowledge his achievement, ascribing it to Wren, but now recognizes it as the work of Wood, a man, in the words of his epitaph in a local churchyard, 'sufficiently qualified for better employments than those he was bound to by his education'.

Significantly, it was building and urban renewal which ultimately provided the opportunity for a better rapport at official level, opening up a crossing place where Town and Gown could meet and cooperate. The first tentative step had been the conduit built by the university from Hinksey to Carfax. Although intended for its own members it was also open to 'any inhabitant of the citye that will desire ... to have a private benefitt to himself, drawing water out of the mayne pipe'. Later, it was through the enterprise of another university figure, the jurist Sir William Blackstone, that Oxford's first piece of planned city development since the Normans was achieved – the building in 1768 of the New Road to the West, linked by Botley Causeway to a new tollbridge at Swinford.

There had long been complaints about the squalid shambles of Oxford's streets and its open markets. After 1771 through a series of parliamentary Acts, a joint university–city body, the Mileways Commissioners, was set up to oversee and raise tolls for the broadening and straightening of roads, the strengthening of bridges and the sweeping away of the old street markets. One major outcome was the New or (as it is still known) Covered Market, built on land owned by Lincoln and Jesus and again administered by a joint city–university committee.

A mutual interest in improved transport and communications also united Town and Gown. Prices and commerce were still largely dependent on the navigability of the Thames. To overcome this a canal was cut, running first to Banbury and then on to Coventry. Again, both city and university backed this project, together with local MPs and grandees of the county. The final section to Oxford opened on 1 January 1790 to peals of bells from the city churches and trumpets of a band of the local militia. Overnight coal prices, which had been nearly four shillings a hundredweight, dropped to a little over a shilling. In the long tension between Fort and Ford, the latter had at last triumphed.

Thereafter growing reconciliation continued into the nineteenth century, eventually crowned by two highly symbolic events – the university's lifting of the St Scholastica's Day penance in 1825 and its wise decision in 1859 – after an Oxford citizen, Isaac Grubb, refused to swear the loyalty oath – to back down and not pursue the matter further. That century also saw the university gradually withdrawing from the extensive powers it held over the city. However, one major obstacle to consolidation under the authority of the city was the plethora of independent bodies each looking after a particular area of administration. On these the university was usually represented, and the fragmentation no doubt reflected its being granted a say in each area. Even when the old Freemen and their antiquated privileges were swept away in 1835, the corporation which emerged in Oxford was largely powerless. The Mileways Commission remained a key agency, to such an extent that the powers of the local Board of Health set up in 1865 were vested in that body.

Finally in 1889 Oxford was made a County Borough and most of the independent bodies were absorbed. Yet even then the university retained the right to nominate nine councillors and three aldermen, a privilege which was not revoked until 1974. Oxford institutions die hard: the Vice Chancellor's Court, which had been such a power in the medieval city, was only finally wound up in 1977.

The gradual transfer of power by the university reflected a growing recognition of the Town as an increasingly separate and diverse entity. From beneath the medieval stones of its centre a new Oxford was beginning to spread out in a circle of redbrick suburbs which Gerard Manley Hopkins called its 'base and brickish skirt'. Economically, though, their inhabitants were still largely dependent on the university. Almost a third of those in the 1831 census were in domestic service or in the retailing or distributive trades tied to the custom of the colleges. The Industrial Revolution largely bypassed Oxford, deflected by university resistance. The dons, whereas they had welcomed the increase in their creature comforts resulting from the Canal, fought hard against the coming of the railways. The Duke of Wellington, then Chancellor of the University, opposed them on the grounds that they would encourage the working classes to 'move about' unnecessarily. Gradually, though, the lines crept towards Oxford, hedged about with restrictions, first to a branch at Steventon, then Grandpont, then finally to Rewley Road, west of the city centre. Yet when a proposal was made to site the GWR workshops here in 1865, the university united in vociferous opposition, despite the serious local problems of unemployment and poverty. 'Everyone knows what evils are apt to result when the University is placed in the midst of a great city and the students allowed access to the population,' wrote Goldwin Smith, the Professor of Modern History, pointing ominously to 'the character of the students of Paris'. Nevertheless, despite all the resistance to change, some change there was. Even a pale version of an industrial working class quarter appeared in the rows of Jericho and West Oxford housing employees of the University Press, the railways or the canal.

As well as these new elements there were other older working communities in Oxford, little enclosed worlds split off from the rest of the city, again almost fortress-like in their isolation. Along Fisher Row was an ancient riverside settlement of families – the Bossoms and the Beesleys – who had made their living for centuries by Oxford's waterways, as fishermen, boatmakers and bargees. Squatting out amongst the Headington quarries was something like an outlaw community – the Quarry Hogs. Churchless, fiercely independent and suspicious of outsiders, they led their own life and settled their disputes internally. A strong and violent culture, almost a counter-culture, held it together, based around communal sheep-roasts, cock fights, morris dancing and a private *patois*. At its heart was a dense cluster of interrelated families, working as quarriers or stonemasons – the Coppocks, Bushnells and Wells – and a glance at the telephone directory still shows a heavy presence of these names in the suburb today.

At the top end of the social scale there was also increasing diversity. Although Oxford had never produced spectacularly rich families, respectable accretions of wealth occurred amongst local bankers, lawyers and brewers, where the university connection waxed profitable. Several local families – the Halls, Tawneys and

Morrells – made substantial fortunes and moved out to country seats (moving also incidentally into Liberal politics and artistic patronage in the case of the Morrells and Fabian historiography in the case of R. H. Tawney). Soon, the new railway classes rolled into North Oxford. Lord Curzon, when Chancellor, noted how 'the central position, the excellent railway connexions, the educational advantages (not of the University alone), and the perennial beauty of Oxford have attracted thither a large non-academic population ... retired civil servants and clergymen, military officers, doctors, solicitors, etc.' The social climate had changed, as one American woman journalist writing for *Harpers Magazine* in 1890 noted: 'In former days ... there was one large university set, with clearly defined limits, consisting of Heads of Houses, Professors and their families ... The social tone was rigid and exclusive in the extreme, and it was hard, if not impossible, for any outsider to get a footing in Oxford society.' Now, by contrast, she found it similar to the suburbs of Croydon or Brixton.

Feeding on the profits of this suburban expansion a new breed of local entrepreneur appeared, the property speculator. Typical was the builder, Walter Gray, originally a Lincolnshire railway stationmaster who had been talent-spotted by the Master of Keble and installed as Steward at that college. Soon Gray branched out into property, particularly in nearby burgeoning North Oxford. An adroit man of business, he lost no opportunity to advance his enterprises. When a rival, the Oxford Building and Investment Society, fell – rightly – under suspicion of corruption, Gray promptly pointed out that all the builders to which it had made loans had used the characteristic pale yellow bricks (still much in evidence in parts of Oxford such as Warnborough Road) made by the brickyard owned by the Society's secretary. After it inevitably collapsed, he was made its liquidator. Thereafter he rose steadily and was made Mayor of Oxford four times and eventually knighted.

No doubt the new social elements did something to dilute Town–Gown antagonism, but the old divisions still lingered. The Oxford tradesman, portrayed as a grasping villain, remained a particular butt of university contempt. One nineteenth-century pamphlet, *Tradesmen and Undergraduates,* intended to warn of the dangers of the credit dangled temptingly by local tradesmen, affably advocated repudiating debts: 'To the *honest* dealer it is doubtless most injurious, but the majority of Oxford tradesmen have long since reduced college debts to a mere gambling speculation, in which ... their loss is more than amply compensated by their profits.' One Head of House complained of 'pastrycooks who had made fortunes cheating members of the University', polluting 'the magnificent entrances to the most beautiful of cities in the Kingdom'.

Traditionally, the tradesman, along with the college scout, had been the representative local figure with whom the university most often came into contact. Soon two others – the Oxford landlady and her husband – entered the arena of encounter and potential conflict. Edward Pusey, the arch-conservative of the nineteenth-century university, had warned that living out, when the undergraduate and landlady are placed perilously 'solus cum sola', would lead to the moral disintegration of the student body. But after 1868 students were allowed to live out of college in university-licensed lodgings, and by 1882 there were 520 such premises, accommodating 1,100 undergraduates. A series of bemused collisions took place between the two alien tribes. One undergraduate in a magazine, *The JCR,* described the landlady's husband: 'After some weeks' residence you will begin to note a weak nervous man lurking in holes and corners of the house. This is your landlady's husband, a docile creature whose role it is to be represented on occasions as a sort of inflexible Jorkins, deaf to reason. As a rule, he has no visible occupation, and may usually be seen smoking an apologetic pipe in the backyard, and wistfully contemplating the three cabbages and a radish known as the kitchen garden.'

This was the traditional, genially contemptuous end of Town–Gown relations. At the other extreme was horrified disgust at the poverty of the city's slums. Conditions in the poorest parts of Oxford – St Thomas's, St Clement's and Red Lion Square next to Gloucester Green – matched anything seen in the slums of the East End or the industrial North. Polluted water and poor sanitation were major causes of disease, leading to cholera outbreaks in 1832, 1849 and 1854. St Ebbe's, a particular blackspot, was described as 'a swamp converted into a cesspool' and open sewers ran past the new rows of Jericho. City water was drawn from the Thames into which untreated sewage flowed, and some idea of the evil state of Oxford waterways at this time is given by the gruesome nickname of the Trill Mill Stream – 'Pactolus' – from the Lydian river whose banks were supposedly lined with gold. This horror was bound up with fear of disease (one of the main university arguments against the railway workshops had been the creation of a 'fever belt' around the city) and possibly also the fear, that suppressed nineteenth-century English middle-class fear, of social anarchy. A handbook entitled *The Dictionary of Oxford* intended to enlighten prospective undergraduates, stated emphatically that even the natural democracy of the Oxford man would recoil from such ideas as 'the enfranchisement of the Carfax Club or politicians of the type of the Jericho Rough'.

Paternalist benevolence was a natural response to conditions in Oxford's working-class districts, exemplified in, for instance, Thomas Combe, the University Printer, who became a kind of patriarch to the new district of Jericho. Similarly, the upright consciences and irresistible energy of North Oxford ladies, often wives and daughters of dons, urged them to set up a Local Charity Organization Society, the pioneer of later Oxford social work. St Thomas's in particular, became the recipient of much do-goodery, the nineteenth-century equivalent of Barton and Blackbird Leys. One Miss Mary Jephson of Gunfield, Norham Gardens, was especially drawn to charitable works in this area, and instrumental in setting up a crèche and invalid kitchen on Osney Lane.

Amongst their husbands and fathers, the dons, the record was more mixed. Some progressive and egalitarian figures such as T. H. Green of Balliol transcended the traditional Town–Gown divide, plunging into local education and politics and fighting hard against the electoral corruption of the 1880s. Likewise, Henry Acland, the Regius Professor of Medicine, pressed unstintingly for better conditions, stressing the link between inadequate sanitation and the city's cholera outbreaks. The gulf between the two Oxfords was epitomized most graphically in Christ Church, as it towered magnificently above the slums of St Ebbe's. Refusing for many years to contribute to the local Poor Law Rate on the grounds that as a cathedral it was extra-parochial, it nevertheless felt obliged in the substantial areas of West Oxford which it owned (derived ultimately from its great windfall of Osney Abbey property during the Reformation) to undertake various small bits of social engineering, including a number of model buildings, one of which, the rather grim Old Christ Church Buildings in the Hamel, still stands today.

The poverty of Oxford's working-class areas sprang from the lack of well-paid, regular employment – the lack, in short, of local industries. The University Press with its 750 employees was still the largest single employer of skilled labour. 'It would appear', the Victoria County History confidently stated in 1907, 'that the County is prevented, as if by fate, from ever attaining to the position of a great industrial or commercial centre.' Yet even as these words were being written, in a garage off Longwall Street, a local man, William Morris, was toying with the idea of building a motor car – a dream that was to transform Oxford.

The economic impact on Oxford of Morris was immense. Within twenty years of his starting production the proportion of the work-force in manufacturing doubled. Morris brought full employment (after some initial annual fluctuations due to the Motor Show cycle) and paid good wages. By 1936 Oxford was in the top three most prosperous towns in England, and Morris's workers, duly grateful, repaid the 'Guv'nor' with close personal loyalty.

Yet with expansion, and particularly with the creation of Pressed Steel, an associated Cowley-based company, the pool of available local labour began to dry up. Migration made up the shortfall – from Scotland, Northern England, and, particularly, Wales. Thirty years after Morris's first car rolled out of the factory, the city's population had more than doubled. If, traditionally, there had been the two Oxfords of Town and Gown, now a third, industrialized Oxford loomed over them. The new citizens led a life utterly divorced from the old Oxford, a Luton-like life of work at the factory followed by the pleasures of mass-produced goods, tinned foods, cheap cars and radio sets and the newly built Regal Cinema on Cowley Road. For a time some of the migrants preserved the traditional activities of their native communities – Welsh choirs and so on – but most soon fell into the anonymous modern lifestyle of the new industrial quarter.

Between the university and the new Oxford yawned a huge gulf. Industrialization, coming so suddenly, caught the university napping. Almost in shock it turned its back on the unwelcome developments to the east. The story is told that when a former civil servant, Sir Douglas Veale, became University Registrar (its chief administrative officer) he looked up a letter which he had sent from Whitehall requesting the university's views on further expansion at Cowley. He found it stuffed in a file with a scribbled note that these developments were of no interest or consequence to the university.

Two things bridged – but only partially – this gulf. The first was politics. Oxford workers had long been the despair of outside labour organizers. 'They did not', wrote one, 'have a sense of class; they did not like to think of themselves as a class, and they had not got the pride of workers but had the feelings of the servants of the rich.' This now changed. The immigrants brought tougher industrial and political attitudes with them.

Oxford's first serious industrial dispute gave rise to a major strike at Pressed Steel in 1934. Thereafter the wards of the new housing estates regularly returned Labour councillors. At the same time leftwing elements were strengthening in the university. Many dons (including, earlier, the founder of the Fabian Society, Sidney Ball of St John's) had become increasingly disenchanted with the old Christian benevolent attitude – the deigning don's wife approach to Oxford's social problems. So, to an extent, left Town and left Gown made common cause, even forgoing a Labour candidate in the famous 1938 election in order to campaign behind an anti-fascist independent candidate.

Yet a certain detachment still marked this alliance. G. D. H. Cole of Nuffield, that tireless proponent of socialism, spoke of Cowley as if it were some remote industrial region ('We have no Mr Ford', he stated, 'but we have Mr Morris; and Cowley, I understand, is not very different from Detroit on a smaller scale'), and the 1938 united front was characterized by Patrick Gordon Walker as a middle-class, university initiative, reflecting 'the views of people who are rich enough to afford the luxury of ignoring everything except foreign policy'.

The other bridge between the two Oxfords was Nuffield's own benevolence. Much of Nuffield's £25 million philanthropy went to local hospitals, but over £4 million was donated to the university. Sums were allocated to support advanced study, a physical chemistry laboratory and medical research, with the lion's share going to the college that bears his name. A son of the Town, he had become a major benefactor of the Gown.

Yet Nuffield's relations with academic Oxford were always marked by a certain distance and *froideur*. He is said to have harboured a prejudice against the university arising from an early unsuccessful joint venture with an undergraduate when he first went into car-making. And, for all the university's expressions of grateful respect, it never took him to its heart. Perhaps it resented the loss of its dominant position; certainly it hated the changes he had wrought in the city. The story is told that when Nuffield was first sounded out about a benefaction by a university intermediary, it was suggested it would be no more than recompense 'for what he had done to Oxford', to which Nuffield, apparently, made a spirited reply, regrettably not preserved.

Oxford's twin aspects of 'Ford' and 'Fort' were both accentuated by the arrival of Morris. The city became a crossroads indeed, the hub of a vast industrial network, but socially it also found itself even more divided. To house its new citizens, an outer fan of suburbs was flung up in Headington, Cowley and Botley. Broken up by Oxford's diverse geography of rivers and floodplains and its ganglion of roads, these further added to the city's fragmentation. The walled city went, in one suburb, from symbol to reality. In Cutteslowe the developer of a private estate adjoining a council one erected a wall in order to protect the select tone of his development. The Cutteslowe Walls became a *cause célèbre,* both inside and outside the city, and gave rise to a prolonged and ludicrous tussle with the Council. There were occasions when the Council would knock the walls down only for the workmen of the private estate immediately to put them up again. Accidentally demolished during wartime manœuvres by a tank (driven, significantly, by a local) they did not come down finally until the 1950s.

The initial reaction to the New Oxford – the Fortress reaction – was to wish it away. The Oxford Preservation Trust which had been founded in the 1920s to conserve the traditional views of the spires, eventually got Cowley in its sights: the motor factories were to be sent packing and replaced with selected clean, light industries. However, it gradually dawned that Cowley was there to stay. But if it could not be got rid of, perhaps it could be contained by a kind of planning apartheid – an approach which became known as the twin cities policy. Oxford would be both the ancient university town to the west and a modern commercial and industrial city to the east, with Magdalen Bridge as a valve between them, a kind of Checkpoint Charlie on the Cherwell. However, little came of this, not surprisingly, as the city's business heart had since the Middle Ages been west of Carfax.

Like the Oxford Preservation Trust, the council was also slow to adjust to the changed nature of the city and its new problems. After the war it decided something should be done, particularly about traffic congestion, but could not make up its mind exactly what. In time-honoured fashion it brought in an outside consultant, Dr Thomas Sharp, a professional town planner. His report, *Oxford Re-Planned,* breathes all the clear-eyed interventionist confidence of the postwar Welfare State era. Radical, imaginative, wrong-headed, it appears in retrospect a bold attempt to reconcile the Fort and Ford visions of Oxford. While also calling for the relocation of the car factories, he declared himself 'neither pro-town, pro-gown, pro-dungaree ... quite simply pro-Oxford' and rejected the twin cities idea as divisive. However, what he called 'the noble central tenth of Oxford' had to be safeguarded. The High Street became a Sharp fetish (according to him, 'the greatest and most typical work of art England possesses'): to protect it a new road would be driven through the northern fringes of Christ Church Meadows.

Predictably his report stirred enormous controversy while bringing little actual result. Indeed its effects were entirely negative in that it focused attention obsessively on the single issue of the Meadows Road. For over twenty years this issue deadlocked Oxford planning: proposal and counter-proposal, inquiry after inquiry followed one another in its wake, jamming and fuming like Oxford's traffic itself. The Council, characteristically, began by trying to duck the issue. Its first plan in the 1950s called only for the completion of the ringroad. But for Duncan Sandys, the then Minister of Transport, this simply would not do. He intervened, reviving Sharp's idea of Christ Church Mall – dubbed by one university wit as 'the New Jerusalem, a city built on Sandys'.

Christ Church was roused to resistance. It issued a writ against the Minister, and flew in experts like the American urban historian, Lewis Mumford. The High Street colleges, however, glimpsing the pleasant prospect of less traffic trundling past their lodges, sided with Sandys. The Council, caught in the middle, dithered and did nothing. Perhaps it could do nothing. Such was the strength of Oxford's connections that the issue went all the way to the Cabinet. At the height of the Suez Crisis it found time to debate the matter and, not unexpectedly (five of its members were Christ Church men) stalled the proposal. The stalling was crucial. The climate of opinion was shifting against unlimited provision for the car, and by the time the Labour Party gained control of the Council in 1972, it felt able to throw out the relief road option altogether and introduce in its place the Council's Balanced Transport Policy.

Yet if the Council vacillated over the Meadows Road, it acted in other areas with almost headlong precipitation. The neighbourhood of St Ebbe's was swept away wholesale. Its close texture of street and pub, of corner shop and workshop, was torn up, and an inner city road driven like an arrow through its heart. Just as nineteenth-century Christ Church and its wretched environs had epitomized the state of the city, so now the college again offered a symbol, sitting like a noble fortress, effortlessly picking off proposals, and plucking high-placed consultants out of the air; while, on the other side of St Aldate's, St Ebbe's, unsupported and inarticulate, was pulled apart at the whim of planners. The demolition process was only halted in Oxford when it reached Jericho and a campaign of community protest brought about a switch to a policy of neighbourhood rehabilitation.

Meanwhile the residents of St Ebbe's were banished beyond the bypass and rehoused in bleak new housing estates such as Barton and Blackbird Leys. The city had gone beyond being a split city, it had now begun to turn itself inside out, its entrails stretched out along roads of ribbon development. Nor was this process limited to the new council estates. Development, checked near the city by the green belt, bubbled up elsewhere, in part in the county towns of Wantage, Witney and Didcot but also in villages like Kidlington, Wheatley and Eynsham which expanded in clumps and strips around the city. Oxford had become Greater Oxford, its settlements and dependencies scattered across half the county in a shower of suburban fragments.

In all, Nuffield could be said to have bequeathed a poisoned legacy to Oxford. The car, manufactured here, has itself re-made the city. It has pumped in new people and new prosperity and engineered a range of new schools and estate developments. But in its wake it has left a fume of social splits and planning wrangles. Oxford planners are still struggling to come to terms with the car, slowly squeezing it out of the city centre street by street through a creeping barrage of parking restrictions and no-go areas, while at the same time trying to absorb and accommodate its daily influx of commuters.

Like a genie suddenly whisked out of a bottle, car-making wrought its violent magic on the city. Now it too is dissolving and disappearing. The Cowley car factory is shrinking, shedding staff and, in the opinion of many, may shut down altogether. So the ultimate irony is that the source of all Oxford's massive changes this century may itself prove as transient as all the other travellers and passers-through in the city of the crossings.

– 3 –

Chips with Everything

'People are Rover's strength', the video tells visitors to the Cowley car factory but on the tour that follows it is the robots that grab the attention.

A Cowley car begins in the Press Shop as a huge bobbin of steel, progressively snipped and squeezed to form its 400 panels. The Press Shop, with its heavy hydraulic presses thumping down, many of them dating from Lend Lease and even earlier, is the world of the Industrial rather than the Electronic Revolution. But later, when the panels are welded, the robots come into their own, swivelling and peering, descending from above like heavy-duty dentists' drills, or clamping sideways like ponderous crabs, before arcing out their tracers of sparks. The bits and pieces are stuck on to a circular jig, a fat surrealist wedding cake of pistons and wires, the crabs pinch once more, spit their fierce fires and a body shell, a recognizable car shape, emerges. Next, on to the checking booth, where the shell is checked to a fifth of a millimetre – a science fiction scene by Francis Bacon, the perspex cells sparkling with the vermilion glow of lasers. Later, as the line progresses, humans increasingly move in next to the robots, but themselves often looking rather robotic. After the Paint Shop (a seven-times repeated cycle of spraying and dipping) wax injectors advance on the shells, helmeted like astronauts and umbilically hooked-up to hot wax reservoirs. Then the robots return, this time sighted with laser vision, to affix the windscreens and windows with undeviating precision. 'They do the same job at four as they did at nine', comments the guide: 'They never get tired or bored.'

The guides spout statistics almost as fast as the robots spurt sparks: 200,000 cars a year (not counting the Rolls-Royce bodies which they still make here); a Montego every minute, a Maestro every 1.75 minutes; a Rover 800 every 2 minutes. Each year the factory consumes 42,000 tons of steel, 4 million litres of paint, £10 million of gas and electricity (it used to be more before the robots moved in). Annually the factory pumps, they claim, £111 million into the Oxford economy. Yet what they do not tell you is that it is shrinking all the time: down from 30,000 workers in the 1960s to about 7,000 today and with further men to be lost when the South Works shuts in the early 1990s.

They paint a bright picture of a clean high tech world, a new human environment in the factory with strategically dispersed rest areas, electronic bulletin boards and worker suggestion schemes. Yet underneath it all – in the workers' sardonic side-glances and the practical jokes they play on the visiting parties – you sense something irrepressible, anarchic and bloody-minded. There are other satisfactions, other solidarities. As you leave, a scrawled graffito lets you know that 'This job sucks'.

Oxford car-making is now nearly a hundred years old. It started with William Richard Morris repairing bicycles in the back room of his parents' house in James Street in East Oxford. He prospered, moving on to a showroom on the High Street and diversifying into motor cycles, garaging and taxis, run from premises on Longwall Street. A natural if untrained engineer, he was already toying with the idea of building a motor car in 1904. But it was not until he took over the old Military College at Cowley in 1913 that he was able to produce his first model, the famous Bullnose Morris. War briefly interrupted production but afterwards business boomed.

Morris's success was based on two very simple ideas. The first was not to manufacture cars in all their detailed entirety but simply assemble them from parts made by other manufacturers in the straightforward way he had earlier built bicycles. 'The basis of Cowley', he declared, 'is buying not manufacture.' To his factory, with its good road links, components were transported and there assembled using the mass production techniques he had witnessed during visits to the USA in 1914. The second side of his genius was an almost unconscious empathy with the tastes and pocket of the average customer. When a slump hit the motor trade hard at the end of the First World War, Morris, instead of maintaining or raising prices like his competitors, took a gamble and savagely slashed them. 'Every time you make a reduction,' he later wrote, 'you drop down on what I may call the pyramid of consumption power to a wider base.'

Yet for all his business genius, Morris (or Lord Nuffield, as he became) was an oddly unattractive character: complex and contradictory but also singularly colourless; full of energy, but plagued by ill health and insomnia; increasingly remote and withdrawn, but keeping a tight grip on all aspects of his factory; penny-pinching over business costs, but lavishly open-handed in his charity. Towards his workers he displayed a face simultaneously generous and authoritarian. His rule could be cruelly arbitrary. If your face did not fit, it was said, you were soon out. His one exploitable chink was apparently his hypochondria. Men up in front of him who pleaded ill health would find their symptoms accorded prolonged and loving attention and invariably be let off. His house out at Huntercombe, now owned by Nuffield College, has been preserved as it was and somehow sums up the man: wealthily spacious and comfortable, but full of the factory-made bric-a-brac of the interwar period and lacking any hint of individual taste or character. Only in a backroom cupboard do you find any suggestion of a personal interest: his original toolbox and – curious evidence of his medical obsessions – a pickled appendix preserved in a jar.

Morris's workers at first were only too glad of the high wages and regular employment he provided. They were generally docile and undemanding, mostly having come from shops or colleges or farms (by 1937 nearly half were still coming into the car factory each day from the surrounding villages). Later, as the factory expanded and its associate, Pressed Steel, got under way, outsiders with a tougher industrial background were drawn in – unemployed miners from the Welsh valleys, Geordies and Londoners from the East End.

What kind of world awaited them on the line? At first when vehicles were pushed from one point to another and men were individually responsible for fairly large areas of car-making, there was some larger satisfaction to be gained. But as the production line automated and tasks were increasingly broken down, this disappeared. Men survived by learning to switch off and focus on other outside interests. Working the line have been many local councillors and magistrates, and they will tell you how they composed their speeches while they turned the same bolt a thousand times a day. Creativity, baffled and frustrated at work, flowered in hobbies, gardens and handiwork at home. If you visit the works social club on a Sunday when the model aeroplane club members mount a display, you will see marvels of minute, loving skill – all the deflected craftsmanship denied to them on the line. Yet there were lighter moments, moments of humorous release, and a long shopfloor tradition of practical jokes. Perhaps the truth was that they felt a contradictory tangle of emotions: resentment, security, the strangely liberating pleasure of cutting off and letting your mind run free, and even pride – a pride in your stamina in taking for so long what the line threw at you.

It is against this background of mechanical de-personalized work that one must set the factory's history of troubled industrial relations. Morris had been deeply anti-union, and indeed unions were not even allowed into the factory until after a long strike in 1957. In place of official convenors management selected its own shopfloor representatives. These people, weak and unable to deliver on their promises, were discredited, and in the 1960s a new breed of hardline militants found it easy to take over and exclude more moderate official unionists. The militants would never compromise, resorting at once to strikes, and deliberately putting in excessive demands in the hope that their rejection would politicize the workforce. 'Management had tried to contain the trade union movement from within the plant', says David Buckle, a former secretary of the local TGWU: 'The result was that they put a tiger in their tanks.'

Cowley was further disabled by financial and organizational weaknesses that led back ultimately to the flaws in Morris's own personality. Despite his increasing absence from the factory, Morris never found it easy to delegate. Meanwhile, flying in the face of his philosophy of simple assembly and relying on outside contractors, he found himself buying up these contractors and setting up an array of subsidiaries. A loose conglomerate resulted which, despite Morris's efforts to weld it into a single entity, never quite cohered.

When Austin and Morris merged in 1952 to form **BMC** (the British Motor Corporation), the incoherence continued, due largely to the hostility of Leonard Lord, head of Austin, towards Cowley (he had previously worked for and been sacked by Nuffield and had left, vowing to take Cowley apart 'brick by bloody brick').

Thereafter the conglomerations and swallowing-up continued apace. In 1966 BMC joined Jaguar to become British Motor Holdings and two years later merged with Leyland (which itself had just taken over Rover) to form **BLMC**. The organizational digestive process belched and heaved, trying to absorb and rationalize these huge motor-making chunks. None of which mattered so long as business boomed and there was that big safe share of the home and 'empire' market to rely on. In the 1960s the only brake on Cowley was government HP restrictions: when tightened, men were laid off; lift them and business resumed its boom. Management's only terror was stopping the line, to avoid which any concessions would be made to the unions. As for the future, no one gave it a thought. In 1969 production reached an all-time high – but disaster was just around the corner.

By the mid 1970s the giant was tottering: BLMC was on the verge of bankruptcy and was effectively nationalized as British Leyland Ltd. Following the practice of those days a commission was appointed under Lord Ryder and duly reported. British Leyland was to be pumped up even bigger until it could stand shoulder to shoulder with its foreign competitors. Union–management mutuality was enshrined in an elaborate consultative structure at plant, area and national levels, generating considerable confusion. Shop stewards found they had been co-opted as managers and could not disclose sensitive company information to which they had been made privy. Perhaps the moment of maximum absurdity came when one Cowley shop steward found himself obliged to challenge locally a decision to re-locate some production at Swindon – a policy which he himself had approved at national consultative level. Meanwhile the strikes went on, no new models appeared and the company's market share continued to fall.

Then in 1979, with a change of government, the wind from No. 10 veered again. There was to be no more cosying up to the unions, no more propping up of lame ducks. The chosen instrument of new policy at Austin Rover was Michael Edwardes. In this there was an irony – Edwardes, a Labour government appointee, had for the previous two years gone along with the Ryder expansionism. Nonetheless, he now set about becoming the surgeon's knife with a will. Plants were shut, overproduction pruned and the workforce slashed. In marched the robots and, after some delay, out rolled a range of new models. Yet perhaps the greatest change was in labour relations. Unions were sidelined, and confrontation, backed up by the threat of rising unemployment, became the norm. Men at Cowley now look back at Edwardes' reign as a nightmare period of industrial dictatorship. Discipline was imposed, management won back the right to manage, but, some would say, at a terrible cost.

Now Cowley has entered upon calmer waters, a new and perhaps terminal phase in what might be called Cowley's late Japanese period. Anglo-Japanese collaboration had already started under Edwardes with the successful rebadging of the Honda Ballade. It gathered strength with the joint development of the Honda Legend/Rover 800 and has now reached the point of Rover and Honda UK taking a 20 per cent share in each other. The strategy seems to have been, if you cannot beat them, let them join you and eventually take you over. The hallmarks of the new era have been an even more intensive application of automation, greater use of training and an educational gearing up of the workforce (Rover now has seven times the number of graduates it had a generation ago). Management has simultaneously become more decisive while softening its style. There is a new scrupulous clarity, an almost oriental politeness, compared to the confusions and brutalities of the past. So perhaps a lesson has been learnt, but is it all too late? On the line they have accorded these changes a muted, slightly bemused welcome, mixed with fear of the future and doubt that management are fully disclosing their hand.

Many fear Cowley is suffering death by a thousand cuts. Much of the time it is working at well under capacity. The South Works is due to close in the early 1990s and the same fate has been announced for the North Works also. True, Rover has committed itself to investing £130 million in a new smaller factory at Cowley, but no new models have been assigned to it, only refined variants of the existing 800. The news that Honda/Rover would be setting up a new factory in Swindon sounded like a death knell in many local ears. There are those who predict that by the end of the 1990s car-making will have vanished from Oxford altogether.

Yet as Oxford's old industrial giant shrinks and totters, a band of new and vigorous high tech enterprises is springing up around its feet. Traditionally it is Cambridge with its high tech belt which is associated with these industries rather than Oxford. Yet the gap between the two cities is closing all the time: surveys have identified 260 high tech firms at Cambridge, but Oxford now has 190, if the great research centres of South Oxfordshire are included. Of those employed in manufacturing in the county, nearly half are in advanced technology industries, ranging from contract research to electronic goods, crystallography, high performance cars to lasers, biotech and robotics, medical instruments or low temperature physics. Despite their diversity of products these companies share a common profile, being small, with a keen centre of highly qualified and motivated staff, international, selling nearly 90 per cent of their products abroad and, above all, new. Most sprang up during the 1980s, and up to a third of their founders had never worked in industry before.

What is most striking to the visitor though, is their atmosphere. They are a world away from the old-style factory with its smoke and din. Enter their airy production offices, and everything rises up brand new and full of clean, confident edges – from the parking lines in the forecourts to the designer office furniture and corporate reports. It is a world of open plan and single status facilities, of chunky polished steel and tasteful veneers in greys or pastels and of staff in loose, casually smart clothes as if it were a company requirement to kit themselves out at *Next*. But behind all this in the background is a constant hum, a hard electric rhythm, the product of youth, high pressure and high ability (in many the average age is twenty-five and the proportion of doctorates as high as a third). There is a tremendous commitment, a willingness to put in hours and delight in teasing out elegant solutions ('I never want to do the same thing twice', said one of these entrepreneurs, 'I will employ someone else to do that for me.') And, despite all the sharp, hard definition, there is something curiously impermanent, almost improvized, like some high quality exhibition booth ready to be hauled down at a moment's notice and flung up elsewhere as the business shifts direction.

For sudden growth is their most common characteristic. Their starting point is nearly always some specialized product, some spin-off from research or ingenious idea that fits a niche market like a key into a lock. As they grow to fill the niche, they swell dramatically, often doubling or quadrupling within a year. Their growth rate is so fast that, like a jet surmounting the barriers of its machs, they experience periodic and predictable patches of turbulence. The first comes when they seek initial backing (and recurs frequently thereafter for they guzzle capital like a high performance car burns up fuel). The next occurs as competitors close in on their original concept. Then they must diversify or die. Fortunately these firms are obsessed with product innovation almost to the exclusion of all else. This helps keep them a leap ahead but in turn leads to other problems. As they reach a certain size, they will hit yet another bumpy patch during which their rudimentary financial and management systems will cease to cope. An inner vertebra of business specialists has to be inserted to stiffen the expanding outer shell. This is generally when the friction starts, as the original tight-knit team is diluted, bringing with it the slammings of laboratory doors and the stormings-off of prima donnas. Afterwards, to gain stability and diversity, they may absorb a related firm and eventually go public. For always there is the need for capital, and allied to it the need for more space, as, once a year, they shed their skins and stretch into new premises.

The computer company, Research Machines, exemplifies this pattern. Its twin founders, Mike Fischer, an Oxford physics graduate, and Mike O'Regan, an economist, are a balance of contrasting talents: Fischer, the scientific force behind the business, intense and a lover of radical solutions, O'Regan his genial and laid-back organizational foil. In 1973 they found themselves sharing a flat in Swindon – 'drop-outs' in O'Regan's words 'in the sense of not wanting conventional jobs but desperately keen to start our own business'. Supporting themselves as labourers, electricians or telephone operators, they one day found themselves commissioned to build a one-off computer for a company carrying out sleeping drug trials. Nine months later, at 7 o'clock on the morning the device was needed, they delivered it to the firm's offices, having so wildly

underestimated the time required that they ended up working
for the equivalent of 3p per hour. Next they moved into selling
microchips by mail-order to computer buffs, all the time, however,
gradually piecing together the parts needed to manufacture another
computer. In 1977 they brought it out – the 380Z, a machine built
largely with the schools market in mind. The DTI adopted it as a
micro for use in schools and for the first time they sniffed the scent
of success. ('We realized there was no logical limit', says O'Regan,
'why shouldn't every school have one?'). But with only eight staff,
they were still tiny, hatched away in cramped courtyards and
backrooms throughout East Oxford, even nesting for a time behind
Tesco in the Cowley Road. The members of the company lived,
slept and even ate the business, taking their meals together in the
narrow terraced houses of the area. Everything was ploughed back
into the business ('It is easy to be poor in a student town like
Oxford', comments O'Regan: 'It's the sort of town where if you
get cash you buy a typewriter, not a suit').

In 1980 they brought out another successful model, the 480Z.
But they noticed a change had crept over the company. It was
no longer the old tight-knit circle. As their success spiralled, so
did their problems. Clashes over personalities and management
styles became frequent. Amid bitter recriminations one director-
shareholder, David Small, quit in 1982. Thereafter the company
resumed a smoother but still steeply upward path. Its growth rate
has been fantastic – averaging 40 per cent a year since 1977 and
in some years twice that. Now with 500 staff (most of whom joined
in the last eighteen months) and a £50 million turnover, they
are fifth or sixth in UK computer manufacturing terms and are
spreading out of schools into business and government ('Why
shouldn't every civil servant have one?' muses O'Regan). They
have outgrown not just their East Oxford cradle but the city
itself, moving out to Abingdon and becoming 'an Oxfordshire
rather than an Oxford company'.

By contrast to the almost accidental, learn-as-you-grow progress
of many local high tech firms, one new player on the Oxford
board, British Biotechnology, exudes the confident air of having got
everything right from the word go. It has chosen to operate in the
newest and highest of high tech fields – biotech – and picked Oxford
over Cambridge as a base because of its comparative under-

development in this area. Having started out making 'designer genes' to synthesize complex proteins for customers, it is now working on a range of products, including an anti-AIDS drug, anti-clotting, cholesterol-inhibiting and wound-healing agents. Its aim is to become a producer of 'mega drugs' and 'a fully blown pharmaceutical in the European arena'. Deliberately and carefully it has built up a large capital reserve to sustain early development losses, drawing on a mix of shareholders, venture capitalists and government grants (it was the proud recipient of the first of the government's LINK grants to stimulate academic–industrial collaboration). The whole business seems slickly professional, from its capitalization programme right down to its spanking new research block in Cowley – ironically only a stone's throw from the ailing Rover car factory.

Another feature of British Biotechnology is its smooth integration with the university. Two of its leading research staff, Sue and Alan Kingsman, also lecture in the Biochemistry Department and through them British Biotechnology both funds and benefits from academic research. This highlights the kind of impetus which can be given to local high tech by the university science area. Traditionally the university has a reputation for setting its face against local industry, from its rejection in the nineteenth century of Oxford as a site for the GWR's railway workshops onwards. Of late though there seems to have been a sea change. Supporting this is a recent survey of Oxford scientists: 79 per cent had or were forming industrial links and 31 per cent had set up their own companies or were considering doing so. One quarter of the founders of local high tech firms are from the university – either dons or graduates.

But the university is not the sole source of local high tech. Through the south of the county runs a belt of research laboratories: Culham, the Rutherford Appleton Laboratory, the Esso and the Hydrological Research centres and Harwell – itself a mini science campus including the National Radiological Protection Board and the Medical Research Council's Radiological Unit. Their drab blockhouses and hangars (many started life as wartime installations) house an Aladdin's cave of scientific wonders. At Culham is based the JET (Joint European Torus) project. It could be compared to a gigantically hot pair of hands squeezing a genie in order to realize a magic wish. Within its enormous Tokamak reactor tiny amounts of plasma as little as a tenth of a gram are whisked and whirled around at incredible speed, squashed by magnetic fields, flailed by beams and rays and heated to ten times the temperature of the sun, all in order to yield a flash of fusion and unlock an endless sea of clean, cheap energy. At the Rutherford they make precision instruments which end up being fired into space on probes or Star Wars devices; among their other wonders are a particle accelerator, and kind of scalextric track in neutrons, some of the most powerful lasers in the world with names like Vulcan and Sprite and a computer so powerful it has to be housed inside a miracle of refrigeration.

These research centres contribute to the local high tech phenomenon not so much by the companies which they spin off but through becoming commercial concerns in their own right, gradually being nudged and edged, like the university, towards the enterprise mode. Half Harwell's work now comes from non-government contracts, and a quarter is non-nuclear, its activities ranging from dating 'Pete Marsh', a Celtic sacrificial victim unearthed from a Cheshire bog, to drying out flood damaged books and carrying out more mainstream research for industry. Indeed Harwell, like Rover, is also on the line, dowsing its old reactors one by one, laying off workers and finding itself forced to scrabble for work and stand, Thatcher-wise and sharper-eyed, on its own two feet in the marketplace.

The Oxford high tech phenomenon now seems firmly based, if scattered throughout county business parks and other odd corners of country villages. Many feel its progress has been badly checked by lack of an Oxford science park. They point out that a science park does more than provide space for new industries or even catalyse technology transfer – that subtle alchemy between lab and enterprise. Above all it furnishes, they claim, a symbolic rallying point, a visible statement of commitment to a new age – something Oxford has sorely lacked until now.

The lack has not been for want of trying. A whole sheaf of proposals have been put forward by consortia, often including colleges keen to sell their green belt land, but have been thwarted by planning or traffic considerations. Now, however, the dream has finally been realized and Oxford at last has its science park –

built out at Littlemore by Magdalen College and predicted to create some 1,000 jobs in due course. And the future? Well, it will probably bring several such parks in and around the city. There is a need to accommodate two opposite lines of development – what have been called the 'inside-out' and 'outside-in' developments, whereby new enterprises are hatched out from the laboratories at the same time that the research arms of outside corporations are drawn in. So there will eventually be a whole staircase of provision, ranging from central 'innovation' or 'incubator' units through intermediate facilities further out and, finally, to an outer shell of county business estates. The Oxford high tech phenomenon, substantial if somewhat held in check, now looks set to boom.

In fact boom was the common experience in Oxford in the late 1980s. Everywhere you stepped in the city you seemed to fall under the shadow of a crane or hear the chug and clang of construction. From the railway a whole swathe of redevelopment swept up Park End Street, over Hythe Bridge and past Gloucester Green's new toytown complex into the centre of the city. To the south a cluster of new blocks sprouted around Folly Bridge. Both Westgate and Paradise Square were slated for extension or rebuilding. The reasons for the boom were clear enough – Oxford's centrality and good communications, its amenities and desirability as a place in which to live and, not least, the cachet of an Oxford business address.

An impressive pile of statistics pointed up the boom. Even in the early years of the Thatcher decade when nationally the economy contracted and jobs fell by 2 per cent, those in the Oxford region rose by over 7 per cent. Small businesses started up at an amazing rate – over one a week, growing by 26 per cent, a rate exceeding the rest of the south east, including London. Indeed by all the indices overheating rather than contraction was the problem. Oxford business rents more than doubled in the late 1980s, reaching the highest rates outside central London. Full employment levels reflected the general boom.

The Oxford jobless total plummeted to a fifteen-year low, 2.5 per cent – a rate which is unofficially regarded as non-existent. UB40, the agency catering for the young unemployed, actually shut up shop for lack of clients. True, there were local unemployment blackspots such as St Clements with its 10 per cent rate, but elsewhere the picture was rosy. Even in Blackbird Leys, traditionally reliant on the car factory next door, the jobless fell from 20 per cent to 5 per cent. Ironically, even Cowley, in the throes of long-term contraction, found it hard to fill jobs and retain staff. In one attempt to find workers it had to draw 85 per cent of applicants from outside the traditional Oxford 25 mile radius 'travel to work' area. Of these, half failed to turn up for interview and of those given a job, another third left after only three months. Natural wastage and the swelling absorbency of the local economy seemed to have taken care of the Cowley problem.

So where has the growth been? The traditional pillars of the Oxford economy have been cars, colleges, hospitals and books, but the new expansion has been above all in services. Oxford has been a microcosm, an extreme example, of the national shift away from smokestack industries to the clean, light land of the service sector, of invisibles measured only in terms of desk space and computer screens. Jobs in these areas grew three times as fast as the national average, even in the first part of the decade, leading to a situation where three-quarters of the Oxford workforce now earns its bread in services and only about a seventh in engineering or vehicle manufacture. Winners of the jackpot were financial services with a whopping 54 per cent rise, but catering, tourism, retailing and distribution followed close behind.

The boom in distribution is reflected in Oxfordshire's 200 trading estates. The largest, Milton Trading Estate, covering 200 acres and including 130 companies, is like a separate township in the depths of the country, complete with banks, estate and travel agents and traffic system, even its own customs post (it is a designated inland port). With its vast warehouses stuffed with sheaves of tobacco and gleaming white-goods from the EEC, it currently provides 2,500 jobs, soon to swell to 4,000. But it is in 1992 with the coming of the European Single Market that places like Milton, nodes on the Channel–rail–road nexus, will really take off – vast commercial beanstalks sprouting and spreading on their green field sites.

Many see a dark lining to the silver cloud of the services boom, and feel that, unlike manufacturing, it provides only shallow-based, insubstantial and unproductive jobs. In one way they are absolutely right. Too many of the jobs are in low-paid or part-time tasks that attract the unqualified or women keen to edge back into the workplace in combination with bringing up their families – supermarket checkouts, fast-food eateries or scrubbing the floors of new office blocks. But shadowed beneath the blossoming of the service sector is something deeper – the rise of what has been called the knowledge economy. Ideas, knowledge and the manipulation of information are themselves becoming products for sale in the marketplace.

In Oxford there are a growing number of companies of this sort, specialists or experts in one field or another. One example is MRC, the Marine Reporting Credit company, which employs a staff of twenty in its Magdalen Road offices. Started in 1988 by an Oxford PPE graduate, Stuart Kenner, it began by providing information on shipping companies but has since broadened its scope to cover other volatile and high risk areas such as the oil industry and to offer general business consultancy services. It employs ex-businessmen, lawyers, economists – even writers. 'It is very much', says Kenner, 'a putting together operation, a lateral thing – rather than possession of a body of theoretical knowledge.' It is curious to know that from behind the dull façade of an East Oxford street, with its terraced houses and pokey old hardware shops, spreads a global information network with hundreds of clients and branches in New York and Hong Kong, that can tell you whether your money is safe in the Liberian freighter sailing on tomorrow's tide from Singapore.

That other traditional Oxford industry, the book trade, also illustrates this phenomenon. Oxford, since the coming of the university, has always been a book city, a city of words. It is a hive not only of publishing houses but of libraries, bookshops, second-hand dealers and all those who make their living by the book – writers, editors, researchers, designers, typographers and proof readers. After London it is the second largest publishing centre in the country and fast becoming the nation's educational and journal publishing capital: among its publishing houses are Oxford University Press, Pergamon, Elsevier, Basil Blackwell, Heinemann, Clio Press, Learned Information and Facts on File. Oxford has also always been a city of printing. The first book came off its presses in 1478 and even then Catte Street was a row of stationers, scribes and binders. But now there are great changes overtaking this area of publishing. In 1989 amidst much harumphing and complaint, OUP finally shut up its printing works and lost its last few hundred learned typesetters and readers. Now printing jobs are hived off across the globe, delivered by disk to cheap, efficient printshops scattered throughout the Third World or edging the Pacific Rim. The knowledge economy has, fittingly, caught up with that most knowledge-intensive of objects – the book. If there is one image that above all sums up Oxford as a book city with its blend of medieval and modern it is to be found in the Bodleian's Duke Humfrey Library. There, amongst the centuries of tomes, wink the green glimmerings of the library's new information network, electronic pulsings and squirmings, like an alien's cradle overarched by the ancient, watching walls.

In publishing, the electronic frontier of the future stretches ahead in place of the old typesetting. Oxford University Press, recognizing that in the 1990s there is more text in computers than on paper, has set up a new electronic publishing division. So far it has issued products from desktop molecular modellers to concordance-creating programmes and an automatic textbook of medicine, but its most prestigious project will be the combined edition of the *Oxford English Dictionary* on compact disk. This will convert the whole history of the language into a vast rumpus room, enabling its owner to race this way and that at will through this monument of erudition, instantaneously sifting its contents in any direction – by type or origin of word, by source of quotation and backwards by definition. By combining search terms it will be possible successively to refine and narrow the aperture of enquiry – to discover, say, all English words derived from Italian, then what musical terms, and finally all such terms first used in the seventeenth-century authors or, say, in Milton. It will exemplify the way electronic publishing is, as Adam Hodgkin, formerly head of the Department and now a freelance electronic publishing consultant, says, 'neither a means for producing nor distributing texts. It is a way of providing new kinds of intellectual objects. That is its fascination.'

Two other advanced projects in electronic publishing are based in Oxford. Blackwell Scientific's Adonis Project is aiming at the ultimate learned periodical – the jukebox journal, in which a potential 35 million pages of articles can be mounted and played off at will from a set of CDs. Meanwhile down in Park End Street (which with firms such as Wang Electronic Publishing is fast becoming Oxford's electronic publishing alley), Attica Cybernetics is heading out into 'hypertext' – a digital information system so rich and flexible it can reproduce combinations of vision, text and sound. 'The palette', says Hodgkin, 'is almost endlessly rich. It is asking for a tremendous range of skills, almost for the editor to become a film director ... so one day they may come up with an encyclopaedia that sings you a South American bird song, a cookery book that *tells* you how to cook a dish or a repair manual that animates changing a spark plug.'

Oxford has always been not just a book city but also a brain city, a city full of people making their living by their ingenuity or their perch in some narrow niche of learning. It is a city on-line with odd talents, whether you want a *Times* crossword devised, a page of cuneiform proofread or a column written on the situation in Eastern Europe. Enter a shop to buy a sweater, and you are likely to emerge burdened with a historical disquisition on Norse knitting patterns. It is full of people living on the sharp edge of their wits, doing no visible work and seeming to live on air alone. When Taine, the nineteenth-century French historian, visited Oxford, he commented on encountering the 'most numerous families' living by coaching or writing: 'Everywhere I met this hand to mouth existence.' The last census of the city disclosed as many 'artists and ancillary workers' as there were unskilled labourers and that a tenth of the workforce were doing jobs so unusual they had to be classed as 'inadequately described occupations'. So it comes as no surprise that in this most knowledgeable of cities, the first faint stirrings of the knowledge economy should be most clearly detectable.

Which brings us back to the other Oxford, the world of Cowley, the car factory and the assembly line. Michael Edwardes once called British Leyland a 'microcosm of the issues affecting British industry'. Its history here has certainly been a sorry industrial case study of how not to do it. But it is a microcosm in another sense. 'Two of the things that the car plant seems to me to illustrate', wrote a former head of industrial relations at Cowley, 'are probably the two worst aspects of our society.' One was 'the poverty of the professionalism of British management', the other 'the class differentials within factories. The class differentials', he added, 'are very clear in a fairly small place like Oxford ...'. Indeed these divisions are ironically symbolized in the city, with the ancient university town and its bleak industrial twin turning their backs on one another in the same city.

'*People are Rover's strength*' said the visitors' video. And, one might add, Oxford's as well. What an irony that so much of the income in this most cerebral of cities should have come from such brain-deadening routine. Now that is changing. But what education, what training will fit them for the new world of the science parks, the specialist consultancies, and the cybernetics of the future? Or will they end up, victims of the skills lag, boxing burgers by the hour for Cornmarket's tourists or trapped within four walls, fed only by the endless flickerings of a video? It is a problem which goes beyond a single city or even country but one which Oxford, with its contrasting side-by-side pattern of old and new, high tech advance and traditional survival, focuses most sharply.

– 4 –

Penniless Bench

For over 200 years there was an Oxford institution known as Penniless Bench. A lean-to next to St Martin's at Carfax, built by churchwardens in the sixteenth century, it soon came to attract a congregation of beggars, thus earning its nickname. Later it was replaced by a pillared arcade where local dignitaries could gather before city meetings but remained, according to a contemporary, 'a great nuisance, a harbour for idle and disorderly people' and was, by command of the council, knocked down in 1750.

Today there are quite a few modern versions of Penniless Bench scattered up and down the city, occupied by the vagrant and disturbed, the street drinkers and the homeless. You can see them slumped in Bonn Square (which they call 'Scratchy Corner'), perched on the broad ledges of the Radcliffe Camera or swaying in the defile of Folly Bridge. They sleep, they sing, they beg. Only rarely are they aggressive; mostly they turn quietly away at a hint of rebuff. The stunning fact is that every night in Oxford, one of the richest cities in England, several hundred are without a home or even a room, either staying in overnight hostels or 'skippering' under bridges, in empty sheds or even public lavatories.

The Night Shelter, which provides a meal and basic accommodation for the over-25s, is, according to its director, Paddy O'Hanlon 'one step up from the cardboard box'. It has an atmosphere, a culture, all of its own – the culture of the mobile underclass. Everything there seems wrapped in an omnipresent fug, a compound of unwashed flesh, damp clothes and stale tobacco, a dull palpable mongrel of a smell, hanging heavy in the air and sticking to surfaces, thick, blurring and cohesive. People slump in battered armchairs, caught in a collective drowse, trapped by time. For derelicts time oozes and trickles, compelling its victims to loiter in queues, traipse through a procession of official waiting rooms, doze in church halls and hostels. As they drowse, a kind of collective under-mind seems to take sway through which mood and emotion can be transmitted and amplified with strange speed and intensity. Beneath the trance-like surface a shifting patchwork of enmities and alliances plays, and a gulf of violent threat can open with frightening rapidity. Here a different language is spoken – in words and in body talk. Pieces of street wisdom are passed round, lovingly handled like old relics; tales are told of outwitting 'them' – the monolith of officialdom – for the most part pathetic fictions, flimsy hutches constructed to shelter battered self-respect. Then there is the round of rituals – passing the bottle, singing (volume, angle of lean and direction of glance all being important elements) and 'raring up' – that theatrical display of aggression, squared-off and fists balled to the world, saying, there is still a scrap of dignity, push me no further.

But through it shines a terrible loneliness and vulnerability. They can switch in seconds from trying to palm off some ancient wrinkled cheque to clinging limpet-like for interest and attention. For all its camaraderie the Shelter culture must not be sentimentalized: it is destructive, downward-tugging and violent, erosive first of friends and health, finally of identity and self-respect. Few can stand exposure to it for long, even the most dedicated 'carers'. The staff, prodigiously capable, a young and transient population themselves, burn out in months or even weeks; find themselves sleepless through tension or suddenly screaming across a counter. Only Paddy O'Hanlon, a sturdy bearded figure, seems to be able to absorb it all without strain, a man so unflappable that his centre of gravity seems locked in the earth beneath him, a paradigm of unshakeable, stout benevolence.

Oxford has always attracted the penniless. City documents of the sixteenth century bristle with references to them and 'the swarme and multitude of rogues, vagrant and idle persons commorant in this place'. In this century Oxford has been something of a grand junction for vagrants. One resident recalls the Woodstock

Road in the 1920s as a 'caravanserai of tramps' who congregated in an old brick field near Osberton Radiators, a Beckett-like landscape of campfires and belongings kept in battered perambulators. Another form of shelter was offered by the empty railway carriages ranked north of the station. Cleaners in the 1950s reported discovering to their astonishment as many as thirty men sleeping in one carriage. A survey in 1967, which became something of a watershed, disclosed over fifty sleeping rough in the city, including one man lodged upright in a telephone box.

Oxford's response to its underworld has always been polarized. One reaction was to turn the back, pass the problem on to someone else – an attitude encapsulated in one terrible tale set down by Anthony Wood, the seventeenth-century antiquary: 'extreme cold weather ... A poore man died with hunger and cold: he began to die in St Clement's parish, but the parishioners discovering it, hired or rather carried him under Magd. Tower in St Peter's parish East to die there and so save the parish two or three shillings to bury him.' On the other hand there has also been a strong local tradition of generosity and constructive benevolence, one mark of which was the string of almshouses in the east of the city, most notably the eighteenth-century Stone's almshouses in St Clement's. The twin faces of this split city – the Ford and the Fort – visible throughout its history, have been turned too upon the needy.

Today the purpose-built Simon House in the heart of the commercial quarter symbolizes that generosity. Its birth was long and hard, beginning with the 1967 survey already mentioned. In its aftermath the local branch of the Simon Community (an organization founded by ex-probation officers) collected several hundred pounds and opened a hostel in an old BR shed off Osney Lane. Local residents, resenting being saddled with the problem, responded with a petition of protest. Indeed the site was widely accepted as not ideal: one councillor even daringly suggested siting it in the plutocratic eyrie of Boar's Hill. When some vacant council land near the Westgate Centre was proposed, local traders immediately rose in arms (ironically, as was pointed out, in view of the fact that some had few scruples about selling liquor to the tramps). 'Dossers on the finest street in Europe' screamed one Oxford newspaper, but eloquent support was lent by Olive Gibbs, a prominent local councillor: ('People are not drunks because they want to be drunks. They are sick. Some of us should say: there, but for the grace of God and one extra gin, go I . . .') Another driving force was the present director of the hostel, Mike Hall, who, as an Oxford undergraduate, had taken part in the original 1967 survey, a charismatic figure who combines a flair for publicity with an amazing instinctive rapport with the street people. Eventually the land was bought by a church trust, and funds were found for the building. When it opened its doors in 1981 such was the press of numbers that within months it was having to turn away the younger, fitter men.

Simon House is now only one strand in the net of provision for the homeless in Oxford. It restricts itself to handling specialized and intensive needs – the old, sick, women, the long-term homeless and ex-alcoholics making a serious stab at restarting their lives – the quality end of the market, if you like. Complementing it are a range of facilities including the Church Housing Association hostels for single homeless men, the Warneford's Chilton detoxification clinic and the Day Care Centre run by the Probation Service.

The system of provision is like a ladder. Stretching up from the Simon House are a series of smaller 'dry' hostels, mostly on the Iffley Road or out in the country, intended to wean the reformed away from their old cronies and the drinking culture. The long-term aim is to give them a chance to regain their confidence, reconstruct their lives and hold down relationships and jobs. From the hostels they can graduate to bedsits (often basic facilities run by a particular group of East Oxford landlords – the Rajah brothers, the Farouks and the Cronins). But long-term rehabilitations are few and far between: perhaps 80 per cent of detoxified Simon House inmates relapse within months.

For the majority the provision is, sadly, simply a form of serial containment. Once when street drinkers bumped up against the system – the police and courts – they would be locked up for a few days, then let out once more on to the streets to resume the cycle of offence and arrest. It was not unknown for desperate officers simply to give them a few bob just to go away and take the weight off the system for a time. Now the broader net of facilities at least succeeds in 'lengthening the cycle', and giving them a longer respite from the street. Pessimistically, the attempt might be seen as simply pouring inadequates from one holding tank and canister to another; more optimistically as giving them a chance to break free of the cycle altogether. Even their relapses, it should be said, tend not to be as grave as their initial conditions, and in any case any time away from drink is a kind of achievement, one that can be built on.

Once Oxford's street people came from a well-defined constituency or rather, set of constituencies. There was the traditional 'tramp', the kind of man Orwell wrote about in the 1930s, and possibly the descendant of the old tinkers, who slept rough much of the time and wandered around looking for odd bits of seasonal work, supplemented by occasional begging. Oxford is a crossroads for these vagrants. It lies on a number of travellers' circuits, one stretching out from London along the South Coast and swinging back through the West Country and Oxford and another passing through Oxford to the Midlands and Lancashire and returning via England's eastern counties. Some complete the loop in a summer season, others may take years. 'Dougie' whom I met in the Shelter was a traveller. A thin, dark, bearded man, he had been for a long time in the army, then gone on the road, picking potatoes in Lincolnshire, hops in Kent and tulips in Holland. But such occasional work was getting harder to find. He was getting on now and thinking of giving up the wandering life. 'But when the weather picks up, I'll probably change my mind and head out again.'

Like Dougie, there are quite a few old soldiers, men conditioned to taking orders, who find it hard to regulate their lives once off the rails of military discipline. Related to these are the ex-lags, of which Oxford, with its prison, receives a fair number. Then there are the old navvies, the men who largely rebuilt Britain after the war and were victims of the 'lump' method of payment – cash in hand with no records kept and no National Insurance paid. Many of these belong to the so-called 'Celtic hard drinking culture' and overlap with another traditional category, the alcoholics and street drinkers. Finally, there has always been one very small set peculiar to Oxford itself – dons who go off the rails and hang about old academic haunts, sometimes half-pathetically, half-comically trying to barge through college gates.

But now whole new classes are tumbling down to street level, blurring the old clear-cut categories. In the hostels you can meet once-capable citizens who, through some prolonged combination of outer accident and inner weakness, have stopped coping and slithered, one collision and disaster after another, to the bottom of the heap. Society in the last decade has spat out its casualties harder and faster than ever. Responsibility seems to be slipping generally away from the state, becoming more diffuse and ending up who knows where. The psychiatrically disturbed are increasingly turned out, like heavily drugged zombies, on to the streets by the hard-pressed hospitals. It has been calculated that Oxford's hostels are looking after the equivalent of at least two long-stay psychiatric wards. There are now more women among the street people, often on the run from violent partners, and many, many more young people.

London is of course the Mecca for the young, with its glittering promises and its reality of cardboard cities and rentboy lives, but there is a steady trickle through Oxford. Fortunately provision for them is quite good here. To prevent them being sucked into the Shelter culture volunteers (including many students) have for years provided accommodation for the young homeless (originally in a church-owned basement in St Clement's known as the Night Cellar, but now in a house converted by the council on Iffley Road called the Bridge). There is a longer stay hostel in Headington, Windmill House, and a drug abuse clinic out in Yarnton.

More alert and less obviously damaged than the occupants of the Night Shelter they are nevertheless amazingly tribal and close-knit, ready to close ranks and form a tight circle of resistance to adult opposition or interference. This mistrust is not surprising. Most have been abused in one way or another. Many of them who drift to Oxford come with big ideas of well paid jobs and their own flats, but, with a bedsit costing at least £40 a week in the city, and without benefit as they are not on YTS, they end up being driven back home or on to London or squatting on someone's floor.

The final new element on the street are locals who are simply without a home. Oxford has a worse housing problem than any equivalent London borough. Given the level of house prices it has been calculated that buying a house is out of reach of 65 per cent of the county's working population. Currently the City Council has 4,600 on its housing list and a further 360 in temporary bed and breakfast accommodation, often of a woefully inadequate character. Moreover its statutory responsibilities cease with families: the single homeless are left to shift for themselves. In the Shelter you can see some of them sitting apart from the rest. They are, you discover, ordinary working men who came to Oxford for work but found nowhere to live. They make a point, rather pathetically, of keeping up standards and being cleaner and better organized than the rest. But the barrier is frighteningly flimsy and after a few months the pressure pushes them towards the other occupants, to drink, dissolve into the Shelter culture and let themselves slide under.

Twenty-five years ago there were fifty homeless on Oxford's streets. Now (including those in hostels) there are ten times that number. Those working in the field feel facilities, despite their expansion, are still deeply inadequate. Instead of shelters they would like to see direct-access bedded accommodation, comprehensive psychiatric screening with the possibility of immediate referral to a detoxification centre. Their opponents believe increasing provision simply increases the problem just as more roads create more traffic, and point to the disfigurement of Oxford's streets and squares by vagrants and beggars. To which the carers reply that Oxford has always had a problem and always will. If tackling it draws in more unfortunates, then so be it. Someone has to look after them, they maintain and, if so, why not Oxford?

The face which Oxford turns towards its homeless is, taken in all, a caring one. Indeed the range of philanthropy in Oxford is striking. Behind it lie many factors. One is undoubtedly the liberal academic conscience of the place (not for nothing is Oxford known as the home of lost causes). Then there is the presence of a large number of floaters, people of varied education and experience, well travelled and often equally well connected – and for that reason ideal fundraiser material. There is a growing number of needy causes, not just the homeless. Oxford is a veritable casket of precious but now increasingly tarnished jewels – libraries, activities, institutions and facilities – in urgent need of help for restoration, refurbishment and even day-to-day running costs. It is not only people who find themselves in increasing numbers on Oxford's Penniless Bench. There is a growing band of institutions propped together there, the victims of underfunding and mounting pressures. Prominent among the needy cases are the hospitals.

Oxford has grown into a great medical centre in this century. A flotilla of major hospitals is based here, each with its individual specialties. The flagship is now the John Radcliffe, the general, accident and emergency and teaching hospital, but there is also the Radcliffe Infirmary, the oldest institution, one still seen by many as 'Oxford's hospital' but now devoted to a range of specialties including neurology, eyes and diabetes; the Nuffield Orthopaedic Centre; the Churchill, specializing in, amongst other fields, cancer and the immune system; the Slade, once a centre for treatment of skin diseases but now caring for the mentally handicapped; the two mental hospitals, the Warneford and the Littlemore; and a variety of lesser clinics and facilities. Within its local health authority (itself one of the largest in the country) Oxford is the capital, spending the lion's share of the budget and containing 13 of the 30 major units. Its hospitals are, moreover, inextricably linked, on almost every ward and level, with the teaching and research of the university's medical school.

Just as Oxford's concern for the poor and homeless can be traced back to its medieval almshouses, so Oxford medicine stretches back to twelfth-century hospitals such as St Bartholomew's in Cowley or St John's, on the present site of Magdalen College. Over the centuries the medical centre has zigzagged around the city, eventually ending up on its edges. The first physicians plied their trade in Catte Street; pushed out from there by the growth of All Souls' they shifted across the High Street to a row of apothecaries' shops. Later they switched again, moving, with the opening of the Radcliffe Infirmary in 1770 and a neighbouring charity hospital, to the northwest of the city around Broad and Beaumont streets. Then began the switch to the suburbs. The Warneford opened its doors in 1826, amply providing, with its Headington manor house and landscaped grounds, for the insane gentlefolk; Littlemore, for lunatic paupers, followed in the 1840s. Fever hospitals, convalescent clinics and military hospitals all sprang up in the green fringes and on healthy rises of the city, providing the seeds of later hospitals such as the Nuffield and the Churchill. Meanwhile, a farsighted Radcliffe treasurer, Rev. G. B. Cronshaw, pulled off a major coup in 1919, acquiring cheaply a 75-acre site in Headington, on which in 1979 the first phase of the John Radcliffe opened. Since then it has begun to trickle in a slow cascade of concrete over the rest of the site. One day it will probably take over altogether from the old Infirmary, and the move to the city's circumference will be complete.

Historically, another mark of Oxford medicine has been the golden touch of patrons and benefactors. Monarchs founded the university's first lectureships in medicine, and Oxford doctors became Royal physicians, often amassing spectacular fortunes through their cures and remedies. One was Dr Jonathan Goddard whose celebrated Drops were apparently so efficacious that Charles II paid him £1,500 for the secret; another, John Radcliffe, a blunt Yorkshireman, became doctor to William III and grew rich, not, it is said, from deep medical knowledge but from his bedside conversations. It was from the money that he left the university that the Infirmary was constructed. In this century Lord Nuffield poured his millions from the motor trade into seven professorships and an institute, all bearing his name, and expanded the Infirmary, postponing for a time the need to develop the Headington site acquired by Cronshaw.

Out of all this munificence and the talents of Oxford's doctors and administrators has come a long line of achievements. Most famously, it was here that penicillin was first isolated in quantity and used on patients by Professor Howard Florey in 1941. Sir Hugh Cairns pioneered the treatment of head injuries, stimulated apparently by tending Lawrence of Arabia after his fatal motor-cycle accident, and later given ample scope by the soldier casualties of the Second World War. Earlier, in the nineteenth century, both the Warneford and Littlemore had keen early practitioners of the enlightened and non-coercive treatment of the insane. Today Oxford research has thrown up everything from the use of simple aspirin to prevent blood clots to new treatments for anorexia, alternatives to hysterectomy operations and the identification of inherited disorders from a pinprick of blood. It is at the forefront of the fight against cancer and leukaemia and of that whole dimensional shift to the micro and genetic levels of medicine, away from the relatively crude cutting and patching of surgery to the very roots of disease.

Nor has medical innovation in the city been limited to the purely clinical. Oxford's hospital administrators have always been a bold and bolshy lot, prepared to chance their arms and put their heads above the parapet. Their initial achievement, the Infirmary, was built as a deliberate political gesture, a piece of defiant flag-waving by Jacobite Oxford to the Hanoverian regime. After the First World War, a time when Oxford's hospitals were in dire financial straits, overrunning their budgets by as much as 50 per cent (which puts today's overspends into perspective), Cronshaw refused to be cowed and continued to push facilities forward. One of his innovations was a local contributory scheme of 2p a week to ensure easy, comprehensive health care. In the event the hospitals were saved (again, interestingly, given the current debate about funding) by a mix of public and private support – Nuffield's generosity *and* the city council's taking health care on to the rates.

Yet the development of Oxford medicine and public health has not been an unbroken march of triumph. In fact, as in most things in Oxford, its progress has been interspersed with long periods of inertia. In the nineteenth century reformers such as Dr Acland had to battle against the apathy of the city authorities to improve basic sanitary conditions and counter the periodic outbreaks of cholera, and it was not until the 1880s that the city had anything like a decent water supply. There have been other periods of stasis and stagnation nearer our own time. After the local hospitals were absorbed as the United Oxford Hospitals into the National Health Service in 1947, they were starved of adequate funds, stunting the university's nascent medical school and delaying for decades the development of the present John Radcliffe site.

Today Oxford's hospitals present a confused picture, a kaleidoscope, jumbled and intensified, of all its earlier characteristics – innovation and energy, stagnation and demoralization, public poverty and private generosity. High tech advances press on apace – as do demands on the system – both threatening to outstrip funds and gulp up the budgets for less glamorous, long-term community health programmes. The local health authority is fighting hard to balance the budget. In desperation hospitals are turning to new ways of income generation or, as in the past, to private benefactors and charities such as the Radcliffe Medical Foundation, set up to fund otherwise unaffordable medical projects in the city. Over everything loom uncertainties in national policy, such as plans for enabling hospitals to contract for services or even opt out.

A look at the John Radcliffe points up the problems. The JR is widely considered an efficient but chilly machine for medicine, huge, complex, impersonal and apparently not much liked by the staff, many of whom hark nostalgically back to the cramped county hospital feel of the old Infirmary. Externally it seems oddly topsy-turvy, with its entrance at one end and car parks at the other. Like a major airport in all its comprehensive variety, it contains shops and restaurants, an industrial block and art studio, sports facilities, a bank, a hairdresser, several social workers and, underneath, a miniature road system. Internally it also has something of the atmosphere of an international airport, its broad corridors dotted with padded seats like those in departure lounges and that same sense of distant bustle and repressed anxiety.

Down on the lower levels are the blood and guts – the hospital's ten operating theatres. Here all is bright, ticking intensity under the scrutiny of cameras; many of the twenty or so daily operations are filmed for research purposes. Cloth-bound surgical instrument packs ('the big ones to get you in, the others for detail', the orderlies bluffly tell you), are sent in sharp and shiny, emerging bloodied in canisters to be dunked, shaken ultrasonically and steam-sterilized before being flung back once more into the fray. But this is the grim old sawbones side of the hospital. Elsewhere its new high tech face gleams down – the giant body scanner into which patients are fed as if into the drum of a huge washing machine, or the new Institute of Molecular Medicine, a kind of hotel for research in whose suites specialist teams plumb the cellular levels of disease.

Medically, almost everything seems represented here, from the sprains and smashes of accident and emergency to the haggard recovering suicides on the Barnes ward, from the comfy contiguity of Maternity's mother-and-child cubicles to the bright, sad colours of the children's wards. The JR is in fact three hospitals – maternity, general and cardiac – and will in the course of time become more. It has virology and haematology, it has histopathology and cytology and a mystification of other -ologies. It houses ten university departments, a suite of lecture halls and the prestigious Cairns Medical Library. It even has a Bereavement Officer, a warm-hearted lady in a cosy bower of cushions who counsels up to thirty grieving relatives a week.

Its statistics are staggering. Every day, if you include students and outpatients, some 3,000 will go to work there and 8,000–9,000 be treated. In the course of a year it will patch up 54,000 accident victims and deliver 6,000 babies. Each week its seven kitchens dish up 190 lbs of frozen peas, 42 kilos of dry jelly crystals, 313 lbs of potatoes and 294 lbs of Smash. Through its pipes stream 26,000 gallons of water every twenty minutes. It holds thousands of sheets and blankets and literally millions of medical records (mostly microfilmed and tended round the clock by 236 staff). 'If this is a hotel,' commented the hospital's Head of Hotel Services, 'it is one hell of a hotel.' Staggering too are its costs: currently it gets through over £35 million a year, nearly a quarter of the local area health authority budget. And here we come to the nub of the problem. The JR is chronically short of cash. In spite of the most careful trimming and balancing the hospital's spending has invariably surpassed its income in recent years.

The John Radcliffe is moreover an institution in the grip of culture change – and no one is quite sure whether this is part of its problem or the first glimmerings of a solution. Once the emphasis was on the quiet pursuit of consensus management. You got everyone round a table and tried to please them all. But in the middle of the 1980s a new breed of hospital general manager was drafted in to take a grip on the diffuse administrative miasma, a lot of whom came from business or the army. Typical of the type is the JR's General Manager, Tony Stapleton, recruited from the retail trade. His early days (recorded with grim hilarity in a TV documentary) were a baptism of fire, with one union striking over private patients on the wards. Since then, though, the unions have become almost somnolently passive and he has had a chance to make his mark.

Around him he has gathered a team of smart young middle managers. They have that corporate look – a combination of crisp shirts and ties with a firm-jawed determination to take those hard decisions, of personal ambition jockeying with keenness to act the part of company team player. Their talk is of corporate strategies, resource management, linkage. Stapleton, a prodigiously hard worker who puts in a twelve-hour day plus time at weekends, is quietly satisfied with achievement to date: the successful privatization of areas like cleaning, progress on staff appraisal and the prospect of substantial funds for computerization which would not only cover clinical data but provide financial information essential to management. Some see this as a step towards opting out and eventual privatization – a proposal which Stapleton does not dismiss, even though the hospital is so tightly woven into the teaching and research facilities which it shares with the university.

Stapleton is elsewhere mounting a three-pronged attack. The first prong is directed at the doctors. It would be a mistake to see the rise of the general manager as an attempt to wrest power from the old culture's gods, the doctors. On the contrary, he is trying to thrust it more and more their way, perhaps on the somewhat Machiavellian principle of curbing the doctors' demands through loading them with responsibility. Doctors always want the best and they want it now. Under the new system of 'clinical management' they will be organized into 'firms' and made responsible for their own budgets, resources and patient take-ons. Secondly, Stapleton devotes much effort to trying to wheedle more out of the local health authority, putting together complex bids – lateral moves in what he himself describes as 'a game of three-dimensional chess'.

The trouble is the funds are just not there: the effort is rather like entreating a dry tap to yield up a fresh trickle. So Stapleton's third strategy – and a suitable one, given his commercial background – is to turn entrepreneur and fundraiser. In addition to going hell-for-leather for more private patients, a variety of other schemes are being discussed, such as putting in an arcade of shops or renting out roof space for aerials. It is 'JR plc', and perhaps fittingly the hospital has adopted for the first time a logo – a coat-of-arms commemorating John Radcliffe, the famous old Oxford doctor and skilled accumulator of fees.

Meanwhile the battle with beds and waiting lists goes on. Each day Admissions performs a frantic juggling act as the staff try to balance bedspace with the press of demands, squeezing a few more in here, postponing the waiting list there and haggling on the 'phone like commodity brokers in an attempt to persuade other hospitals to shoulder the overload. In 1989, for the first time since the hospital opened, it was forced to abandon its open-door policy. Cover has been down on most wards because the hospital is suffering a shortage of nurses, not surprisingly given the pay on offer and the full local job market. Indeed it has been forced to mount 'headhunting' expeditions to Scotland and the north east to try to recruit more staff. Everywhere you turn in the hospital you find amongst the nurses tight-lipped exhaustion, sagging morale and talk of a possible explosion of discontent. It is a grim picture, and people in the city shake their heads, look back at the old Radcliffe and wonder what has become of 'their' hospital.

Oxford's benevolence, however, has never been totally absorbed by its own problems. While it is directed down to the needy on its own streets and channelled invigoratingly into its hospitals, it is – through organizations like Oxfam – dispensed to the broader world.

Oxfam often feels its stature slighted within the city: Oxfam staff in their darker moments feel they are taken for granted here and are also aware of co-existing uncomfortably with the cultivated and cloistered cynicism of the university. Cramped into a coven of corridors and offices in Summertown, the giant grumbles, especially since a deal to buy land and build new headquarters on the other side of North Oxford fell through. There are periodic demands amongst the staff to pull out to some low rent location on a trading estate or by a motorway. But it will probably stay put. For its feet are firmly planted here: constitutionally a number of its trustees must come from the city, and it gains also much Oxford sustenance – from the experts in the university and from its vast local army of volunteers, be they women dusting the flour of family commitments from their hands, retired colonial administrators straitened in their North Oxford niches or the large band of international radicals in East Oxford.

Indeed Oxfam sprang from a marriage of two very Oxford elements – the Fabian liberalism of the university and the Christian, and specifically Quaker, conscience of the local churches. Significantly, two of its early leading lights were Gilbert Murray, the Oxford Professor of Greek, and Canon Milford of the University Church. After a preliminary gathering in the Friends' Meeting House in St Giles, the first formal meeting of the Oxford Committee for Famine Relief (as it was then known) was held in 1942 in the Old Library of the University Church, its minutes being duly recorded in an old exercise book – a relic still preserved with wry reverence by Oxfam staff today. The intention was to help the starving in war-blockaded Greece, and it raised some £3,200, all of which was donated to the Greek Red Cross.

Interestingly, given the recent disagreements surrounding its non-political stance, it was born amid such dispute. A subsidiary intention of the Committee was to campaign for the lifting of the naval blockade in Greece – a controversial aim in those wartime days and one which it failed to achieve.

Now Oxfam is a giant amongst charities but at the time it was only one of a number of famine relief committees. (There was, for instance, a Hudfam). When the war ended, the Committee might well have been wound up, but refugees proliferated throughout the world – between the ruined cities of Europe and in divided Palestine – and it was decided to press on with the good work. In 1948 its first shop opened in Broad Street, and its success set a pattern for the future. These were known as 'the clothing years' when the Committee concentrated on sending second-hand clothes overseas. One can see in all this a reflection of North Oxford frugality, of the dons' wives with their large families carefully turning collars and sharing out the hand-me-downs amongst their children.

After 1960, when for the first time cash raised equalled clothing in value, there came a change of direction and identity. The organization moved its headquarters and transformed itself into a major development agency under the new name of Oxfam. These were the idealistic years when Oxfam groups and shops multiplied throughout the land. In the 1970s came worries over inflation, a period of consolidation and increasing deployment of technology and expertise. In recent years causes such as Kampuchea and the Ethiopian famine have stirred consciences ever harder and propelled Oxfam even more into the public eye.

It is now the biggest voluntary aid agency in the world with thirty-five overseas offices. Part of its work – the part that grabs the publicity – is disaster relief. Its 100,000 square foot warehouse at Bicester is on a 24-hour seven-day alert, stocked with emergency kits able to do everything from feeding 250 people to vaccinating 5,000. There are ready-made shelters, high-energy biscuits (of necessity the most fattening biscuits in the world), water purification kits, mountains of blankets and – I noted, in a corner – 750 fake Lacoste tracksuits, made in Taiwan, confiscated by British customs and now on their way to Zaire.

But disaster relief is only part of its work. Its main job is in long-term development projects, over 2,500 of them, ranging from building up grain banks in Burkino Faso to setting up literacy classes in Bangladesh. Behind these there is always a distinctive Oxfam philosophy – never impose from above but work from the grassroots up, supporting and encouraging local initiatives. There is an old Oxfam adage which nicely encapsulates this ethos: 'Give a man a fish and you feed him for a day; teach him to fish and you feed him for life.'

In the course of its existence Oxfam has raised over £354 million, over £67 million in 1989 alone. On average, 80 per cent goes on aid, 5 per cent on education and campaigning, and the rest on fundraising, administration and shop development. An enormous chunk of its income comes from its 830 shops, distribution to which is also handled from the warehouse in a slick automated operation overseen, along with Oxfam's mail-order business, by an ex-Habitat manager. The shops are essentially the scaffolding around which Oxfam's national structure is organized. There are six to eight of them in each Oxfam district. Four districts make up an Oxfam area, twenty areas one of the two regions into which the country is split, the whole organization employing 1300 staff and drawing in 75,000 volunteers. At the centre is the Summertown head-quarters, itself with some 500 staff, and on top of the whole structure sit the 50 trustees, a body not unlike an Oxford college, self-electing and self-perpetuating and – like a full college governing body – meeting three times a year.

Is there an Oxfam institutional culture? It has a definite image, that of bright, articulate, ideologically pure people, vegetarian, feminist, naturally inclining towards Greenpeace and Friends of the Earth, bloody-minded but deeply committed, the assertive end, if you like, of the Herbivore Tendency. While there is some truth in these labels the Oxfam culture runs deeper and is, in any case, now moving in new and different directions. Much of Oxfam's ethos can be traced back to its Quaker roots. There is, for instance, an emphasis, almost an insistence, on speaking out, testifying and bearing witness. This can lead to a disease identified by one Oxfam worker as 'meetingitis' (although it does not seem to prevent it responding swiftly to emergencies). Oxfam committee meetings can drag on and on. Going to a vote is considered a cop-out and the secretaries taking the minutes are said to be adept at listening for the inaudible click when consensus occurs. Other discernible Quaker elements include a determination to work in whatever way and in whatever situation for the common good; a deep-seated opposition to war and the armaments trade and a canny Quaker businessman's stewardship of others' funds. Above all there is a puritan frugality of style, shot through with a cold silvery humour – a smiling but faintly chill air of holding the moral high ground.

These are the traditional ingredients in the Oxfam mix but it has now become a much broader church. The place fairly judders with varying energies and visions, and is informal to the point of stroppiness. An Oxfam staffer will think nothing of sharply contradicting his (or more likely, her) boss in a meeting if need be. The issues are felt to be simply too big for run-of-the-mill hierarchical yes-manship (or yes-womanship). It is probably the most varied employer in Oxford. There are all sorts on the staff – engineers, lawyers, politicians, journalists. There are also lots of women – 67 per cent of the personnel, thus earning the organization the nickname 'Oxfem' amongst certain of its members. However the women will point out with due Oxfam stroppiness that only 37 per cent of top management posts are held by them. Then there are the volunteers, who range from humble packers to translators and agrarian experts. The volunteers who run the shops are different again. They are often known as the 'Three Ms' – middle-aged, middle-class and middle-of-the-road. There are sporadic attempts to involve them in the ideology side, the campaigns and so on, but the Cardigan and Tweed Skirt Brigade just shrugs them off and gets on with what it is really good at – selling bric-a-brac and making Oxfam lots of money.

Oxfam has always been a people sort of place 'a bridge of people' as one writer called it. Now, however, it has reached a size where things have had to become relatively more structured and formal. Old hands say that the vitality still springs but ... something indefinable has been lost. There is a trend towards experts, technocrats and efficiency. What is more, within the broad church are now detectable certain sects and schisms. One divide is between what might be called efficiency experts and the organizational idealists. The former want Oxfam to be a super-efficient corporate conduit of expertise and resources, with all else subordinated to that end. The latter look to the organization to exemplify and embody its ideals in its own structures and press for such things as the representative employment of minorities, codes of working practice and lifts for the disabled.

Also ranked against one another are those who might be called the diffusionists and the centralists (who often overlap with the efficiency experts): those who aim for greater autonomy, not only in the field but also amongst the fundraising branches, and those who favour continuing control from Summertown. You can run up against surprising anger towards headquarters amongst the grassroots. Perhaps this is in a way not surprising. Oxfam after all is an organization about anger – anger at hunger, poverty and all the violent disparities in the world. Containing it is a particular problem for those returning from the field. They come back from helping people survive on the edge, out of the barest rim of existence, to the caring comfort of North Oxford. 'You have to be able', said one worker, 'to live in two worlds, decide on an acceptable minimum lifestyle and stick to it.' Usually the anger is carefully suppressed, channelled and pressed into service. Sometimes, though, it festers and gets deflected on to the staff at headquarters.

Recently two other divergences have opened up, different but, in a curious roundabout way, related. In the past Oxfam's fundraising was, if never sedate, always highminded and pedagogic. There was something called the doctrine of the Educated Pound: you taught as you took. There was a kind of moral symmetry about it all: the ends and the means were in balance, the fieldwork and the fundraising a harmonious whole. Money was raised through covenants (a modern equivalent, some thought, of the old Quaker tithes) or the honest eighteenth-century commerce of the shops. Now in some of the Summertown offices you can meet harder, glibber men who bow down before bigness and have no compunction in harnessing Mammon to the Oxfam cart. They look lovingly upon telethons and pop spectaculars like Geldof's Live Aid, talk excitedly of the 89,200 red noses sold in Oxford alone during Comic Relief Week and of dropping the 'd' from 'fundraising'. One even breathed the heresy that 'the fundraiser is more important than the fieldworker. He is the one who makes it all possible.' Horror!

Mammon loose in the Meeting House, vulgar materialism rampant in the moral club!

The second divergence is over politics. Oxfam has been traditionally – and, as a charity, necessarily – apolitical. But in recent years it has taken an increasingly partisan position. The organization's primary aim is 'to relieve poverty, distress and suffering' with the subsidiary goal of educating the public 'concerning the nature, causes and effects thereof ...'. Through this small back door a host of troubles has swarmed. The politicization started unexceptionably enough in the early 1980s with the attempt to rally opinion over Kampuchea. It continued through the Hungry for Change campaign whereby members were urged to lobby MPs and bring about a switch in government policies over the Third World. It gathered momentum with Oxfam's support for the Sandinistas and culminated in an ill-judged attempt to influence government policy on South African sanctions. The organization looked set to become half-charity, half-political pressure group. At which point the Charity Commissioners stepped in and issued a stiff little reprimand to Oxfam for exceeding its brief.

Oxfam's creeping politicization illustrates the rise in the organization of a more militant spirit at the expense of the old Quakerish reticence. It may also reflect the impact of the present director, Frank Judd, an ex-Labour politician, who has set up a new office with the title of Public Affairs and Communications Services, to coordinate Oxfam's public campaigning. But the shift also reflects something larger, something *out there* to which Oxfam is simply responding – a change in the moral climate. Everything in the 1980s became more hard-edged and sharply defined. Institutions had to huckster their wares ever more stridently in the marketplace, fight harder to defend their new positions and adopt a more prominent profile. Certainly as far as Oxfam is concerned the point seems to have been reached where the Red-Nosed and the Politically Hard-Nosed tendencies come together.

In recent years Oxford has become a fundraising Mecca, the begging bowl capital of Britain. There is Oxfam and the Radcliffe Medical Foundation; there is the Playhouse Trust to get that theatre going again and Music At Oxford, raising about a quarter of a million pounds annually in local business sponsorships. Other organizations include Summertown's 'Young Enterprise', aiming to foster business acumen and commercial links in schools, Southern Artlink on Walton Street, complete for a time with an executive seconded from Marks & Spencer, and, out in Witney, the wonderfully named 'Chapter One – Ketchum Capital', targeting organizations in trouble due to withdrawal of public funding. Dwarfing all is the university's £220 million Campaign for Oxford and its associated appeal on behalf of the Bodleian Library. The poly has also jumped on to the sponsorship bandwagon, acquiring funds for an Asda Business School Professor and a Chair in Estate Management backed by Chestertons.

Now there are more and more institutions huddling on Oxford's Penniless Bench. They have come to resemble each other more closely as they have been nipped and pinched by the keen commercial culture of the last decade. As responsibilities have slithered from the state, public and private agencies such as the hospitals and the hostels for the homeless are shouldering greater burdens and facing new tests of identity. In their pursuit of resources – as with the JR and Oxfam – all are becoming more vociferous and more entrepreneurial in approach. The begging bowl held out at the start of the 1990s is bigger than ever before and held out with greater urgency. Taken together, Oxford's charities and public sector institutions and the demands which they are scrambling to meet, present a collective portrait of benevolence *à la mode*.

– 5 –

Education PLC

The business of education is, when you consider it, Oxford's biggest industry after the hospitals and the car factory. Jot down all those people teaching in the university and its thirty-five colleges; include all the supernumeraries and auxiliaries, the librarians and lab technicians, the administrators and the porters; add in the polytechnic and the College of Further Education; the crammers and correspondence colleges; the language schools, the mayfly swarm of summer schools, the secretarial colleges, the outsiders and sidlers-in – and not forgetting the schools, from primary to upper – and you will probably be left with a figure not far short of 10,000. There is extreme diversity of institution. Some seem inextricably interwoven with the life of the city, others simply stuck on. But one thing they share: they are either succeeding or surviving in a much-changed environment, beneficiaries or victims of the '80s enterprise culture. Their common concern therefore is cash.

Let us begin with the schools, in particular those of North Oxford, an especially rich pond of educational endeavour. There is Frideswide's Middle School, there is the Crescent, there is Greycotes, Wychwood and 'Phil and Jim' (St Philip and St James). There are schools which have national reputations like the Dragon, famously and scruffily successful, or the High School for Girls, a formidable Oxbridge forcing house. There are schools which are part of the warp and woof of the suburb, others, like Summer Fields – an Etonian feeding factory, with a distinguished roll of alumni, including Harold Macmillan – which serve a few select areas of Belgravia ('Very Pimm's-on-the-lawn', according to one member of staff). There is tremendous individuality: each has a social micro-climate of its own. But, cutting across all this variety, is the big, big divide between what educationalists term the 'maintained' and 'non-maintained' sectors, state and private. So, picking a pair from either sector, let us zoom in and, as examiners say, compare and contrast.

With its small Gothic spire and tidy squares St Edward's (or 'Teddies' as it is affectionately known) rather resembles Keble College – a model village version, thoughtfully laid out for the convenience of visitors near the top of Woodstock Road. The resemblance is not accidental: both Keble and St Edward's sprang from the High Church Oxford Movement of the last century. Teddies started life under a cloud – of incense. When it opened, the *Oxford Chronicle* warned prospective parents of the 'proclivities' (religious ones, that is) of the teachers 'who at the recent laying of the Foundation Stone simply plagiarized Rome'. Late in the century, as the ritualist glow diminished, the school seemed set for a slow fade into nonentity. What saved it was patriotism plus good housekeeping, a well-beaten mix of Lord Kitchener and Mrs Beeton. In the Boer War a Rifle Corps was founded, and old boys' derring-do on the veldt lovingly chronicled in the school magazine. Later still, as the school's massive memorial plaque records, they fed themselves in satisfactorily large numbers to the machine guns of the Western Front. Gore and glory duly matched, the school was thereafter set on a sound financial and material footing by one Kendall, a headmaster remembered in the school on account of his constructional zeal as 'the Master Builder'.

Traditionally Teddies' image is one of friendly, boisterous heartiness. Geography could have had a hand in this. Its sports fields, a positive prairie of pitches, occupy an area almost as large as the rest of North Oxford put together. There is even a full-sized golf course on its grassy steppes. 'It's out there somewhere', sniffed a disgruntled groundsman, when questioned, waving an arm airily at the far horizon. Being a groundsman at Teddies must be a dispiritingly ceaseless occupation – rather like being a painter on the Forth Bridge.

At any rate, be it due to the plethora of pitches or for some other reason, all boys at Teddies play sport each afternoon until they reach the Sixth Form. Afterwards you can see them in the hall, red-cheeked and relaxed, tearing into mighty chunks of bread and chocolate. Likewise in the staff common-room the masters, men of mighty frame, similarly red-cheeked and relaxed, effortlessly brush one another aside in their keenness to get at the tuck and just as eagerly cold-shoulder the visiting outsider. In the big afternoon sports push at Teddies it is all hands to the ball.

If the sports field has so far defined St Edward's so does the sports jacket. Everywhere you turn is a sea of tweedy flocculence – chunky, classically well-cut, with huge buttons glowing like lacquered conkers and always for some reason several sizes too big. These sports jackets are not mere garments but a species of stout woollen body armour, a carapace for the callow. And you can understand the need for self-protection. Teddies has not been, perhaps, a school for the sensitive or the solitary. Kenneth Grahame survived there by rowing and by kindling within himself a vision of a private childhood world which later found expression in *The Wind in the Willows*. So, by a kind of roundabout passing movement, at least one work of literature has been a product of Teddies.

But this is unfair. This picture does not do credit to the present. The library at Teddies may once have been only a place you clattered through on your way to the sports field but no longer. Under the new head, Mr David Christie, a Gorbachev-style reformer, something like educational *perestroika* is under way. Once its arch-rival, Magdalen College School, was the place where the dons sent their clever, cocky sons: Teddies got the thicks, the outsiders and the non-Oxfordians. But that is less true today. Christie, in a spirit of *glasnost*, explains that he wishes to earn 'due credit in the mind of North Oxford for what St Edward's actually does'. Now the emphasis is not only on academic performance, (it gets fine results) but more on a spectrum of achievement and provision of a broad palette of extra-curricular opportunities, from archaeology to role-playing. Such wide-ranging pursuits mean the boys (and staff) are caught up in a scrum of activity from seven in the morning to nine at night. Like a factory with a bursting order book, Teddies hums and thrums at all hours, turning out well-rounded products. One hears stories of Teddies boys caught misbehaving in the town. How do they find the time, you wonder.

Perhaps like the POWs in the German Stalag they tunnel out from underneath their vaulting horses during the afternoon exercise sessions.

Cherwell Upper School is only about a mile away on the other side of North Oxford but might as well be in a different universe. There you are plunged into a world that looks, sounds and even smells and feels entirely different. By comparison it is ... well ... so down-to-earth, so *ordinary* and so much of a piece with modern society. If Teddies is sports jacket, Cherwell is denim and velcro fastenings. These are kids who look as if they could have come in from the nearest Tesco. And, the school being co-educational, there are more girls around. (Teddies has them at present only in the Sixth Form.) In the common-room the teachers sprawl, reassuringly standard-size issue, the elbow-patched and rather frayed figures one recalls from one's own schooldays.

To describe them one gropes for the appropriate bouquet of adjectives – energetic, exhausted, heroically dedicated. Over the digestives and chipped beakers, all is frantic pedagogic networking. There is no smooth collegiate taboo on shop talk here. Everyone, it is clear, is busy liaising with everyone else, all the time, at all levels and in all directions. The compulsive communicators converse via a kind of private intercom system, *acronym-speak*, one of the fractured, mutated dialects increasingly practised within professions. Are you coming to the ROA (Records of Achievement) meeting tonight? No, I've got an HOD (Heads of Department) or an HOY (Heads of Year) or a mysterious something called a PCE. Well then, semaphores back the first speaker, let me have your SSSs (Student Summary Statements, that is, not of course, the Self Study Skills packages). As you drain the last of your Maxwell House, you begin to feel you have swallowed an overdose of alphabet soup.

'They mix up everybody in everything here', was one pupil's analysis of why he loved the school. Certainly, if athletics remains a slightly dislodged deity at Teddies, the genius of Cherwell is *involvement*. All is activity and participation amid the relentless quest for relevance. Everything is knitted together, tied into outside life and rooted in the community. In the classroom gone is the old formal discipline and the old chalk and talk, the imposing teacher, the silent, obedient taught and the respectful gulf between. Instead the teachers seem, if they can, to contain their classes like a bubbling flux within the flask of their own personalities or that of their teaching methods and materials. No wonder they look so exhausted afterwards in the staffroom.

The two schools are as different as chalk and cheese. What informs it and encodes it is, of course, the great British unmentionable – class. How nervously people edge and fidget their way round it. This reticence came across at a Saturday morning open day for prospective parents at St Edward's. It was a marvellously middle-class occasion, something between a christening and a product launch, wreathed in flowered hats and shy, uncertain smiles. Groups of lost adults shuffled round, shepherded by grinning, sharp-suited boys. The parents, if tackled during the visit about why they wanted to send their children here as opposed to a state school, became evasive. Voices lowered, eyes swivelled for the nearest exit, and messages were stuttered out in code ('It turns out the kind of boy parents are looking for'). You had run up against the Twitch Factor, the Middle Class Cringe Syndrome. There is a bridge over the canal on the far side of St Edward's that somehow symbolizes the exclusivity of it all. Tread on it from the Teddies side and it lets down smoothly, permitting you easy access to the canal footpath and the broader world; but then, as you step off it, it lifts sharply back, neatly barring passage to the outsider.

These divisions are all the more ironic because Cherwell itself is now substantially a middle-class school. This is no depressed, under-achieving inner city sump. Its catchment area takes in council estates such as Cutteslow and New Marston but it also includes the solid villas of Summertown and North Oxford. Going comprehensive has, at Cherwell, originally a secondary modern, been a great success story, unlike some local grammars which initially dipped under the impact of egalitarian education. Under the tutelage of a wise old head and his successors, Cherwell got in good teachers and has steadily improved its performance. Now it has the best results in the county and an enviable Oxbridge entry record, and is, by consequence, greatly sought after by the middle-class parent.

An awful lot of dons now send their children there, contributing no doubt to the pupils' characteristic articulacy and assertiveness. ('I am afraid the mathematics are pretty basic,' I overheard one don child flouncing, as she dropped off a model for distributing surpluses to the Third World). Such parents can be divided into two categories: first there are the conviction comprehensiveers, some of whom could afford to go private but whose consciences choose public; then there are those who would like but cannot afford to go private and cut their convictions accordingly. There is also a third class who soldier on with the struggle to educate their children privately until the Sixth Form and then, judging it relatively safe at that point to commit them to the blackboard rough-and-tumble of the state system, transfer them.

Cherwell's rise is all the more remarkable given its relative poverty – or, in education-speak – 'under-resourcing'. The contrast between the two schools is again illuminating. For what the county spends annually per child at Cherwell, the child could be sent as a day boy for a single term to St Edward's. Cash and class – the twin faces of the same coin! Step into Teddies and you soon realize someone has been there before you, polishing and preparing and opening up doors – Money. Money has trimmed the lawns to perfection, has built a superb new Art and Technology block, hires companies of actors at the drop of a hat to organize workshops on set plays. Money is up to all sorts of tricks at Teddies. Round at Cherwell Money makes himself scarcer. Everything has that run-down, uncared-for air now generally associated with any public or civic facility in this country. Work on the main building, a hideous concrete box, halted when the 1974 oil crisis hit us. Now a shanty town of temporary huts and prefabs round the back houses its swelling numbers. And this not in some urban wasteland but in the heart of the richest suburb of one of the richest cities in Britain.

Yet for all their disparities, change is pressing in on both schools from outside, prodding them paradoxically in roughly similar directions. The biggest changes have been educational ones. Continuous curricular revolution might be a fair description of Cherwell in recent years as it has striven to absorb one innovation after another – one year the GCSE, the next the new National Curriculum. Perhaps this underlies the acronym-speak practised by the teachers – they are too pressed to do anything except fire abbreviations at one another. Now Cherwell is faced with the prospect of opting out, of earning part of its income from the number of pupils it can dredge from the demographically shrinking pool of teenagers or the services it offers back to the county. The Head might go along with it if he got a new school building out of it. Cherwell too is being edged and nudged towards the independent commercial model, towards marketing itself like the private schools.

The enterprise school! The prospect is made real in yet another construction on the grounds of Teddies – the Douglas Bader Sports Centre (named after the famous old boy). There, Money, smart entrepreneurial elf that he is, having put up the facility, is hiring it part-time to outside groups in order to raise ... still more money. There, where lurex-leotarded housewives twist their torsos to the tunes of Kylie and her clones, you can meet a new breed of keen young fitness specialists. They dismiss the old ideas of character-through-sport and talk instead of aerobic capacities and shaping life fitness programmes. What a sea of incomprehension they must meet from the old common-room sports jackets. Out with the old empire-building, White-Man's-Burden-shouldering virtues, in with the sauna and the solarium. The supermarket and the special offer has come to the schoolroom. One Cherwell governor recently predicted local schools might end up offering prospective parents discounts on shower units as one school in Nuneaton had done. Roll up, roll up, grab your vouchers. We are all, it seems, going private now.

Education is indeed an Oxford boom industry. In many of its educational establishments the hard glint of the profit motive out-dazzles all else. Throughput is all, and the whole process is about as ceremonious as a battery farm, or a factory in which a set level of beans has to be squirted into endless rows of empty cans. One independent tutorial college recently boasted of being able to take a pupil from nought to A level in thirty-one days flat. In others there is a decent overlay of pedagogic principle or style. In none is this overlay thicker than at the crammer, Edward Greene's Tutorial Establishment.

Although Greene's has only been in existence for a little over twenty years, it positively creaks with history, traditions and olde-worlde atmosphere. Pass its portals in Pembroke Street and you are swept back to an earlier, nay Dickensian age. It is the snuggest of academic snuggeries, a warren of wood panels, corridors and carefully preserved pokinesses. At every turn is the blaze of real

fires, the artful disarray of pipe racks and cedar spills, of copies of
The Field and *Country Life*, and dogs – old English sheepdogs
everywhere, an impenetrable layer of them draping all available
surfaces, in brass, plaster, wood and even real, foot-impeding flesh
and bone. You expect to see Mr Pickwick himself come bouncing
in, jovially twinkling round the nearest corner. Instead round
bounds Mr Greene, himself a somewhat Pickwickian figure, pink-
faced and portly, in three-piece pinstripe and a gold chain so thick
it looks as if it could draw an anchor let alone a hunter. There is
something about him redolent of casks of Madeira, antique snuff
boxes, rinded rounds of Stilton and thick smoked hams that hang
heavy from the rafter.

Beaming with affable precision, he introduces his staff and
explains the mysteries of their nomenclature: there is the Preceptor,
the usher who works at an upright desk timetabling examinations
(a task that would tax the station master of a major terminus, such
is the depth and complexity of their entry); then there is the Bursar
who keeps a kind of roving eye on things; a chauffeur, who bears
an uncanny resemblance to Bob Geldof, steers the establishment's
huge box of a Bentley around town; and then there is Reg, a handy
little man who fixes up all manner of useful locks and contraptions.
It is all wonderfully chummy and cosy.

Everything at Greene's radiates affectionate attention to detail,
not least *The Brochure*, a bibliographical labour of love that would
not look out of place on the shelves of an antiquarian book dealer.
Its covers are so luxuriously stout that it looks as if they could
deflect an armour-piercing shell with ease and so dense in typo-
graphical ornament that the text undulates before the eye like a
prancing pony. Mr Greene has been at some pains to get this right.
When OUP could no longer do his letterpress as required he turned
to a printer in his native Scotland. But the cover is handmade in
Sweden, the engraving added in Norfolk, and, last of all, it is
stitched together on an antique device especially imported by Mr
Greene for that sole purpose.

If all this gives an impression of Greene's as an unserious institution, it would be a false one. It attracts some 350 pupils a year,
mostly boys, mostly from private schools and mostly doing A-level
resits or getting in some extra cramming in their hols. Its formula
of intensive individual tuition really works. A third of its A-level

entrants get As or Bs. While one traditional staple, the Oxford scholarship exam entrant, has declined, it continues to pull in another staple – the oddball or dropout who finds it hard to adjust to the restrictions of ordinary schooling. Moreover, like all crammers, it is getting more students who see it as a kind of alternative Sixth Form college. Pupils, however, are not taught on the Pembroke Street premises; they migrate to wherever their individual coaches live and teach, be it a finely furnished study or a threadbare garret. Most are in digs, often in the terraces of Rose Hill or East Oxford (or Cowley St John, as Mr Greene prefers to call it). But their welfare is by no means neglected. A pig-roast welcomes them, followed by a schedule of boat trips, complete with bands, and fortnightly teas in the ornate setting of the Shake-spearean Painted Rooms in Cornmarket, presided over by the school Dame, Mrs Smedley.

Greene's is the Rolls-Royce of Oxford crammers. It used to be said that the loudest thing in a Rolls was its clock. The loudest thing in Greene's is a pen nib scraping zeros on a cheque stub. It charges serious money: if you took three A levels for a year and had five hours of tuition a week it would cost nearly £13,000. For there is money to be had by stuffing learning into empty adolescent heads and the growth of the crammers in Oxford in recent years goes to prove it. Greene's was the first but there are now about a dozen, including d'Overbroeck's, Brown and Brown's, Cherwell, St Aldates and Wolsey Hall, many of them started by ex-Greene's employees. When it comes to crammers Oxford is cramming them in but Greene's, by virtue of its high standards and its highly wrought, almost rococo style, still stands head and shoulders above the rest of the usher pack.

Similarly, amongst the language schools and independent colleges there is another institution that lifts itself above the purely commercial level – St Clare's College. If Edward Greene's is a Rolls, St Clare's is a high-class European model, not a vulgar Italian sports job, but something solid and well made, say a Saab or a Volvo. Yet strangely it has always suffered from an image problem, having been branded as a kind of superior European finishing school that had for some reason swapped its Swiss chalets for the Gothic gables of North Oxford. In fact St Clare's is deeply drenched with idealism. It was started from a bedroom in 1953 by two women friends, one of whom was wheelchair-bound. Pan-Europeanism and reconciliation were in the air. Continentals were to be brought to Oxford, have English drilled into their heads and get introduced to members of the university.

Essentially it was a language school but with a moral annexe. Now in addition to English classes, it offers liberal arts semesters to American and other foreign students. But the jewel in its crown is its International Baccalaureate programme, a pre-university course similar to A levels but far more wide ranging, involving the study of both sciences and arts and insisting on proficiency in foreign languages. It is aimed, says the Principal, at 'whole person education'. In fact, the air of postwar Euro-idealism still clings about the place, something strict and clean and earnest, smacking of Swiss or Scandinavian sanatoria, or sunlight and psychoanalysis health regimes. Rising from the ruins we shall rebuild the damaged old Euro-patient and cure him of his complexes with citizenship classes and large doses of *Welt Kultur*! Its ethos ('freedom with responsibility') recalls that of Kurt Hahn, the founder of Gordonstoun, but without his emphasis on morality-through-fitness. All students are expected strictly to observe its regulations regarding staying out late (the worst thing at St Clare's is to tell a lie) and to do something called CASS (Creative, Aesthetic or Social Service). St Clare's teaching is excellent and its Eurovision utterly admirable and impressive, if a touch tinged with tweeness.

Image problems – those of the international jet set – have also dogged its students. They have been called unfairly the Eurobrats of the Banbury Road. The Principal prefers to refer to them as 'the children of the internationally mobile'. Certainly this is no Order of Poor Clares. Hang out in their favourite venue, the Dewdrop in Summertown, and it is the teeth that strike you, that perfection of expensive orthodontics framed in those open European smiles. There is something deeply rich and glossy about them as if they had been lapped all their lives in social fabric conditioner. But these are not tanned and vacant airheads, the *jeunesse dorée* of Gstaad or St Tropez. They would be more at home in Brussels, Bonn or Geneva. They are the children of the new Eurocracy, the sons and daughters of diplomats, politicians, academics and the employees of internationals. The opinions they offer in the conversation classes at St Clare's would not shame the leader columns of *Le Monde*.

In all, St Clare's rather resembles one of those solid old-fashioned publishing companies whose backlist and money spinners support its prestigious titles. Its reserves of language students and those substantial chunks of North Oxford, amassed through decades of careful buying, support its pride – the International Baccalaureate course. What it dreads above all is becoming just another language school. It wants to maintain what it sees as its 'mixed economy' and apprehension enters the Principal's voice when she refers to the recent massive influx of Japanese wanting to learn English as 'the Japanese invasion'. Like the oriental imports threatening to swamp our automobile industries, the yellow peril also threatens the Euro-idealist core of St Clare's.

St Clare's acts as an omnibus of the independent educational sector, rolling up language school, pre-university courses and graduate-level liberal arts all in one. Elsewhere you encounter a greater degree of breakdown, one area of which is the liberal arts colleges. These, usually the offshoots of foreign campuses of American institutions, fall into a further two categories. There are the stand-alone colleges and then those tied in some way to the university. In the latter students get access to college facilities but receive their own tuition outside the university system (although often carried out by university tutors). It is a deal which satisfies everyone: the foreign institution gets access and privileges and the right to put an Oxford address and photograph into its annual catalogue, the college gets cash and the university gets a clear conscience, because there is no formal deal involved. Stanford University, which has both its own premises on the High Street and a tie-in to nearby Magdalen, straddles both categories.

In a class of its own, though, is Warnborough College, the self-styled 'American college of Oxford'. It is an independent and privately owned college which offers education in the American mode, complete with semesters and course credits. To visit its Boar's Hill premises under a flapping Stars and Stripes is to breathe deeply the spirit of free enterprise and confident corporate promotion. 'Dare to be great', its doormat shouts at you as you go in. Once inside you find yourself confronted by large framed

photographs of luminaries such as H. G. Wells and Gandhi –
alumni or former governors? But no: the link is rather more
tenuous. They were guests, it emerges, in one of the Warnborough-
owned houses, Yatscombe, when it was owned by Gilbert Murray.
Also represented amongst the photographs are such right-wing
heroes as Ronald Reagan and Sir Joh Bjelke-Petersen, Premier of
Queensland. Rather less imposing than the photographs are the
cramped student bedrooms, the Lilliputian library and the tiny
refectory. Outside in the garden stands a trailer of the sort one sees
in laybys selling hot snacks to the students, and a variety of
earthworks, for the college is, in the spirit of self-improvement,
constructing a football pitch and other extensions as part of a
£500,000 fundraising drive amongst its alumni.

Complaint has dogged Warnborough throughout its brief
history, due in part to ambiguous and overambitious advertising.
In the 1970s it was constrained to insert into its brochures the
disclaimer that it had 'no official connection' with the university.
In 1987 a group of American students walked out complaining
about the tuition and the facilities, and the college was as a result
the subject of a muckraking BBC radio documentary. Subsequently
it hired a public relations consultant and acquired accreditation
from a body known as the Chartered Institute of Washington, one
of a plethora of such agencies in the USA. This step, however,
did not prevent a German organization, the Reisezirkel-Jensen,
branding its English language teaching in 1989 as 'very bad and
absolutely insufficient'.

In fact the question of the accreditation of Warnborough College
raises the larger issue of academic regulation – one which has
particular relevance to Oxford and its educational establishments.
Until 1980 the DES was responsible for such academic control;
then in a piece of Thatcherite de-regulation it shed its duties to a
body called BAC, the British Accreditation Council for Independent, Further and Higher Education. (It also, incidentally,
turned down Warnborough when it applied.) BAC is a voluntary
organization and was thus unable to clamp down, for instance, on
the spate of bogus universities selling fake degrees and giving
Oxford as their address, such as Sampson University or the All-
England University of Oxford. Fortunately, the new Educational
Reform Act has put a stop to these particular abuses but there is

still a major regulatory gap. Oxford may have lost the blackest spots besmirching its educational panorama but it is still a scene with an uncontrolled infinity of shades of grey.

For if, on the forecourts of Oxford's private schools and colleges, Greene's is a Rolls and St Clare's a Volvo, there are also plenty of other models: some cheap economy jobs, efficient and serviceable, others clapped-out old bangers, complete with doctored clocks and logbooks and beneath whose bonnets you dread to peer. One cannot help pitying the poor foreign student, lured by brochures replete with dreaming spires, dimity Cotswold views and hints of learned comminglings in the cloisters, only rudely to awake to find himself lodged in a cramped bedsit on a city council estate somewhere out beyond the ring road, left to loiter in his spare time in MacDonalds and the Apollo Downtown Manhattan, and receive tuition of, to put it mildly, variable effectiveness.

TEFL (the Teaching of English as a Foreign Language) is a very big part of the education business in Oxford. There are some 180 language schools operating in and around the city, nearly all of them one way or another working the name 'Oxford' into their titles. Of these only about a dozen are permanent establishments. The most prestigious lump themselves into a body called ORSE (the Oxford Recognized Schools of English). These tend to be dotted in and around the Banbury Road, a veritable Babel-alley at 3.30 each afternoon when the schools spill their yellow-anoraked and blue-backpacked contents on to its pavements and bus stops.

A good example of these schools is the Oxford Academy of English on Bardwell Road. Started as a family concern it now employs 53 staff and has at any one time about 120 students, from a score of countries. Although its 3–4 week general English course is still a staple, the move is towards contract courses laid on for foreign firms such as Lufthansa and embassies as well as towards deliberately angled specialities such as English for use in medicine. It also exhibits all the entrepreneurial pull-yourself-up-by-the-bootstraps energy of many of the schools. Having recently extended its facilities the director talks of crossing a new threshold and of setting new standards for the 1990s, standards so high that they will earn praise even from those notorious nitpickers, the Germans and Swiss.

The North Oxford language schools have thrust themselves into the society of that secluded, leafy suburb like vulgar but successful tradesmen. Frowned upon and constantly resisted by their neighbours, they are ever anxious to improve, to extend and convert, and cram in the latest and best in TEFL-ware. There is a relentless, if invisible, planning battle going on all the time in the neighbourhood, its objective not a trench or a salient but a few extra bedrooms squeezed in here or a garden shed converted to a classroom there. Also, despite all the language schools' commercial ebullience, they suffer from the status-insecurity of the *arriviste*. It would require a Henry James of institutions to do justice to their snobberies and fears. Just as St Clare's dreads dropping down to the level of a mere language school, so the top language schools quiver at the thought of being lumped together with their lesser brethren. Piously they join in the choruses to crack down on their weak and inadequate colleagues and force them on to a register, policed by a code of conduct.

But even about the best of them there is something sharp-eyed and hard-hearted. If you feel sorry for those foreign students lassooed by the cowboys, you cannot help also pitying many of the staff who work for them – harassed, marginal figures, underpaid, under-experienced and generally overworked. The schools, like the crammers, recruit from Oxford's academic floaters and the semi-detached, the in-betweens, the has-beens and the undecideds, the nervous, the redundant and the squeezed out, and generally the vast, pale, inky tribe of dons-*manqués* in which the place abounds. These Banbury Road Irregulars are an odd assortment of new-hatched graduates, academic wives and sweethearts, divorcees, loitering postgraduates and those at a loose end just back from abroad. Forced by the fist of economic necessity, they find themselves driven up to the teaching line, to become TEFL fodder, grimly facing across their desks the serried, unknowing ranks of foreign nationals.

Out on Headington Hill stands an institute that has no accreditation problems whatsoever – Oxford Polytechnic. Such is its eminence that the body which 'validates' polytechnic degrees, the Council for National Academic Awards, has granted it a kind of self-governing 'dominion' status. It is the polytechnics' polytechnic, carrying out research on behalf of other polytechnics on how they should teach their students.

Yet with its pale concrete columns and 1950s polyurethane panels, it looks a most unassuming institution. It is a different world from both the university and the independent colleges. There is none of the air of fortified distinction of the former and, as yet, little of the crude commercialism of the latter. In term it fairly throbs with bustle and clatter and concern, like a major railway station at peak rush hour or a busy general casualty department on a Saturday night.

It is a pragmatic world of hardwearing institutional carpet squares, battered wooden banisters, scuffed formica table tops. It is full of corridors jammed with batteries of pigeon-holes, photocopiers squeezed under stairways, dens of offices – and noticeboards, noticeboards everywhere, slotted with baffling NHS-style colour-coded directions, swathes of computerized exam results, announcements for protest meetings, Saturday night ENTS or urgent pleas for accommodation. Crowds of students clump past in their regulation jungle boots and rugby shirts or drape themselves over counters to engage in a continuous institutional dialectic, demanding grant cheques, timetables, or just information please.

Meanwhile, the lecturers, in their cords and safari jackets, wander through in a state of near permanent dishevelment, as if they have just emerged from a violent, if friendly, tussle to get the kids to bed in their East Oxford houses. Everything is sim- ultaneously crushed but open, cheap but cheerful, harassed but good-humoured. The subtext, as at Cherwell, is involvement, but also – perhaps even more so – access.

Like Cherwell, the polytechnic is a great local success story. It began humbly and provisionally enough in 1865 as an art class in a borrowed room on the ground floor of the university's Taylorian Institution. Almost at once it found itself kicked downstairs to a basement, when Professor Ruskin formed his School of Art, which, he stipulated, should exclude the 'Artisan Class' and only be open to 'members of the University and of the Upper and Middle Classes ... desirous of studying Art for Art's sake, children included...'. Later science was added to the curriculum and, in 1891 it passed under the City Council (being transferred to the county in 1974). In the 1950s it climbed the hill to Headington and became a fully-fledged polytechnic in 1974.

Now it spans two campuses – the main one at Headington and the former Lady Spencer Churchill College of Education at Wheatley, which it absorbed in 1976. Organized in five faculties, the largest of which is the odd but fitting composite of Business, Languages and Hotel Management, it spends about £28 million a year; has over 6,000 students (half female, a fifth part-time, and a tenth from overseas); and offers a broad swathe of BAs, BScs, BEds, postgraduate diplomas in urban planning, certificates in health visiting, DipHcs, HNCs and MNDs. People press to get in. There are twenty applicants per average place, 50 per cent more than in any other polytechnic. Indeed to other polytechnics it is now almost what Oxbridge is to other universities. It is considered socially 'smart' and gets in a high proportion of middle-class and privately educated children.

What particularly distinguishes the polytechnic is the modular system of study which it pioneered. Its supple, open structure allows students to range across disciplines and, Meccano-wise, to construct their own degrees. It is said that if you delved into the polytechnic's Registry you would find no two identical degrees. You find historians also studying accountancy and biology, caterers taking modules in the history of art. Everything is wonderfully horizontal and democratically open; like a gigantic game of academic hopscotch in which you can leap as fast or slowly as you like between squares of your own choosing.

It is also firmly bolted on to the world of work and the local community. Not only does its modular system make things easy for part-time and mature students in the area, it also, through its Access scheme, enables them to study at their nearest College of Further Education, while another scheme, Pickup, provides refresher courses for those in employment. As well as being a participant in the Oxford Consortium, a training organization serving local companies, it has developed a range of specific courses for employers, such as the bookselling course for W. H. Smith or the graduate nursing programme for the local health authority, and earns about £1 million a year in industrial contracts. A further mark of its contribution to Oxford was that for every pound it drew from the local authority it pumped twenty back in wages and purchased services.

But now, in terms of control, the polytechnic is increasingly cutting free of its locality. Once its funding dropped down through a series of bureaucratic chutes and hoppers with controls and filters at every stage – originating in the DES, advised by the NAB (the National Advisory Body for Higher Education), passing through the Department of the Environment and ending up in the local authority. In 1989 it became an independent corporation. Now the polytechnic makes its 'bids' directly to a newly created body, the Polytechnics and Colleges Funding Council, and its funding will also reflect more immediately its success in attracting students to its courses. At a stroke it has been quasi-privatized, converted into a semi-free enterprise operation, plying its trade in the educational marketplace. The local authority is now just one more outside 'client' and the new 'owners' are the governors, a tighter operational team of thirteen with increased business and industrial representatives as opposed to the old sprawling consensus and co-option body of forty. Something of the altered atmosphere of the polytechnic comes across in its new statement of aims. Formerly the emphasis was on providing a distinctly different form of higher education; now it is on serving cost-effectively the 'economy and society', and, significantly, the old reference to preparation for 'citizenship' has been dropped.

The staff are divided over the new dispensation: some welcome it, others feel apprehension, others still 'a despondency', in the words of the Director, 'that the prospect which they embarked on as idealistic young people is now turning sour, that it is heading into a money-grabbing, quasi-private company region that they did not sign up for'. One dean on the modular course felt quality and the 'social side' of the poly, its provision for disadvantaged and part-time students would be bound to suffer in the race for numbers and more income. A new hard-nosed attitude is detectable, say some, from the directorate. In the 1980s the poly took considerable steps towards cost-efficiency, increasing student–staff ratios and cutting the amount spent per student. Now, with the shift to devolved management, the staff fear the screw will be turned yet tighter.

The Director, Clive Booth, who often chafed in the past under

local authority control, says he welcomes the changes 'with a
mixture of excitement and trepidation ... if we fail we shall have
only ourselves to blame'. Indeed he views this as an inevitable
further stage in the polytechnic's progress – its steady growth to
maturity and standing free, like the university, on its own two
feet. More, he believes that both polytechnics and universities are
pressing forward on a convergent path. Just as there is a new
PCFC, there is a UFC, a Universities Funding Council. It can only
be a matter of time before they merge. A hierarchy of institutions
will emerge with the polytechnics and less research-oriented universities indistinguishable from one another. Oxford will no longer
be a city with a university and a polytechnic but a twin university
city.

Roll up, roll up, we are all going private now! Survey the Oxford
educational spectrum and the overwhelming impression is indeed
one of convergence. The university, like the polytechnic, is becoming much more industrially and vocationally minded, building
research partnerships with companies and setting new degrees in
management and business studies. Both are increasingly dominated
by the need to market themselves and generate income. Then again,
the state secondary schools, like the polytechnic, are being tempted
towards opting out, taking the first tentative steps down Privatization Road, and moving towards their independent colleagues. The language schools, crammers and foreign colleges are
no longer the despised fringe of the educational scene but the new
entrepreneurial models. It is a changed landscape, under a harsh
new sun, full of educo-enterprise hybrids, crawling and twitching
their way to viability.

Once the Oxford educational scene was like a slice across the old
social class system. You had the university, like an aristocrat, head
and shoulders above the rest, lifting its nose beyond the horizon
and not talking to anyone locally except to address them as
servants. You had the privately employed professional classes –
the Teddies, the Dragons and the Radleys. Then there were the
social *arrivistes* and the foreign parvenus of varying degrees of
acceptability – the language schools and independent colleges –
and, finally, there were the solid, lower middle-class functionaries –

the poly, the state schools and the CFE. Now everyone finds themselves out there on the street, busking for a living in the bitter breeze of the marketplace.

GOWN

OXFORD Gown

– 6 –

Concrete and Cloisters

Oxford is a capital of learning, and at its heart is the university. But where is the university? It is a perplexing question, not only for the many visitors to the city. So in approaching the university let us follow the visitors' footsteps and start with the colleges.

In all, the university contains thirty-five separate colleges, each armed with its own history, traditions and character, each buttressed with its own statutes and endowments. Each is a self-governing, self-perpetuating corporation. Its fellowship elects new fellows who in due course will elect new fellows in their turn.

They are immensely varied, ranging in size from Nuffield, with some seventy students, to New College, with nearly six hundred. The wealthiest – St John's, Christ Church and Magdalen – are possibly a hundred times richer than the poorest – Keble, Hertford, St Edmund Hall, St Peter's and the former women's colleges. In buildings they range from Merton's tiny, medieval Mob Quadrangle to the eighteenth-century elegance of Magdalen's New Buildings, the red brick Victorian-ecclesiastical of Keble and the 1960s concrete and glass of Wolfson.

Formerly, all were single-sex institutions, with five of them (Lady Margaret Hall, St Hugh's, St Anne's, Somerville and St Hilda's) women only. Now all are co-residential except Somerville and St Hilda's. One college, All Souls, has no undergraduate students at all. The seven most recent (Nuffield, St Antony's, Wolfson, Linacre, St Cross, Green College and Templeton) are postgraduate colleges and tend to specialize in specific subjects. The rest try to represent a range of subjects though they have undeniable specialties and bumps of excellence, often made known only by experience or word of mouth.

It takes time, or a particularly generous benefactor, for a college to become a college. So there are proper full-dress colleges, colleges-in-waiting and a large dangling retinue of institutions of uncertain status. The oldest college – University College – was founded in 1249, the youngest – Green College, a medical foundation endowed by a Dallas millionaire – in 1979.

Each college has a distinct character, a compound of its history and its buildings and its members, past and present, and their achievements. Christ Church, for instance, is deemed grand and Establishment and called 'the House' (as if it were a stately country home, although in fact the nickname derives from the words on its crest *Aedes Christi*, 'the House of Christ'); Balliol has a reputation for being severely highminded, radical and committed to achieve-ment; University College is said to be 'friendly'; and Magdalen is thought rather frigidly aesthetic and cosmopolitan.

Accurate or no, these labels reflect that the colleges have very different identities. Anthropologically, they are an archipelago of separate little tribes. Just as the latter centre on hut and hearth and the fundamental processes of eating, drinking and sleeping, so the colleges value the shared pleasures of the common table. Like tribes they observe a seasonal round of events – from the drinks of the Freshers' Blind in October through the boat bumping races of spring and summer – and their academic and sporting triumphs and Old Members' later successes form their equivalent of tribal trophies.

A college is not simply a place or organization where certain kinds of teaching and research take place. Like a tribe, its identity is intimately interwoven with its surroundings – its sticks and stones and trees and totems. It is its pictures and its ornaments, its buildings and its gardens. Again resembling primitive cultures they are highly inward and secretive, enclosed in buildings designed to shut out the wider world, riddled with quaint rituals and ceremonies and full of private words and codes and shibboleths and slang. 'When laudable old customs alter', said the eighteenth-century Oxford antiquary, Thomas Hearne, ''tis a sign learning decays' and Oxford colleges, clinging to their customs, are guided by his precept to this day.

But for all their weight of tradition, colleges are also surprisingly adaptable creatures, mimicking or borrowing from outside models when it suits their purpose. Their overriding rule is to survive. The first Oxford colleges were pretty clearly modelled on the religious houses of the time. They were in fact little monasteries, but with other elements built in. In their layout they combined not just monastery cloisters but the walls of a medieval fortress and the central courtyard of an inn or country manor.

In Oxford they represented an evolutionary advance. The predominant organizational lifeform in the early university had been the academical hall – lodgings, where groups of undergraduates, often from the same region, would lodge under the protection of a 'principal', originally also a student, licensed by the university's elected chief officer, its Chancellor. The colleges were different creatures: tiny communities of advanced scholars dedicated to prayers for their founders' souls and the education of their kin. Their most important feature was the independence conferred by their statutes and endowments, and gradually these advantages told. They prospered and expanded, swallowing up the halls, so that by the mid sixteenth century, only eight survived. Only one – St Edmund Hall – was hardy enough to last until the present century, finally converting to collegiate status in 1957.

Soon they took over a new role – educating the sons of the nobility for their place in society. Beginning with New College and Magdalen in the fourteenth and fifteenth centuries and inspired by the New Learning of the Renaissance, the colleges secularized and humanized themselves. Reflecting the backgrounds and destinations of their new charges, the colleges turned themselves architecturally into palaces and courts, crenellating their walls and loading themselves with ornament and detail.

By the eighteenth century the colleges had changed once more into a strange cross between coffee house, club and theological training college. Oxford became almost the training wing of the Church of England, producing parsons by the pew. At the same time, it remained a resort for the wealthy sons of the middle classes, many of whom – celebrated as foppish 'loungers' and 'smarts' – idled away their days here.

Thereafter shades of the rising public school closed round the 'loungers'. Discipline and organization were tightened up, and college spirit bloomed, informed by hearty schoolboy values. Men who offended against college spirit – pale-faced scholars or flowery aesthetes – were likely to have their rooms and pictures wrecked. A high, bright star rose in particular over Balliol, which had been among the earliest colleges to throw open their scholarships. Jowett, its Master, who confessed to 'a general prejudice against all persons who do not succeed in the world', said he hoped to 'inoculate the world with Balliol'. The college had adapted once again. Squaring up to the White Man's Burden, it had become an imperial training academy.

The present century has seen a whole shoal of changes: a gradual relaxation of undergraduate discipline, increasing participation by them in the running of the colleges and a steady if still unrepresentative broadening in the intake of pupils from state schools. In one respect there has been something of a swing back to the colleges' original role, that of institutions of advanced study: seven of the nine colleges founded since 1920 have been for postgraduates.

But the most dramatic change has been the introduction of co-education, which started in 1974 when a group of five colleges was allowed to go mixed. A gradual, phased changeover was envisaged for the rest depending on the success of the 'experiment' but other pressures soon made themselves felt, not least the provisions of the Sex Discrimination Act, and the rest joined in a sudden rush to amend their statutes.

Today, if there is one overriding organizational model it is the Enterprise College. The colleges are in the process of turning themselves into little limited academic companies, using their plant and resources in as cost-effective and streamlined a way as possible and maximizing their assets and profits. Fundraising appeals, property deals and science park projects, summer schools, conference bookings and other 'hotel' activities are the focus of much ingenuity and effort.

The new entrepreneurial edge of the colleges cuts into both domestic and academic spheres. Just as you contract for services in the kitchens, so there is also a switch to academic contract employment, to greater deployment of temporary lecturers not permanently tenured to the foundation. Skills are bought in as required, whether for teaching first-year philosophy students logic, or acquiring a hundred pre-cooked meals. The preoccupation is more and more with such matters as 'product range', 'market gap analysis' and 'brand image management' (although the colleges would never openly use such terms).

There is increasing competition among the colleges to market themselves. The sudden onset of co-education in the late 1970s did not spring entirely from a commitment to social and sexual equality: it was also informed by a hard-edged realization that students would favour mixed colleges in their applications and any remaining single-sex college would be cutting itself off from a large pool of talent. Similarly, behind the increasing pressure to get good results and achieve a high ranking in the Norrington Table (the annual table of colleges drawn up according to their Finals results) is the fact well known to dons that a high ranking guarantees a surge in applicants.

For some time colleges have entered into arrangements with foreign colleges and universities whereby they accept 'affiliates' who stay for anything from a term up to a full academic year. Now, however, the colleges are entering into a whole new dimension of relationships with overseas institutions. It has dawned on many foreign business heads, especially those in the Far East, that the colleges, with their teaching strengths in history and literature and the central niche they enjoy in our society, are not only excellent centres of study but also ideal facilities for cultural acclimatization – solaria, if you like, where the oriental corporation man can go global and soak up the necessary Western values. Increasingly, Japanese companies are entering into arrangements with colleges whereby they open overseas offshoots and run courses for nominated students. Kobe Steel, for instance, has reached such an agreement with St Catherine's College, and it is no secret that there are many others wanting in some way to buy into the colleges.

So far, throughout all these gradations of association with outside bodies, a due degree of scholarly decorum has been maintained. A distance has been kept between the college's mainstream academic activities and the encapsulated areas of its summer schools, affiliates, foreign offshoots or whatever. The prospect no one at Oxford is as yet prepared to entertain is that of guaranteeing an outside body places in return for financial benefit. But the pressure to do so is undoubtedly there, especially from Far Eastern clients who are far franker than their Western counterparts in demanding the quid-pro-quo.

If all this makes colleges sound cold-eyed commercial creatures, bleak factories of academic enterprise where the balance sheet and the property portfolio rule supreme, it would be false. Paradoxically, the other side of the colleges – the cohesive, familial side – has also reasserted itself with a new vigour.

Three factors in particular have played a part in this change. One has been the nightly retreat of the dons who nowadays mostly come in to do their teaching or whatever, and then head off to their homes in the evenings. So the new college spirit is generated and sustained by the handful of dons who stay on, by the college servants – a class not to be overlooked – but mainly by the students themselves. College life now could be said to represent a return to the medieval halls of Oxford, where student companions lodged together and ran their own affairs with a few servants and under a chosen principal.

However, the new college spirit is different in character from that of the past: less conformist and authoritarian, more tolerant of individual variety and with a new emphasis on openness and flexibility. Undoubtedly central to this has been the coming of women. Their acceptance into men's colleges, widely predicted in advance as something which would undermine and eventually destroy those institutions, has paradoxically brought about the opposite and given them new life. Penetrating these all-male preserves, the women have not only made them brighter and more colourful, but also have embraced many of their most traditional activities. This is true, for instance, of rowing, so that the river each afternoon in term is practically jammed with women crews, heaving in unison to the peremptory commands of their coxes.

But it is also a softer, more homely life that the women have brought to the colleges. In the college of a generation ago, as in all male institutions from schools to prisons, there was something hyper-charged in the very air. It enclosed a small, sharp field of awareness, very competitive and conscious of the pecking order. Beneath the surface boisterousness and bonding it could reproduce within itself an absurd parody of the stereotypically feminine –

brushfires of backbiting and bitchery, sudden intense ignitions of friendship or ludicrously solemn unbarings of the soul over late night cups of coffee. Now, a whole principle of balance has been introduced, the unhealthy layer of insulation between college life and outside stripped away and much of the internal hysteria – that rising spiral of over-competitiveness – earthed.

The final factor affecting the colleges lies out there, in society and the fate of the modern family. As they absorb more students from broken homes or disturbed emotional histories they are turning themselves into a kind of surrogate family, the old communal tribalist bonding converting itself into a support group against the fractured complexities of the modern world.

The colleges, in the course of their long and serpentine history, have passed through several stages – medieval abbey, Renaissance academy, Anglican seminary, nineteenth-century public school and imperial forcing house – only to become in the latest twist of their evolutionary spiral an odd blend of modern multinational and New Age commune. There are many who predict the colleges' eventual decline and absorption into an ever-encroaching, centralizing university but they have shown themselves over the centuries to be amazingly hardy, protean beasts. It would be a bold man prepared to wager on their eventual demise.

But where is the university in all this? On paper it certainly exists: it teaches 10,000 undergraduates and 3,600 postgraduates, has 2,600 academics and researchers organized in sixteen faculties, employs 2,900 clerks, librarians and technicians and spends going on for £129 million a year. But it is not a specific building or place. Oxford University is a structure, almost a metaphysical entity, hanging shimmering over the colleges like a vast and intricate web of spidery filaments.

The mysterious interlockings of college and university are absorbed by the dons and those who work for them like the tenets of a theological system. It is in their bones; they dwell lovingly on its Byzantine niceties. To outsiders it is a source of endless confusion.

The colleges form part of the university but remain at the same time independent of it. The relation between the two is often presented as a smooth synchromeshing; in fact it is endlessly intricate, almost, some would say, labyrinthine. As a rough rule of thumb, it is the colleges which pick undergraduate students and look after their accommodation, teaching and social life, while the university administers examinations and degrees and is responsible for central facilities such as laboratories and libraries and for advanced study and research.

Historically, the university came first – in the original bands of students who collected in twelfth-century Oxford to pursue their studies. They gathered in democratic assemblies called Congregations, elected their own Chancellors to represent them and with great pertinacity won recognition from Pope and King. The university then was an individualistic sort of set-up. Students would attach themselves to a particular Master of Arts, attend his lectures and progress towards their degrees, gradually assuming the role of teachers in their turn. (Today, one side of the university's responsibilities still preserves these early activities, in the matriculation of students, provision of lectures, the setting of examinations and awarding of degrees.)

Thereafter power slid from the university into the hands of the colleges. In the sixteenth century the Crown, seeking to extend its power over the university, imposed upon it an outside Chancellor (generally a magnate of the realm) and set up a ruling body, Hebdomadal Board, comprising the heads of all the colleges. Effectively Oxford had gone from the medieval democracy of its Congregation to something like oligarchy. During the eighteenth century colleges waxed fat: as their incomes rose they were able to undertake a lavish programme of new building. But for the university the picture was quite different: accounts attest to libraries bare of readers and laboratories sooty with neglect. By the early nineteenth century, one critic, voicing the outrage of many liberals, attacked Oxford as 'a sinister conspiracy of colleges to usurp the functions of a university'.

Then the pendulum swung back. A royal commission descended on the university in 1850 and a second one twenty years later. These broadened the representation on Hebdomadal Council, opened up some colleges' fellowships to competition and suppressed others to create a new Central University Fund to pay for new posts and facilities. In this way the other side of the university's role came about – forwarding research and advanced study and administering the libraries and laboratories that support them. It seemed as if the centre of gravity had moved irreversibly towards the university and that the colleges might gradually decline and wither away. But the resources freed by the Commissions failed to produce the level of support envisaged. This financial check sharpened and polarized opinion within Oxford. The younger tutors (a group known as 'Young Oxford') formed the Non-Placet Society (so called from their exercise of the veto in Congregation) to defend their position and resist the proponents of advanced research and the scientists (known as the 'Museum Vote'). The tutors won the day, and, by making the colleges the focus of their loyalties they ensured the structure of Oxford as we know it today.

Nevertheless, during the present century the university has continued to expand and consolidate, a process accelerated by Oxford's decision after the First World War to accept central government funding. Increasingly it became the leading partner in spending and in supporting posts jointly funded with the colleges. Nowadays its annual expenditure is about twice that of all the colleges put together, and on average it pays for over two-thirds of jointly funded arts posts and four-fifths of those in the sciences.

Internally, Oxford University is an extraordinary mosaic of an institution, complex and fragmented almost beyond belief. Its major split, of course, opens up between the central university and the thirty-five colleges. Supporters of the status quo talk of the harmonious meshing of the two, of them being the warp and the weft of the fabric of Oxford. In fact the threads tug and twist in all directions. Representing the colleges in theory is a body called the Conference of Colleges. But in reality this is little more than a talking shop, much despised and with little power to act or co-ordinate. More important as 'clutch plates' between the university and the colleges are the various committees of college tutors, such as those of Senior or of Admissions Tutors. But these concern themselves only with specific limited areas and, besides, as one senior university figure commented, 'like all clutch plates, have been known to slip'.

Moreover, the central university is itself full of duplications and divisions of power. The Chancellor, its titular head, is a venerable figurehead, usually drawn from the ranks of distinguished ex-

politicians. It is the Vice-Chancellor who counts. But his powers
are distinctly limited. Whereas most universities appoint permanent
vice-chancellors, Oxford limits his reign to four years lest the
colleges feel too threatened by the creation of a permanent central
power base.

The university's 'parliament', Congregation, is not an elected
senate, again as in most universities, in which the professors exercise
significant sway, but a gathering where all dons can attend and
vote. Any twelve members can obtain a debate if they circulate a
signed flysheet, and if they pass a veto (still known as 'Non placet')
it will immediately be binding on university officers. Further exemplifying Oxford's divisions of power are the bodies elected by
Congregation to run the university's business: Hebdomadal
Council (its full name referring to its pattern of weekly meetings
but more generally referred to as 'Council') which is responsible
for the overall administration of the university, and the General
Board of Faculties (known as the 'General Board') which concerns
itself with academic matters. In theory Council should be the
greater power, but in practice power is split between them and is
now in fact thought to lie with the General Board which controls
most of the university budget. General Board jealously guards its
powers, graciously admitting the Vice-Chancellor to its meetings
but not according him the power to chair them.

Beneath these is an intricate, interlocking set of 130 committees,
boards, trustees and other bodies on which interested dons, in an
elaborate game of academic-administrative musical chairs, take
turns to serve. These include, in addition to the key bodies such as
the Delegates of the Press or Curators of the Bodleian Library,
such curiosities as the Delegates for the Nomination of Candidates
for Ecclesiastic Benefices. Finally, as if all these divisions and
diffusions were not enough, the university has in its Proctors and
Assessor a squad of Ombudsmen, licensed to intervene in any
committee meeting and whose role stretches back to representatives
of the resident MAs in medieval Oxford.

How in all this labyrinthine complexity are decisions reached
and power manipulated? It was much easier, of course, in the
Oxford of forty years ago. A much smaller institution then, it was
rather like a club where everyone knew everyone else. Whenever a
decision had to be taken or an outside threat headed off, a group

of like-minded men (and they usually were men) from the richer and more powerful colleges got together behind oak panels and over a suitably dry sherry agreed on the necessary action. The word went out, colleagues were squared and brought on board and that was that. Now not only is the university far larger, it is infinitely more diverse and specialized with its proliferating array of departments, facilities, research programmes and taught courses.

As such it offers a formidable challenge to the academic politicians. Let us trace their typical trajectory. First they win their spurs in their individual colleges or departments. They gain a taste for power and decide to make the jump to the larger university, signing motions, collecting committees like connoisseurs and up to their mortar-boards in paperwork. They rise, get elected to the heights of General Board and maybe achieve the final accolade of high office. But as they close their hands on power, its pleasures slither from their grasp. In other universities it is possible to build a power base and extract loyalty or instil terror by intimated offers or withdrawals of favour. But Oxford is so *gaseously* diffuse. The academic politico has little hold or leverage over others. For many it is all too much. They fade from the scene, burying themselves in their books or their apparatus and muttering about getting some *real* work done, or – in a bout of pique – move off to other institutions where they can get a firmer grip on the rudder of power. From there they lambast their alma mater for its inefficiency, whilst still in many cases continuing to live in its environs.

By contrast those who hang on and work the machinery of the university develop skills of a high but invisible order. Most dons only master those bits of the controls nearest to them and know little of the rest. The successful politico passes through a prolonged apprenticeship learning how to manipulate the whole bank of them. Nor does he ever forget the unseen current of influence and information that runs through the circuit board of Oxford's High Tables, but constantly re-charges himself from its power.

Both these images suggest something coldly modern and technocratic. The successful politico is more like a master sorcerer intoning the right spells to open the right doors. Mesmerist, illusionist, conjuror and shape-shifter – these are his roles. Hypocrisy ranks high amongst his arts. Just as the leaders of the Labour Party are said once to have held its rickety coalition together by saying often opposite things to its various factions, so the master sorcerer must match his words to his audience – playing hard-nosed rationalist for the scientists and cosy-comfortable conservationist to the colleges and their arts dons.

Whatever his private thoughts he must never impugn directly two of the most sacred cows in Oxford's meadows – the collegiate and the tutorial systems – and he must never imply that Oxford has anything to learn from the outside world (Oxford always leads and gives ...). Finally, like all good sorcerers, he must have the power to make himself invisible. If the pride he feels in successfully mesmerizing and manipulating the disparate interest groups of Oxford becomes too apparent, the other dons, sniffing an unhealthy accumulation of power and a burgeoning cult of personality, will wake from their temporary trance, turn against him, and he will surely fall.

Today the university's presence is most concrete (quite literally) in the sixty or so departments and laboratories of the Science Area. With its anonymous brick buildings and glass and steel cartons it could be a business park on the bypasses of Slough or Brentwood. It seems a world away from the gracious climes of the colleges. But at present science in Oxford holds a position at least equal to the arts. It accounts for nearly 70 per cent of the university's departmental spending, some 45 per cent of its academic staff, over 40 per cent of its students and the bulk of its buildings and support staff and services.

Science at Oxford as elsewhere has simultaneously become both more Brobdingnagian and more reliant on sensitive and small-scale interplays, with important developments very often taking place at the edges where two different disciplines touch together. To catalyse this subtle chemistry demands skills of a new and different order. So a new type – the Science Manager – has come to the fore. The Science Manager is far, far removed from the traditional Oxford don, and even from the old laboratory director. He (or she) has rather to be a networker and lateralist, knotting creative links and fostering fruitful associations. Research teams may have as many as sixty members, split between several labs and maybe local research facilities and clinics. Within them individuals will play a variety of roles. A key one is that of postgraduate zealot, fired with enthusiasm for the project and capable of prodigious effort. It is not unknown for these researchers to work twenty or thirty hours on the trot, sleeping on a camp bed to be by their apparatus, before returning, pale and hollow-eyed, to their bleak bedsits, crumpled sheets, naked burning single light bulb and battered shelf of sci-fi novels.

The Manager nurses all these gifted individuals, soothes the prima donnas and acts as a flexible and genially absorbent cushion for the tensions of the team. Yet it would be a mistake to see the Manager as someone who has converted clapped-out scientific talents into the gold of personal skills. The Manager has to be seen as still cutting away there on the coal face to keep the respect of the team.

The Manager, moreover, has to be Janus-faced: to look inwards to his team and outwards to the world. He increasingly has had to become adept at loosening the purses of grant-giving bodies. Recently, for instance, government policy has been to centralize the research-funding agencies and to give them a more direct and industrially-oriented role. The Manager accepts this, dressing up his projects, often quite cynically, in whatever fashionable clothing is required. Whatever is scientific flavour of the month he will provide it. Privately, he may well harbour doubts about this, but publicly he will play the game: whatever is government taste he will pander to it in order to build and maintain the efforts of his team. Often he develops such political skills that he feels confident enough to climb the high plateau of university governance. Or he might go in another direction, move outside and become enmeshed in the world of business.

But science needs more than exciting new structures and approaches. It needs, above all, money. It is the lack of money that has propelled Oxford increasingly into the political arena in recent years. Like the other victims of higher education cuts it has proudly displayed its bleeding wounds. In the Thatcher decade there was a steady drop in its UGC grant and home student fees with the result that the proportion of its budget from central government fell from about a half to a third.

The anti-Thatcher stance of the university was in one way highly ironic because it has applied her policies vigorously. As a result income generation has increasingly become the name of the game. In the Thatcher decade income from contract research and overseas fees has more than doubled. In the science departments a whole spectrum of relationships has been forged with industry, ranging from consultancies to licensing or collaborative deals of one kind or another. The university has recently set up an independent company, Isis Innovation Ltd, to exploit breakthroughs resulting from Research Council-funded projects in its science departments. It has already sold several patents and helped set up a company, Oxford Molecular, to sell chemical modelling software.

Of course there is nothing new about Oxford scientists exploiting their breakthroughs commercially. Sir Martin Wood, founder of Oxford Instruments, the leading local high tech company, is the grand-daddy of them all in this regard. He came to the Clarendon Laboratory in 1955 and was unable to find the powerful magnets he needed for his research. He began making them – first for himself, then for others. Now, Oxford Instruments is a group of eighteen companies with a turnover in the £100 million range and products which range from the massive magnets used in whole-body scanners to a device for the cheap etching of silicon chips.

Some, like Colin Webb of the Clarendon Laboratory and founder of Oxford Lasers, continue to straddle both academe and business. In 1971, having had his idea of a nitrogen laser turned down by several British companies, he was advised by Sir Martin to start up his own business. In the event he chose not to but later regretted this and was determined, when he developed an eximer laser in 1978, not to lose the initiative again. Now he heads a thriving enterprise whose products include lasers for everything from cancer diagnosis to large scale TV projection screens.

Currently, however, 'partnership' is the buzz word. This goes far beyond the old-style commercially contracted research, whereby university scientists got a brief from industry, did the work, submitted a report and then moved on to the next project. Now there is far more collaboration and interaction: companies are getting into fundamental, long-term financing of departments or moving to set up independent two- or three-way companies. Examples include Oxford Glycosystems, set up to exploit the potential of oligosaccharides (complex braids of cellular sugars studied by Professor Raymond Dwek and Dr Tom Rademacher) the profits from which will be shared between the discoverers, the university and the outside backers, the US chemical giant Monsanto.

Probably the most striking instance of this phenomenon so far at Oxford has been the £20 million programme agreed between Professor David Smith's Pharmacology Department and the US drug company Squibb. Half will be spent on a new building, half on basic research in neuroscience. Squibb has the right to select for support specific projects in return for exploitation rights on which Oxford will get royalties. The most unusual aspect of the deal, according to Professor Smith, is the funding of long-term basic research from which new drugs may only emerge on to the market place in ten or fifteen years' time.

In theory everything about partnership is hunkydory: the companies get access to leading edge research and gifted scientists they could not hope to find amongst their own staffs, while the university departments obtain the funding to press on with their research. But partnership also has its pitfalls. In such deals the university is heading into uncharted commercial territory. With contracts come responsibilities. And there are academic fears about intellectual freedom, the rights to share the fruits of research with the broader academic community, and about the dangers of being diverted from long-term 'basic curiosity' questions to short-term profitable goals. In a university like Oxford with its pure science traditions many academics would feel unhappy if commercial funding represented more than a proportion of total income. They stress that, while a valuable supplement, it is no substitute for generous public funding to support long-term academic research.

The most visible manifestation of the university's new entrepreneurial ethos lies, however, not in science but the £220 million Campaign for Oxford, which was launched in a splash of publicity in October 1988. The event resembled a mixture of a college reunion, a Buckingham Palace garden party and one of those public relations exercises when a nationalized industry is privatized.

It was by any measure an extraordinary event. Here was this pillar of the British Establishment embarking on a slick, media-smart campaign, in a word, *hyping* itself. Nor was its extraordinariness limited to a matter of style. The launch represented a tremendous gamble. Oxford, without any established tradition of large-scale alumni giving, was setting in motion the largest fundraising campaign ever undertaken by an educational institution outside North America. At a time when its back was financially against the wall, it was preparing to hazard a considerable chunk of its own funds in the hope of recouping its fortunes.

The campaign set out to raise £220 million over the first five years. Financially, it has so far been a roaring success. By its midpoint it had succeeded in raising some £150 million. This figure includes £65 million from research grants plus £20 million from the partnership deal between the Department of Pharmacology and the Squibb Corporation. Many feel that the inclusion of such research money smacks of sleight of hand – Oxford would have raised that income anyway irrespective of there being a campaign. However, such misgivings aside, the campaign looks as if it will easily meet its targets and indeed probably overrun them before its five years are up. Moreover, Oxford will not only have concluded a successful campaign, it will have concluded a successful international campaign, with over half its money raised from overseas, most notably from the USA and Japan.

Its financial success apart, the Campaign for Oxford has another major success to its credit: it has succeeded in giving a far more definite identity to the university as opposed to the colleges and has etched its profile far more sharply on the public mind. Previously the university was perceived – if at all – as an addition, almost as a general utility or facility. There was the Bodleian Library, there were the labs, there was the anonymous administrative centre in Wellington Square, but together these had about as much corporate identity as an electricity company. Alumni affections and associations clustered around the traditional symbols, the colleges with their old ivy-wrapped walls and cloistered quadrangles. Now, in part through highly professional publications, an image has been projected of the university as a place full of lively developments and debate and possessing a forward momentum of its own.

Yet for all its success, the campaign – like most things in Oxford – squirms with contradictions when looked at close to. The leading lights of the Development Office talk bravely of bringing about a sea change in the university and mobilizing it in new directions. Yet the money has largely gone on filling existing gaps and propping up the status quo. There have been innovations – visiting professorships in performing arts and so on – but most have been icing for the cake, glamorous but marginal. One don compared them to urban developments where the suburbs are enhanced but the centre with all its problems remains untouched. Deep down the vision of Oxford which the campaign promotes is thoroughly traditional – a living icon of collegiate and tutorial systems with a gilding of modernity. For all the campaign's surface razzmatazz, the old Oxford shibboleths have stayed firmly in place.

The campaign is, in the eyes of many dons, no more than a giant financial sticking plaster applied to Oxford – a useful short-term palliative but no substitute for a rigorous self-examination by the university. Ultimately this must focus, they feel, on what kind of university Oxford should be. A number of competing visions are identifiable. The first, which might be termed 'True Blue Oxford', envisages a relatively small university, predominantly undergraduate and supported by its traditional pillars of the tutorial and collegiate systems. But ranked against this version are at least two other models.

One is 'Enterprise Oxford' supported by a minority of radical right-wing dons, which would like to see the university run on commercial lines, offering whatever courses, however vocational and non-traditional, appealed to the market. Limits to growth would be ignored and under this vision the university might swell to twice its present size, even possibly establishing a second 'green fields' campus in the country, given space and planning constraints in the city. Then there is another school: 'Institute of Advanced Studies Oxford' envisages a university of the fourth level, a largely postgraduate institution admitting only those with first degrees from other universities. If undergraduates were to be let in, their instruction would be almost a sideline, carried out by a lesser breed of instructors on short-term contracts.

A further vision, 'Oxford 1992', incorporates some of the above elements but broadens its sights to a wider international dimension. This foresees Oxford becoming a world university, the Harvard of Europe, attracting large numbers of foreign scholars and sharing vigorously in exchanges and other joint programmes. In a way it looks back to the world of an original medieval university – that Latin-speaking community whose scholars wandered unconcerned across frontiers in search of learning.

Finally – lagging somewhat in the rear – is 'Accessible Oxford', aiming at a more socially and regionally representative university open as much to students from comprehensives as to the smoothly finished products of independent schools. Long promoted by left-wing dons, perhaps in contrition for all the paddings of privilege they enjoyed at Oxford, it has recently risen to the top of the agenda. The proportions of provincial and state school-educated entrants, gradually increasing until a few years ago, have begun slipping, and many dons fear that – especially with the prospect of student loans acting as a further deterrent to less well-off students – Oxford is slithering steadily back to its old position as an exclusively middle-class and predominantly southeastern institution.

But these preoccupations form only the external facet of the current debate. The attention of the dons is now also turning increasingly to the inner workings and skeletal structures of the university and how best to coordinate the movements of this sprawling beast that so closely resembles, with its many vertebrae and dispersed brains, one of the dinosaurs in its own Science Museum.

The internal problem remains – as it did for Lord Franks in his famous report – to reconcile 'decision with democracy'. Some would like to centralize the flow of power within Oxford far more, streamlining its various bodies, and, passing up the pretence that it can be run by a series of transient Vice-Chancellors, to create a permanent academic presidency on American university lines. But most dons would see such measures opening up an us-and-them divide between the colleges and their dons and the central admin-istration (which many already see as a dangerously oppressive Kremlin in Wellington Square). They also fear that it would rob the Vice-Chancellor of the requisite irresponsibility in responding to outside, government bodies – that essential breezy out-spokenness which a temporarily seconded don can bring to the job. By contrast, some look for an even greater degree of democ-racy, and they have put forward a range of measures to counter this trend. Then there is a third party that believes that Oxford should face the fact of its fragmentation and indeed institutionalize it, becoming not a university but a 'multiversity', split into super-faculties in seven subjects each with substantially devolved powers.

So there is at present much muffled mulling-over of possibilities behind the oak panels of senior common rooms and in the corridors of the university's administrative offices. In the event no one vision of Oxford, or of the way to run it, is likely to prevail. The result is more likely to be a typical Oxford response, a cautious, conservative fudging together of various possibilities, permitting a gradual evolutionary growth, a slow crab-like advance. Nor should one be too contemptuous of the uncertainty of these compromises, for they reflect no more than the inchoate and unpredictable nature of the intellectual pursuits that are the university's *raison d'être*.

It is the university's sprawling multiplicity that sticks in the mind. In its miscellaneous totality Oxford is a microcosm. Like the rest of 1980s Britain, it presented a picture of an old-fashioned, deeply traditional society in the process of being painfully recast. A generation ago the call was for expansion, increased meritocracy, the opening up of Oxford's privileges and most equitable deployment of the largesse of state support. Now the pressures are for greater cost efficiency, a sharper responsiveness to market forces, for relevance and evidence of a real contribution to the economy. Plunged into the new entrepreneurial atmosphere, it has both bitterly resisted outside pressures, acting as doughty champion of the status quo, and blithely welcomed them – as in its fundraising and various 'partnership' deals. But in no area has it remained untouched.

And in a curious way Oxford has the chance to present not only a microcosm but an example. Its divisions and overlaps, its steady denial of power to the forces of centralization are in one way its fatal flaw, discouraging and dispersing its larger efforts and initiatives. In another, however, they are its chief glory, fostering flexibility, variety and the freedom at local level to experiment, innovate and run one's own affairs. It is strange to say it of such an Establishment pillar, but behind the marmoreal image it is the ultimate Green institution, rich in all the Schumacherian, small-is-beautiful virtues of devolvement. So in a world casting about for new orders and for new ways of reconciling centre with periphery, national and supranational, Oxford, if it ever succeeds in harmonizing its wondrously devolved and diverse structures, could provide from within its narrow walls a larger lesson to the world.

– 7 –

Through the College Lodge

A Thursday in early October, the day the students pour back in their thousands from the Long Vacation. The date sticks out on the college calendar – as if military mobilization, moving house and the Christmas post all fell in the same place and on the same day. It is a suitcase-lugging, staircase-clambering, paperwork-clutching sort of day. Estate cars, laden with trunks and stereos, straddle pavements and narrow cobbled alleys. Dons breeze through cloisters, some returning repeatedly to the Lodge to check their mail as if testing their connection with reality, others vaguely floating in the quadrangles like dirigibles that have slipped their moorings. Lost parents wander passages clasping electric kettles and trailing flexes . . .

From the previous Sunday the students have begun to drift back, the first stray leaves on a wind that by Thursday is gusting to a full-blown gale. Among them the Freshers, all their senses nervous and new-peeled, the Second Year, confident heirs about to seize their full inheritance, and the Third Years – now a class diminished and apart in the run-up to Final Examinations, reduced to dismal daily comets winging in from digs or college annexe.

It is a time of old and new, of familiar and strange, of hope and apprehension. The college kaleidoscope has been twisted into a new combination. Undergraduates step gingerly in new rooms as if trying out new shoes. They hover at the feet of staircases, compare notes: on whom has the vacation shed a deeper lustre, whose metamorphosis has been the richer, who is better placed to move ahead? The return to college is both the crossing of a threshold and a shutting off; there is a sense of life both left outside but also sealed up within, supercharged and superheated. All day this tube of expectation and emotion squeezes through the Lodge, under the sharp eyes of its porters.

7.00 in the morning: the Head Porter unlocks the main gate to let in the first of the college cleaners. Cheery women, they step into the Lodge as if climbing on to a ship's deck, sign on, clatter their keys and then head off to the individual staircases that form their cleaning kingdoms. Not long afterwards the first student surfaces: a freshman striding around the quad, encased in a suit. (The porter grins, knowing how soon he will swap it for corduroys or denims.) Next, a don descends to complain about noise last night in a nearby room.

Then the first post: mail shoals into these few quadrangles from around the world – letters and parcels for students, requests for references from former tutors, academic enquiries, a copy of the *Daily Texan* for a long-gone summer school student, applications from schools, business transactions arising from college lands or property, acceptances from Old Members to a feast. Other subsidiary blizzards of paper – communications from the university's Registry, lecture lists, cards from societies and clubs – will arrive later through the university's internal service (called the 'pigeon post'; price 2p an item).

Bestriding this blizzard is the porter, constantly sorting and popping papers into pigeon holes (one lot outside for the students, one lot in the Lodge for the dons. The latters' are a rich honeycomb of individuality, oozing with impedimenta – balled-up gowns, a sherry bottle, proofs for correction, books for review, squash rackets, crampons, a motor cycle helmet, even a ham.)

Soon the phone begins its bleepings. The porter answers, all the rich gravy of collegiate formality entering his voice: 'And to whom may I be speaking, sir?' Throughout the day they fence and field a range of enquiries and intrusions from the world without. A florist calls with an order: lacking the appropriate paperwork, his bouquets are refused ('Never sign for anything unless you're certain', grumbles the porter, 'if you do, then it's your job'). A wine merchant drops by to ask who buys the college wine. He is

taken aside, a deal is struck, and he departs, grinning, with a pair
of names.

Others make more determined and sometimes dangerous
assaults. Over the drunks and derelicts of the town, the college
seems to exercise a strange sway. They wander in, sometimes singly,
sometimes in groups, and sing, steal or simply sleep it off (three
were once found, roosting in the organ loft). The porters can bring
to bear a whole battery of rebuffs ranging from 'May I help you,
sir?' (meaning, 'What are you doing loitering here, you suspicious-
looking person') to that ultimate deterrent, a truncheon, kept
hidden under the desk.

An arsenal of records and ledgers arms them in their daily fight:
meticulously named and numbered freshmen's photographs (kept
for up to twenty years), duty rotas, the 'greenlist' of current
students, postbooks, books for bookings, key books, works department books, beer cellar books and, most important of all, the
'Lodge Bible' containing instructions on anything and everything
('How to deal with a bomb scare: try to find out where the bomb
has been placed. Say, the college is a large place, please could you
not be more precise. Notice the caller's accent and try to estimate
his class ...').

At 10.00 the day-porter comes on duty. By now the Lodge's
glass partition is shooting back and forth. Student faces swim
up, are dealt with, disappear, only to re-materialize with further
problems. 'May I have the key for ... where can I buy a gown ...
a phonecard ... paracetamol ... Who is my tutor?' (this from a
postgraduate) ... (then, worst of all) 'I have lost my key.' There
are continuous crises: undergraduates, as if mesmerized by
Oxford's rich shimmer of possibilities, cannot keep a grip on anything: keys, Bodley cards, purses and wallets, all go missing. There
are breakages, accidents; one undergraduate – unbelievably for
October – gets stung by a bee, and proving allergic has to be ferried,
swollen, to the nearest hospital.

Each new undergraduate receives a level stare to try and fix the
face and then intimidatingly precise instructions on how to find his
room. Some – the anonymous legion of names who stick in their
rooms and work – the porters will never see again. Others will
become familiar characters in the drama of the Lodge – known
rogues ('Watch it, Fitzgibbon, you're on thin ice. The Dean will

see you later ...') or even friends. Porter-undergraduate exchanges are often like a kind of game, marked by a certain joking, bullying warmth, by deliberate dodgings and misunderstandings ('Where is staircase nine?' – 'Where it always is'; 'How do I use the pigeon post?' – 'Well, you see those tame pigeons in the corner of the quad, first you catch one, then ...').

Most of the hours in the Lodge are spent in a hurly-burly of business as the porters are bounced between competing calls and queries. But every so often strange lulls open up, passages of quiet water. The porters snatch a bite ('They give you the food but not the time to eat it', grumbles one), they read or bodge and potter at some hobby of their own. Like Rosencrantz and Guildenstern in the Tom Stoppard play, characters caught in the interstices of a larger action, they toss matters up and down, examine them from below and meditate on the unfathomable ways of the college (First Porter: 'What would become of the college if prohibition ever came in?' Second Porter: 'Nothing. They'd find a way of getting around it.')

They compare notes on one another's performance: one is too much a toady to the dons, another a bully, while a third loses in fussy detail the larger contours of his role. The Lodge is many things – rampart, switchboard, sorting office, information booth and first aid station. It is also like so many other British institutions, a little theatre or stage on which the porters strut and play their parts. Underlying all their musings is the question: what constitutes the perfect porter and what is his proper role?

The development of the role of servants in the college is in itself interesting. They came to the fore in the nineteenth century. Earlier a college might have had a small permanent core of cooks, barbers and gardeners, but much of the domestic work would have been done by the poorer scholars, who would be called on to serve their better-off fellows in hall. These declined in the eighteenth century and it became the practice for young gentlemen to bring their own servants up to college with them. Gradually this custom also died out and the college servant or scout assumed centre stage. Their role was at its fullest in the early decades of this century. After the First World War, with the introduction of electric lights and fires

and piped hot water, it went into a decline, one that steepened
more sharply following World War Two.

The life of college scouts was hard. Each scout looked after
about eight 'sets' of rooms. His day began around six o'clock when
he lit the fires, brought hot water and served breakfast and then
cleaned and swept the rooms. After a short late-morning break he
served lunch, usually bread and ale, to students in their rooms.
Following a further break, he would return in the late afternoon
to clear tea things, stoke the fires and serve in hall. His final return
might not be until after nine and on occasions even later if he was
detained to serve at private supper or drinks parties. In vacations
he would almost certainly have been laid off, although some of the
more concerned colleges arranged work in resorts and hotels.

Yet their life was not without its compensations. The scout was
paid more than most Oxford workers, until the coming of the
motor industry, and enjoyed a high status in the city. Scouts had
their own club (on Iffley Road), their own rowing team and a
number of favourite pubs in the city in which they held court. A
scout could do odd jobs outside the college, keep lodgings with his
wife and perhaps even own and rent out a second house. He could
also benefit from the continuous, semi-corrupt trickling down of
tips and perks which oiled the antique machine of the college – a
half-crown here and there for 'bearing a cut' (cleaning up an
unpleasant mess) or holding out a gown in a university ceremony.
Traditionally scouts were entitled to 'broken' goods from their
undergraduates – half empty bottles and other leftovers. One
Bursar of All Souls, Sir E. L. Woodward, noted 'a perpetual kind
of dishonesty ... they wouldn't steal money at all, but they'd steal
cigarettes and help themselves to drink ... this had always gone
on, and it was a thing you always expected them to do ... it was
like the army, a perpetual, very mild pinching'.

The importance of the college servants should not be underestimated. They formed an informal power structure, 'a buffer state
between undergraduates and the Governing Body' as one famous
Chief Porter, Fred Bickerton of University College, put it. If too
tight a rein was applied college spirit might be damped; if too lax,
discipline might begin to unravel. There was also a kind of double
standard. Undergraduate misbehaviour was officially frowned on
but could be secretly enjoyed, especially if it was witty or audacious.

Then again it was like a game of chase in which both sides could take pleasure, the undergraduates as they attempted to evade detection, the scouts, deans and proctors as they tried to catch the culprits.

So their relationship with undergraduates was complex: part servant, part warder, part father-figure and friend. Many undergraduates have kept in lifelong contact with their old scouts. They were also, let it be said, part informer and potential petty blackmailer. Theirs was the power to relate misdeeds (such as a woman in a room overnight) to the dons or – for a price, say a large termly tip – to keep quiet.

Their relationship with the dons was just as complex. Far from being *de haut en bas* it was two-way and could, as Classics don Dacre Balsdon commented, be marked by a certain discreet manipulativeness: 'Dons appoint servants and could in theory dismiss them. Yet over the dons servants have a hold even stronger than that; they are their source of comfort. And while dons love learning, many of them love comfort even more – those at least who are bachelors and whom the servants have completely at their mercy.' The servant–don relationship was and still is a curious blend of deference and contempt: deference for the don's learning and position and respect if he shows savvy in college dealings and has certain outside achievements to his credit, say in sport or the army; contempt if he is pliable and otherworldly.

The college servants still see the college from a unique and intimate angle. They amass a curious subterranean, backstairs knowledge of what is going, put together from back-door glimpses and gossip, hints and half-overheard conversations. 'I enjoyed it all but, as I say, it's like birdwatching,' said another Chief Porter. 'If you watches, you can see anything happen, you know. Course, you see, all the dons, as they are, they're up there on high looking down. But I'm at the bottom, looking up, and that's a different view altogether.'

In their private lives the college servants often reproduced a topsy-turvy version of the life they tended in the colleges, mimicking donnish mannerisms or aping their tastes (often, let it be said, with goods purloined from the colleges). Sometimes this phenomenon took a more intellectual form. Many scouts are known to have been great readers, regularly leafing through volumes of Milton or

Shakespeare. This was admirable but had a pathetic twist to it. Had there been broader educational opportunity in those days who knows but that some of these scouts might have taken their place alongside the dons they served.

Envy or bitterness might seem predictable responses to a life of college service but there is precious little evidence of this. On the contrary, most identified strongly with their college, taking pride in its history, its sporting prowess and the fame of its dons and old members. They carried out a psychic substitution whereby they repressed their own personalities, subsumed them in the stones and activities of the institution. You might spend your time mopping up pools of undergraduate vomit and live in a cramped Jericho terrace but through the college you counted. It validated and magnified you. It was a bit like being a member of a feudal aristocratic household: serving the family, you joined it.

This is not to say all college staff were pallid self-effacers or imitators. Far from it: many were formidable characters in their own right who became well known in the university. University College for some reason seems to have produced more than its share of these individuals. Fred Bickerton who wrote a highly literate memoir of his life as Chief Porter has already been mentioned. His successor, Douglas Millin, also became famous for the firm grip which he kept on the Lodge. When one new broom of a Bursar, a retired admiral, asked him to itemize his duties, he gave a reply that passed into college legend, telling him that his jobs stretched from 'cutting a bloke down who's hung his bloody self to finding a safety pin for a lady's knickers that's fallen down'.

A local lad, he came late to the college, having first served in the army to escape trouble from his father and stepmother. The best times had been just after the Second World War, when a lot of ex-servicemen came up, hungry for knowledge and eager to pitch into anything: 'If you were in trouble on the gate, the drunks and that coming in, you'd only got to shout for somebody and they were there, and they would get stuck in.' Discipline was strict, far stricter than today, but imposed informally on the old military basis of not getting caught. 'I used to get on well with the blokes; get them on their own, give them a right old rollicking, and say, Now next time, we'll go and see the Dean. Well, I never used to catch them again, which is the way it should be.'

From then on it had been downhill all the way: 'Everything began to change when tradition and what discipline there was went out the window if you understand me. About the late 60s when we had all this here shermozzle, when that Tariq Ali used to be about here.' Much of the blame he laid at the dons' doors. In the old days they knew what was what, caught out all 'the baalambs' who broke the rules and kept a firm if civilized hand on things. Now they just buried themselves in their books: 'I feel sorry for some of these young dons ... Some of them have got no interest in the college outside their own work and small circle. They forget that if you chuck a stone in a pool it makes circles.'

If Douglas represented discipline and was the father-figure in the Lodge, there was little doubt in the college who flanked him as mother. It was the College Secretary, Gwynne Ovenstone. 'She wasn't appointed to the College Office,' according to the don who spoke on her retirement after forty years of dedicated service, 'she in fact created it.' A woman of great humour, determination and organizational ability, she terrified the dons in her charge. 'She knows so much about us. She forgets nothing and guesses a great deal more.' Particularly frightening to the dons was a collection of magnetic ladybirds she kept stuck to a steel filing cabinet. These represented the fellows, and their rise or fall indicated their changing positions in her esteem. Dons would shuffle awkwardly into her office, nervously eyeing the ladybirds, before asking a favour or blurting out a fault.

During forty years and with 5,000 undergraduates she wove the fabric of the college through her powers of allocating rooms and directing who shared with whom, knotting and cutting social threads like one of the Fates. Three students she let in through a typing error, but so sure was her touch that they inevitably prospered, winning respectively a First, a good Second and a hockey Blue. She became the college's collective memory, even able to trace its bloodlines and genetic codes. When it was once remarked that a certain undergraduate was doing well, she exclaimed that so he should, he had been conceived on staircase twelve.

Like Douglas, she found the 1960s a distinctly trying time: 'You had to see through their hair before you could talk to students. A lot of them were not awfully nice. They seemed to arrive from school determined not to like it.' However, things, along with fringes, have looked up since and she now finds undergraduates eager once more to throw themselves into the life of the college. Co-education was initially a target of her disapproval, but she later warmed to the idea when she found it smartened up the men and produced seventeen marriages into the bargain, no doubt generating in due course further undergraduates to join the large family of the college.

Nowadays, as workplaces, colleges present a mixed spectacle, one marked by great change but also surprising survival and continuity. In the direction of change several factors have been at work. The dons are a far less permanent and prominent presence in the college and consequently less of a focus for individual cosseting and service. There has been a general shift towards informality with undergraduates preferring cafeteria-style arrangements or self-service kitchenettes over formal dining in hall. In fact many undergraduates find themselves altogether uneasy with being waited on and the whole idea of the gentleman–servant relationship.

Colleges now are run far more as crisp hotel-style operations, with professional domestic bursars, and greater emphasis on income-generating conference business (often representing as much as 15–20 per cent of college earnings) and occupants slotted in and out of rooms with ruthlessly timetabled efficiency. A recent trend has been to contract out areas of work. Governing Bodies have long seen the college kitchen as the sink of waste and corruption, riddled with petty pilfering, overbuying and kickbacks from favoured suppliers. Increasingly they have adopted the solution of putting it temporarily under outside control. Once the Augean stables have been cleansed the contractors are got rid of and it is brought once more under college control.

The character of the staff has also altered. Gone is the old male scout looking after a staircase of 'his' men, his place taken by a new tribe of part-time women cleaners. Gone is the old pattern of lifelong service, burnished bright with drudging dedication. In part this reflects larger changes in Oxford. At one time, if you were Oxford-born and working class, you worked in the colleges or in the trades or services that fed off them. Later you had a choice between the college and the car factory. Now, as more offices and industries have been drawn to Oxford, the choice is wide open and colleges with their traditionally low rates of pay often find themselves scrabbling for staff.

Let us look at the staff of one largish college in more detail. To care for its 450 undergraduates and some 40 dons, it employs 50–60 full-time and part-time domestic staff. Four work as porters in the Lodge, four look after the Senior Common Room and serve on High Table and fifteen in the Works Department are responsible for the college's buildings and gardens. Twenty-two scouts (all but two of them women) come in to clean part-time. There is a full-time caretaker who lives on the premises, a chef, four underchefs and a floating population of 'potmen' and other domestic dogs-bodies. All of these are managed by the Domestic Bursar (a Fellow but with no academic interests) with the help of an assistant and 70 per cent of an accountant (the Treasurer, shared with the Estates Bursar's Office).

Forty years ago the staff was much smaller, closer and more flexible, reflecting the fact that the college as a whole had only half its present number of members. Yet it was a pretty loose kind of family whose members looked in several directions. The Chief Porter felt he answered to no one but the Master of the college. The Senior Common Room steward drew his authority from the dons. The scouts were commanded by the Head Scout (now a purely honorary title, awarded to the most senior of them). Today it is all centralized under the Bursar, with the exception of the contracted-out kitchens and the mildly debatable area of the SCR, whose wine cellar and menus are still fixed by a chairman elected by the dons.

Hours and routines vary greatly. The scouts work three to four hours a day (for which they are paid just over £2 an hour). The Lodge porters alternate weeks of working 10 a.m. to 5 p.m. or 5 p.m. until 1 a.m. while the chief porter covers the early morning period, 7 a.m. to 10 a.m. and living on the premises is in addition on call twenty-four hours a day. At weekends the Lodge is manned by undergraduates. Forty years ago Lodge duties were far more demanding: 'Sometimes I used to do from six till ten in the morning, come back at nine at night and stay all bloody night till eight next morning', recalls one retired porter. 'Then I had the rest of the day off; and next day I'd work all bloody day from six in the morning till ten at night.' But some still work very long days. The SCR steward started at eight in the morning and apart from a two-hour break in the afternoon did not get home until after ten at night. Nor is lifelong service entirely a thing of the past. Several members of the college staff have had forty years in the college, and one recently retired scout more than fifty-six.

College servants are in fact caught on the cusp of change. The old knot of loyalties is being unpicked and replaced by something more conscious, more detached and modern. If it was once a feudal household it is in the throes of conversion to a cash economy. Psychologically, the staff have been propelled into an in-between, indeterminate position. Welcoming the gradual percolation of modern conditions and wanting them to go further, they still look back nostalgically to the old, close world of the college.

The Senior Common Room steward fell into this category. He had worked there for twenty-five years and looked ahead to spending the rest of his career there. Once there had been a traditional, family atmosphere: 'Each year you'd get a speech from the Master, it would buck you up, make you feel part of something, and you'd buckle down to it for another year.' Now, he felt, that had gone and adequate conditions and levels of pay had not yet fully taken its place. Utterly dedicated personally to keeping up standards and maintaining the gracious habits of Hall and High Table, he spoke of the 'glow' he still got from a formal college dinner: 'Thousands of pounds worth of silver on the tables, the candles twinkling and the portraits and the wine and all – there is nothing to beat it.' He instinctively looked up to the dons as superior beings and accepted the hierarchy of the college, half rationalizing this to himself: 'They *are* demanding and it is right they should be. They went to school and college and saw the way other dons live and want to live like that themselves. They *are* different to the rest of us.'

But the college is in flux, emerging as a peculiar hybrid of old and new, and there are those who find it easier to identify with the new rather than the old. I talked to one domestic bursar who was in this position. A highly astute and professional woman with a degree in management and a long career in catering and hospital administration, she had pioneered a whole range of innovations and boosted the revenue-earning activities of the college. But something about its mellowed, tumbled-down familial quality frustrated her, its sheer ornery contrariness and knotty, persistent resistance to rules and rationalizations. She felt, one suspects, subtly rebuffed and sidelined by the very spirit of the place. In particular she found some of the dons maddeningly demanding: 'They are life's difficult customers, appallingly selfish people who think their role is to be the centre of the universe. Oxford breeds this kind of arrogance.'

Others in the cast of college servants achieved a happier synthesis. If in the past they squeezed themselves into the mould of the college, suppressing their personalities beneath its enduring dignity and traditions, now like innovative actors they have improvised a new role, one both more suited to the changing nature of the college and more deeply expressive of themselves. An exponent of this new kind of balance was a lodge porter, a bustling, friendly bear cub of a man, overflowing with ideas, anecdotes and trenchant observations. He had fled to the college as a refugee from a series of unfulfilling or overdemanding jobs – including running his own business – and found himself redeemed by its routines and its essential humanity: 'This is the very opposite of a Leyland (motor works) job. Here you're a person not a number. Or put it another way, it is a way of getting on with people without having to take money off them.'

The college had given him security but also endless involvement. He loved to plunge into the frenetic activity of the Lodge, its endless interactions and collisions, and then sink back at the end of the day into the calm of his bachelor house in Barton. An inveterate fiddler, hobbyist and computer buff, he constantly came up with new ideas, including a scheme for computerizing the Lodge records and linking them into a college-wide information network.

He had taken to the college as if it were some great extended family, becoming familiar with its every face and foible. He was 'Mr Popular' as one of the other porters remarked drily, but there was nothing ingratiating or subservient about him. Rather he was to the undergraduates a well-liked older brother or uncle; his greatest joy, he told me, was being asked to play bass guitar in a student band.

Another individual who had found his niche in the college was a Scottish caretaker whom I accompanied on his rounds one morning. Previously he had worked as a hospital porter in the northeast of England but had been lured down to Oxford by its promise of plentiful employment. He had developed a deep affection for the life of the college and for his work there but at the same time still retained a flinty Northern separateness and a canny insight into the occasional indulgences and hypocrisies. Most of the dons he found 'OK' with one or two difficult or standoffish exceptions but he could not resist poking fun at one fellow who had made a great show of distributing apples to the college staff. They were in fact half-rotten windfalls from the garden of a college house ('Man, they had more than they knew what to do with!').

Filling in that morning for a gap in the ranks of the scouts, he went from room to room, vacuuming, polishing, emptying waste paper baskets. At times his progress turned into a delicately tactful little minuet of backings-out and averted glances, as he came across more than one person sleeping in a bed and quietly closed the door and stole away. He was, he told me, supposed to report them but in practice turned a blind eye to it, often assisted by the mutually accepted signal of a prominently displayed waste paper basket outside a bedroom door.

The night before on one staircase had been a wild one. There had been an unauthorized party (undergraduates are supposed to get permission in advance) and a lot of damage. As we stepped gingerly through splattered kebabs and a thicket of broken chair legs and upturned fire extinguishers (released in an idiotic fury of fun) he spoke with iron relish of the penalties which would be meted out to the offenders. For he knew the form of his undergraduates like the back of his fist – who was decent, who a 'rogue' and who might try to pull the odd 'flanker'.

But then our talk took a new and surprising tack. He began to speak of the tensions and problems of modern student life, how he and his wife felt sorry for many undergraduates and invited groups of them round to their quarter for counselling.

The college caretaker as psychotherapist! It is an astounding development, but then college servants are often astounding people. They are already called on to play a variety of roles, so why not – when colleges are increasingly receiving students as vulnerable and damaged as they are gifted – therapist too? Let no one underestimate those who serve in the colleges. John Betjeman said as an undergraduate he found the college servants 'more

1. The Steps of Learning: the Radcliffe Camera and All Souls

2. An East Oxford Landmark: the Penultimate Picture Palace

3. Here Be Dragons: a Typical North Oxford Residence

4. A Present-day Penniless Bench in Oxford, at the North Gate

5. On the River: an Oriel Oarsperson

6. The Walls of Jericho: Lucy's Ironworks from St Sepulchre's Cemetery

7. In the Land of Don: Lincoln College Library

8. Through the College Lodge: Tom Quad, Christ Church

interesting and more efficient and human than the dons'. They are a vital component in a college, subtly setting its tone and temperature and ensuring the sweet and harmonious meshing of its parts, and to the permutations of their contribution there seem few limits.

Late afternoon in the Lodge. A lull as the day porter gathers his bags to leave. Earlier there has been a Bursar's Lunch, an opportunity for the college to fête its old staff and contacts in the city. A retired porter comes to sit in the Lodge, waiting for his taxi. Now, the other porters whisper, he is a sick man, not long for this world. But somehow he has managed to struggle in, determined not to miss his treat, his last small slice of privilege. He leans back in a corner, in a daze of food and drink and pain, eyes closed but seeming to take a vague, unfocused pleasure in the small doings of the Lodge. After he has tottered away to his taxi a momentary hush falls on the porters as if they realize that their parts too will reach an end. Then a college team clatters through returning from a game, a fuse blacks out a quadrangle and electricians have to be summoned. The pace picks up and with it the porters' mood. Yes, their individual strands in the college will come to an end one day but its fabric will continue to be hourly rewoven.

With the Hack Pack

He had just been labelled 'Pushy Fresher of the Year' in *Cherwell*, the student newspaper. But he did not seem pushy at all – in fact, positively languid, with his drawled vowels, ivory complexion and delicately waxed moustache. But as he described his day, a slightly rowdier note entered in. *Rise about ten – usually woken by friends braying in the square. Breakfast, then drinks. No lunch – it's far too sordid in Hall. Then out in the afternoon beagling. Tea, more drinks. Dinner in Hall – it's better at night. Finally end up in The Bear, getting tight, tooting hunting horns and generally making pests of ourselves.* And so – after a final celebratory pee over the walls into Christ Church – to bed.

And his politics? Well, he was 'an ultra-right wing Catholic monarchist' and had, to his triumph, just pulled off the difficult coup of getting expelled from the university's Monday Club for being too right wing. But when I pressed him about his background he became evasive, muttering something about 'a small town in Lancashire' and 'a father in the Army'. He was in fact putting on an act, was as artificial as one of those exquisite fake-antique shops that sell herbs and scents in tiny bottles and jars. All the same, his work rate was enormous, matching any other student toiling with a pile of books. He was a kind of caryatid or temple column, motionless but sustaining an immense weight. Just one second of relaxation and the entire edifice would tumble about his ears. So 'pushy' was the right word after all. He was a strangely modern, entrepreneurial figure, a kind of human factory, with himself as the chief product of its assembly lines, ready to be pushed and promoted in the student market-place of style.

Traditional Oxford undergraduate culture lasted as a coherent slab from the nineteenth century to the Second World War, and – in a weakened, fissured form – a little beyond. The slab was above all homogeneous, its constituents being almost entirely male, middle class and public school educated. The few outsiders did well to keep their heads down or adopt masking social camouflage as soon as possible. (A book on undergraduates published in the 1920s stated if anyone was likely to be ragged it was 'the bird of strange plumage, unfashionable in attire and ill-at-ease in manner ... The poorer scholar from the more private and unmentionable schools making his uncouth and lowly entry upon this scene.') Undergraduate culture centred on the college: only the Union politicians, top athletes and most outrageously vulnerable aesthetes – who clustered for greater protection into common cultural caravanserais – ventured out into the broader universe of the university.

Yet for all the solidity of the undergraduate culture it was riddled with strange contradictions. Individuality was prized but at the same time conformity was all-important. Achievement – academic and extra-curricular – was admired as long as it was not the product of low, sweaty diligence. Discipline, with its nightly lockings-out and compulsory chapel, was strict on the surface but in reality allowed considerable latitude, particularly if you won over your scout (either by charm or substantial gratuities).

Then again a whole tribe of contradictions danced about the taboo of homosexuality. This was a murky corner of the quad where hearty and aesthete edged surreptitiously towards one another. Many undergraduates perpetuated temporarily the practices of the school dorm. 'When we go down, we become normal' declared one book written by an undergraduate. Almost incredibly the Classics don Dacre Balsdon felt able to declare in the bestseller he wrote on the university in the 1950s that 'a vice from which present day Oxford does not suffer is homosexuality'.

After the Second World War a brief revival of traditional undergraduate culture flared, but there was a terminal glow in it all, the dying warmth of an Indian summer. It was on a par with all the other paperings-over that came to mark the brave New Elizabethan era of the early 1950s. But the cracks had gone too deep, and in the wake of Suez, amidst larger crashings and crumblings, the old undergraduate culture gave way altogether.

Soon the postwar Welfare State generation began to roll up with its suitcases in increasing numbers at Oxford station. As the old social coherence split, so there was a swing to the left, one which sharpened in the course of the '60s. Just as Spain had been a rallying point for the student leftwinger of the 1930s, so Vietnam supplied a dominant, symbolic issue. Some have seen the 1965 teach-in at the Oxford Union as the high-water mark of this leftwards tendency; others the student disruptions and the occupation of the Registry in the early 1970s.

Youth culture suddenly came up in a sunburst over the horizon of Oxford, dowsing everything in its Day-Glo glare. There were massive superficial changes in personal style. Absurd and trivial as these seem now, at the time they were felt to be the signs of a spiritual revolution, the harbingers of a whole new era. (*Oxymoron*, a student magazine of the late 1960s, went into a paroxysm of excitement over a pair of flares: 'There is a male boutique in Little Clarendon Street,' it enthused. 'This fact, clearly the most important thing to happen in Oxford this century, does not seem to have attracted the attention it merits ... You will be fascinated to know', continued the student journalist, 'that I have my eyes on some mauve cord trousers that are just fantastic. It's a gas, man ...'.) Out went sports coats and grey flannels, sensible career plans and mature relationships. In came jeans, bell bottoms, Afghan coats and beads, long hair and beards and pot, going to India and, as the Pill was downed in increasing quantities, sleeping together.

Needless to say, traditional elements were outraged. Dacre Balsdon, having captured in one book the clean-cut, well-shaven features of the old Oxford, felt impelled to bring out a second, *Oxford Then and Now*, in which he lashed the new 'capelloni, all Esaus and hairy men'. Gwynne Ovenstone, secretary of University College, still shudders with distaste when asked about those now distant days. Then the wave, to her relief, passed, seen off by the oil crisis of '74 and the subsequent stagflation with its diminished job prospects for graduates and corresponding pressure to conform.

A new era was ushered in by Mrs Thatcher's victory in 1979.

For the emerging Oxford graduate the stick of unemployment was eventually replaced by the carrot of serious money to be made in the City. The word 'Brideshead' summed it all up. Following the immensely popular TV serialization in the early 1980s of Evelyn Waugh's *Brideshead Revisited*, everything in Oxford was branded with the word. A vision took hold of smooth lawns and white flannelled elegance, against a backdrop of prints and dreaming spires, as the long champagne party of an Oxford summer term slid by ...

In the eyes of the press conspicuous consumption, snobbish superficiality and mindless pranks were the order of the day. There were interviews with Oxford's Bright Young Things and stories about societies such as the Assassins with their nasty habits of smashing up restaurants and the Piers Gaveston's alleged sexual orgies. It all culminated in the lurid coverage afforded to the death from a combination of drugs and alcohol of a Tory minister's daughter, Olivia Channon, and the alleged debaucheries of her circle. Oxford, if the media were to be believed, had gone full circle. The Fast Set of the 1920s had returned and were once again alive and well in Turl Street, 'baying', in Evelyn Waugh's phrase, 'for broken glass'.

How accurate was – and is – this picture of Oxford undergraduates? There remain a small proportion of privileged socialites, known as the 'Sloanes'. Sloanes form an invisible college, a hermetic social universe all of their own. They arrive, with a compressed chip, so to speak, slotted into their rather empty skulls, pre-programmed with contacts from school and family background. While other new undergraduates are going out, meeting people and opening out their lives, the Sloane remains in his (or her) room, a perfect, silent chrysalis of Sloandom. Then it wakes, the chip is activated, and it starts to stretch out along the twigs of its network. A small confetti of expensively printed invitation cards will mysteriously shower into other Sloanes' college pigeon holes, inviting them for cocktails or to a dinner party. Then through the first circle of programmed-in Sloanes, they meet other ones. But never very many, for the Sloane pond is a small one.

How does the Oxford Sloane differ from his London brother? The answer is, almost not at all. They make few or no concessions to the fact that they are here. They treat the college as a superior country house hotel in which for some unaccountable reason they seem to be taking a prolonged holiday, and the dons as some sort of superior servant or ingenious butler. Doing the minimum of work to scrape by (a good second would be a source of deep shame to a Sloane), they try their damnedest to conceal the ability that must have got them to Oxford in the first place. They are in fact profoundly embarrassed by this stage in their lives: like oil and water, Sloanes and academe do not mix, or not for very long. Giving the mind a miss, they are deeply into the body, and their talk is all of horses, boyfriends (or girlfriends), cars, foreign holidays, clothes and losing weight. They are, needless to say, very Green Welly and very White Flannel.

You can spot them hurling back malts in the Union Bar, wetting one another with beer in The Bear, buying their heavy leather shoes at Duckers or their waistcoats (say 'weskits') at Halls or joining select dining clubs such as The Bullingdon or The Grid. But they spend as much time as possible away from Oxford – partying in London, shooting in Yorkshire or skiing in Gstaad. To help them gad about, they will have a nippy little runabout – a Golf, a Peugeot or a Suzuki Jeep in Welly Green – which they refer to affectionately as the 'runt' in their family's litter of cars ('I'm taking the runt for a trip up to tine'). While in Oxford, they do no sport apart from a little beagling and never, never hack at extracurricular activities. To do so would be low and imply you needed to try, to sweat. Instead, they get heavily, swinishly drunk and then have awful accidents and smash-ups (the personal damage they happily endure with all the stoicism of their caste).

But Sloanes represent only a tiny fragment of the Oxford student world. That world, unlike the old monolithic undergraduate culture, is a huge federation of fragments, a great honeycomb of cells, cliques and special interest groups, congregating around anything from politics to pop music. Where once there was a single consolidated cliff of social success, now there is a plurality of separate hierarchies. The Oxford undergraduate landscape has been weakened and eroded and now reproduces more closely the features of society outside.

The federation of fragments – the 'big bourgeois colony', as one undergraduate called it – are reflected in a new range of compromises. Exemplifying these is college life. While relishing the social support system and close academic attention afforded by the colleges, many undergraduates would like to see an even greater degree of freedom and flexibility built in. Indeed ambivalence marks their attitudes on a larger level to the privileged environment of Oxford. Many go into profound culture shock at the sheer *difference* of the place – its thick encrustation of history and tradition and such things as wearing gowns, saying Latin graces or going to formal Hall. Indeed they feel there is an arrogant misconception of the status of the university, that the very notion of excellence is élitist and that Oxford should be just like other universities: strong in some areas, weak in others.

There are others who strongly defend Oxford's specialness, but a third category is schizophrenic. Its members, although inclined to kick against traditions, are tempted to act up to them for the glittering backdrop they can provide to the passing social role. They decry exclusivity, while secretly preening themselves on getting into Oxford in the first place. They want to get their fingers on all the privileges and advantages going – including a clean social conscience – and can step in an instant from shelling out hundreds of pounds for ball tickets to supporting the Broadwater Farm defendants.

Summing up all the contradictions and indeed trading profitably upon them, is the figure of the Casual. The Casual is an odd, self-serving mix. For most of the time he speaks the generalized media cockney familiar from 'The Sweeney' or 'Minder'. He dresses down, wears denims and trainers and generally tries to look as much like a plasterer's mate as possible. In town-and-gown terms he has gone native. He puts away loadsa lager in the pubs of St Clement's and the Cowley Road, hangs out in dingy backstreet betting shops (hinting always at his formidable hold of betting form) and likes to be spotted at the dog track, the ice rink or the local speedway, bawling out his support for the Oxford Cheetahs. With every nerve in his body he strives to give the impression that he clambered up to Oxford from a council estate in Brentford or Brixton or punched his way out of the tarmacked playground of a tough inner city comprehensive. In fact his parents are polytechnic lecturers, concerned doctors or liberal-minded lawyers, and his comfortable upbringing amply stocked with books, foreign holidays and brain-stretching adult interaction. At times he drops his usual accent altogether and speaks in a quite different voice – crisp, clean and classless. For the Casual can alternate voices or adjust the admixture precisely at will – or, more likely, unconsciously as he automatically adapts to a particular context.

In fact like nearly everyone else at Oxford the Casual is a high-powered, middle-class self-starter, but one with an especially extensive social tool kit. If he uses it properly (and you can be sure that he will) he will eventually surge up through the media world where his sure-footed agility and instinctive sense of style and audience will give him enviable purchase on its slippery summits.

Another character in contemporary Oxford who trades in contradictions is the Sister. Every college has to have at least one Sister. You cannot miss her stamping across the quads, hair brutally cropped, in denims, combat jacket and a pair of enormous bovver boots. And you can hear her also, only too clearly, speaking as the elected Women's Officer of the Junior Common Room. She is a prodigious paper mill. The female fresher on arrival finds her pigeon hole blocked with bulky pamphlets from the Sister on Being Assertive, on Self Defence, on overcoming Bulimia, on Getting an Abortion and on the apparently insuperable difficulties of 'coming out' at Oxford. If they did not have problems before, they soon learn that they ought to have. The Sister's 'Glossary of Non-Sexist Terminology' has sold or rather been put on sale in every NUS bookshop in the land, and there is nothing more calculated to enrage her than the words 'Master' or 'Fellows'. Her deepest enemy is the Dean, a silky equivocator whom she nags for dragging his feet on a college code on sexual harassment. The beer cellar is, to her narrow eyes, a deep sty of chauvinism, and a personal compliment paid there little short of an assault. The First Fifteen would, she thinks, benefit from an immediate programme of chemical castration. Everywhere she turns in Oxford she sees – and she is doubtless right – male power structures.

The very fabric of the college is a masculine affront to her sensibilities (all those male monkish quads, portraits of paternalist exploiters and phallic spires and turrets) so, naturally, she gravitates towards Jericho and 'a women's collective' (that is, a few girls sharing a flat). There, under shelves groaning with ill-made pots, hand-drawn pictures of overweight women dancing under a full moon, a blown-up photograph of Virginia Woolf and row upon

row of Greer, Millett, Orbach and De Beauvoir, she receives her
boyfriend (a minor Casual) and tells him that, despite their non-
submissive relationship, she really favours 'sexual separatism'. He,
pale frightened individual, nods eagerly in response.

She is a one issue woman and that issue is women. Give her an
engineering problem and she would suggest a feminist solution.
Everything from the Amazonian rainforest to vegetarianism has to
be squeezed through that narrow aperture. She sees herself as a
commando in the sexual combat zone, storming the citadel of
chauvinism. The trouble is that at Oxford the foe is everywhere
but will not give fight. If only her tutor would molest her, what
scalding cataracts of righteous indignation could she release! But
he, weak academic dormouse, could not molest a dunked dough-
nut. So she does her best. She daubs female symbols on the Private
Sex Shop, pickets W. H. Smith to remove their girly mags and
organizes an Oxford JCR ban on Page Three tabloids. Her proudest
moment came when a Towny once called her 'darling' in a Carfax
chipshop and was punished for his over-familiarity with a karate
kick to the groin.

The Sister invents her big confrontational issues, carries them
round like a large placard and as a result misses the real issues
under her feet. For this reason she is largely ignored by the majority
of women students who see her approach as clangingly inap-
propriate. For them Oxford chauvinism undoubtedly exists but it
is a subtle and silkily spoken creature. From male tutors women
undergraduates feel that they are more likely to have to combat a
vague failure of rapport rather than sexual groping. Similarly, what
they resent about male undergraduates is not so much harassment
as patronizing protectiveness or rude overfamiliarity. Public school-
educated undergraduates, incidentally, are seen as the worst
offenders in this regard, covering up their unfamiliarity with women
by gauche agressiveness. By contrast, a natural alliance seems to
be struck between women and the other Oxford outgroup, the
working-class or state school-educated male.

Like the women, another category which often feels it is in an
anomalous marginal position at Oxford is the postgraduate. They
feel in fact triply alienated. As they struggle on, eking out an
existence on meagre grants, sidelined from success, they may see
their former undergraduate peers rising in the material world,

swarming up the salary increments, collecting career points, cars, houses, wives and children ... Then again, being older and more wrapped in their studies, the postgraduates are at a distance from the general hurly-burly of student life. Gone are those 1960s days when the postgraduates were the active young priests of academe, revered and radical. Now a mildewed air of marginality and irrelevance hangs over them. Why, think the undergraduates now, do they loiter in the cloisters? Why aren't they out there, gaining? Finally, the postgraduates are in an exposed position regarding the college–university structure, often scanted of resources and attention and in an unhappy halfway house between Junior and Senior Members, with more standing than the undergraduates but no permanency or power. Although a few colleges like Magdalen successfully integrate them into the mainstream of college life, they mostly gravitate towards the fringes. But they are numerous, and their numbers are increasing all the time: fifty years ago they were less than one in ten of students, now they are more than one in four. They are the lonely crowd of academe.

Out of their loneliness and earnestness is born an intense searchlight of intellectual–moral stringency. With few academic jobs to look forward to, given the continuing squeeze on university budgets, they are driven only by a love of learning, a dedication to disclose and scrutinize. They are like the early scholars of medieval Oxford, those learned starvelings burning with scholastic zeal. They embrace rigorous and abstruse systems of thought eagerly, joyously impaling themselves on their philosophical severities and schematizing their studies according to their arid diagrams.

Not surprisingly their alienation bonds the postgraduates tightly together. Often a group will band together to rent some tiny house in Osney or East Oxford. Then, within its narrow walls, what intensities of shared life, what protractions of analysis over the brown rice and cheap nutritious casseroles, what hurlings and counter-hurlings of arcane argument. The ideal postgraduate household becomes a little backstreet Bloomsbury, a highly charged circle of friendships, sensitivities and meaningful relationships, positively vibrating with the high seriousness of it all. Each circle generates internally a mythology and language of its own, projects its members on to the bare walls of its surroundings as a cast of larger-than-life characters. Never again will life have such sharp definition, such crucial moment! Later, like all connections tied in a time of youth and great intensity, their links will last over lives and continents.

So, socially, the postgraduate world is like a pond full of tiny transient circles spreading, meeting and overlapping. Their intersection points are the middle common rooms, the bars of the Kings Arms, the tables of Brown's and George's in the market and, above all, the Upper Reading Room of the Bodleian – a place not so much a library as a salon suffused equally with eroticism and erudition, an alert theatre of silence, scene of rehearsed gestures, of carefully staged entrances and exits and, over the desk partitions, penetrating glances significantly prolonged . . .

Just as the medieval clerks apprenticed themselves to a more learned *magister*, so the postgraduates enthusiastically seek out discipline-gurus, either in person or through their works. The slightest utterances of the guru will be submitted to miracles of minute, loving analysis by the students, who will, moreover, sedulously ape his attitudes, mannerisms and even dress. Should the disciples be reproved by their supervisors for the obscurity or extremism into which they have been led by their discipline-gurus, they will accept the reproof with all the pride of the stigmata. Their doctorates are not just quests for the Holy Grail but almost martyrdoms, transcendant ordeals, transfiguring agonies of intellectual effort, after which they can descend from the peaks of high seriousness, becoming, if they are lucky, dons, or going down into the happy normality of everyday life.

Postgraduates are not the only ones to make a fetish of their academic work. Oxford undergraduates today differ from previous generations in that they work far harder. Once they fell roughly into three groups: a minority who devoted themselves to getting a First and an academic career; another minority who did next to nothing, lotus-eaters in Oxford's rich orchard of social and extracurricular activities who counted themselves lucky to get a Third; and in between the amorphous mass who took comfort in the prospect of the undivided Second Class degree. These veered between dabbling in outside activities and periodic blitzes of work. These blitzes or essay crises were a kind of college ritual, almost a rite of passage, well publicized in advance and requiring the hovering attendance of a circle of solicitous friends. The under-graduate would stay up all night and emerge triumphantly at dawn, with violet-ringed eyes and a sheaf of scrawled pages clutched between caffeine-quivering fingers.

Now work is high on the altar. Whereas for earlier generations a First was almost a disadvantage if you did not intend an academic career – a sign of the sort of over-crystalline intelligence that meshed ill with the harsh grind of real life – now it is a distinction much sought after. Now spending ten hours a day working in the library is considered chic, and people become celebrities for this.

A number of factors have tightened the academic screw. For one thing entrance standards have risen steadily. Then there is more to be covered, particularly in arts subjects which have retained their broadranging survey structure (sometimes called the 'Cook's Tour' approach) whilst trying to accommodate new areas of study as well as the mass of material churned from the mills of academe. Nowadays undergraduates are likely to have three tutorials a fort-night, as opposed to two in the past, and will probably need to spend up to four days preparing for each. Finally, there is the pressure cooker effect of the Norrington Table which ranks colleges according to their Finals results. Colleges, only too aware of the importance of their position on the Table, are increasingly driving undergraduates to hike up their performance. But there is more to it than internal pressure. Some change in the external wavelength seems to be making students respond with a new and harder vibration. It is as if the need has been generated in them to show how capable they are, like some finely engineered and flexible machine, of sustaining prodigious effort over long periods and making sudden and successful switches of product.

But to make your mark it is not enough just to immure yourself behind a wall of tomes. Simply to do that would be to risk being branded a 'nerd' or a 'dork'. Student sport saw a phenomenal leap in popularity in the aerobic '80s. But really to be seen as a success you have to plunge also into the extracurricular activities and join what are known as the 'Hack Packs'. 'Hacking', a term originally applied to the vote grubbing of student politics, the patient building of a power base in return for a later sharing out of favours, is now used of almost any activity: you even hear of 'Religion Hacks'.

A variety of glittering prizes dangle before the aspiring Hack.

The brightest probably are in politics, but there are also the well-established arenas of student journalism and drama. Generally the Hack is drawn to forms that involve performance and projection. What fuels the Hack in addition to confidence and drive is the hunger for recognition. There has to be some glamour and glitz, some stage or platform on which to parade and a sizeable audience or readership from which to win applause or recognition. The Hack always has his or her eyes set not just on the immediate rungs of the success ladder stretching above him in the university but on London and the real world. The Hack's twin dream is (a) the *coup* – sudden stunning success, say, a prizewinning production or article and (b) the *offer*, a large generous hand reaching down from the outside world and opening to disclose a glittering career.

As such there is bound to be competition. The world of the 'Hack Packs' is not a large one. 'Basically Oxford is run by 250 people,' said one undergraduate. 'Most people do not get involved and of those that do, 75 per cent have given up by fourth or fifth week of Term.' It is all a matter of confidence and drive. The magic word which you hear time and again is not 'class' or 'background' but 'confidence', the X factor, the added extra, the high performance fuel that propels you into high achievement. In many it is a social manufacture, the product of public-school training, but other undergraduates from less privileged backgrounds also learn the trick of somehow synthesizing it inside themselves. Many undergraduates become addicted to the adrenalin economy of Oxford: 'An environment is created here', said one student journalist, 'that makes you push that bit harder. It's like a supercharger effect, that moment on a merry-go-round when they speed it up and you get that exhilarating moment of accelerator switch.'

A Hack variant is the Technician, sometimes known as the Realistic Student. Technicians focus heavily on the nuts and bolts of their particular brand of hackery. If the Technician is, say, a student journalist, he or she will be as interested in the question of layout or typography as in getting a prestigious byline. All well and good, you might conclude: they are immersing themselves in student activities for the fun of it and getting a lot of practical experience into the bargain. But that does not quite capture the high seriousness of it all, the zeal with which Technicians tend the altar of their craft. They display an almost oriental suppression of the self in pursuit of the common objective. The Technician is pre-corporate man, an executive-in-ovo waiting only for the moment to embed himself into the womb-wall of an organization.

The rise of the Technician is all to do with the flow of current between Oxford and the world. Once Oxford politics, drama or journalism were felt to enjoy such a commanding presence that their practitioners could step airily off into whatever they liked. Now the current is switched the other way, the world is injecting its own large cold doses of realism into Oxford. The increasing professionalization of student activities has undoubtedly much to do with the harsher economic climate of the 1980s. Certainly, Technicians are horribly mature, well organized and mapped-out. And sometimes, just sometimes, you cannot help missing the old flaring egotism, the flimsy kite bravely flown, flapping its message of 'me, me, me ...'.

By now the Oxford Hack Track has reached a commonly agreed, almost codified form, its contestants' moves as programmed and predictable as a robot on an assembly line. The Hack's first term is spent socializing – not just having fun but picking out the contacts, the cogs, the powerbrokers. At first the Hack concentrates on his own college but then works outwards into the university (shedding social mistakes and unprofitable contacts as he or she goes). By the summer term of the first year the Hack will be hanging on the fringes of a chosen Hack Pack, gratefully seizing any routine assignment morsels hurled in his or her direction (canvassing, legwork reporting, painting scenery etc.) and often attaching him or herself as a cub Hack to a stronger member.

The end of the first year is a crucial time. Doubts assail the Hack: it all seems impenetrable and is it worth it anyway? At this point the Hacks must grit their teeth, clutch hard their tiny charge of confidence and press on. The summer vacation will be spent by the Hack anxiously pondering and plotting the next move like a general on the eve of a manœuvre. Now confidence is not of itself enough. A quantum of creativity is called for, the window of opportunity being so brief and the stairs so smooth with use. In the second year the Hack launches the offensive – eventually standing for editor, president or whatever in the second or third terms. The Hack leaps snarling into the snapping centre of the Hack Pack and with luck emerges with something chunky for the CV clenched between his or her teeth. In retrospect the Hack will be surprised at how almost ludicrously easy it has all been and will view competitors not with wide-eyed fear but familiar faint contempt. Then in the third year the Hack program clicks into its terminal sequence. The Hack stops being a Hack and becomes a Nerd. He or she retreats to a darkened room, works for sixteen hours a day, and emerges at the end of it with a First or a nervous breakdown or, quite often, both.

But what of the old student idealism, eager to call the whole world into the court of its conscience? No doubt there is as much individual idealism around as ever, but as an outlook – a profile or style – it too has been patented as a hacking thing, the possession of a clique: the Idealist Hacks. Idealist Hacks still rattle off the alphabet of concerns from AIDS to the Third World. They are the ideological long-distance wiring specialists who can connect up a rise in college rents with conditions in Soweto.

In student politics it is on the OUSU ladder that you mainly find the Idealist Hacks. The OUSU offices in Little Clarendon Street are a little cell of the old linkmanship, complete with its packages and checklists, holding out bravely in the sea of social apathy. For on the Oxford scene generally the Idealist Hacks are now somewhat marginalized figures. From their cramped quarters they glower down at the Oxford Union, all Victorian assurance, still lying centrally athwart Oxford and the Establishment generally. If only Oxford were like other universities with a simple facility to pull everything back together again! Wretchedly isolated, they scan the horizon for allies – the NUS, the Polytechnic Union, even the City Council (on one of whose many proliferating committees they are pathetically grateful to get a seat). For support they even look back in time to that *annus mirabilis*, 1968, sprinkling the OUSU Handbook generously with red haiku lifted from Paris and Berlin student walls of that year. For this reason other students regard the Idealist Hacks almost as a curiosity, a kind of nostalgia society that collects the memorabilia and attitudes of a long-gone era.

Hacks rather resemble those old 1940s rockets consisting of two tanks of gas, whose contents, when combined and burnt, explosively propel them to their target. For if ambition brims in one of the Hacks' tanks, anxiety simmers in the other. Anxiety – Oxford phobia or Oxford neurosis – has of course long been a powerful element in Oxford student culture. The undergraduate suicide has a lineage longer than the Boat Race or the tutorial system. The sheer pace, the compressed intensity of undergraduate life, a kind of high speed Cresta Run whose intoxicating acceleration can turn all too easily into a terrifying blur. Even the college as providing a steady base can have its negative aspect, acting as a psychic reflecting bowl, further trapping and concentrating the neurotic intensity.

But this is the old traditional Oxford angst – almost the angst of artificiality and privilege. The new Oxford angst, by contrast, is pressed in from the world, through the psychological problems students import from increasingly broken family backgrounds or through fear of failing – similar to the Hack's fear of falling off the success ladder into obscure mediocrity. There is an underlying depression and disillusionment. The playroom of the under-graduate is still a brightly painted place, littered with toys and excitements, but it has become also a strangely airless, sunless place, all too clearly the anteroom to a slot in society. 'At Oxford we all now live in the present tense,' commented one undergraduate. 'No new ideas burst forth into the mind of a generation,' another has written in bleak, almost Chekhovian terms: 'No one was free enough to invent or to dream or to hope. We were all enslaved by something heavy in the atmosphere, something cloying, hanging over the city like a dark, grey cloud.' A romantic overstatement perhaps, but with a kernel of truth. Today's Oxford undergraduates are perhaps amongst the most privileged casualties of the 1980s culture: somehow they have been persuaded to postpone – perhaps permanently – the chance to wander, to make their mistakes, and to dream.

– 9 –

Into the Land of Don

Dons admirable! Dons of might!
Uprising on my inward sight
Compact of ancient tales, and port
And sleep – and learning of a sort.

Hilaire Belloc, *Verses* (1910)

The dons, the permanent fellows of a college, are the core of its continuity, the guardians of its identity and labours. A certain image of dons is printed in the popular mind: crustily conservative, remote, somehow simultaneously formidable and ineffectual – *donnish*, in a word. But dons' styles and characters, like their colleges, are changing, as change presses in from beyond their walls.

Actually, there is probably no more diverse collection of beings in any one place than the dons of an Oxford college. More than intensely varied, they are usually also divided. As John Betjeman commented in *Oxford University Chest*, the hatred of one don for another is a 'yellow crafty thing that lasts a lifetime'. Within each college it is the Governing Body which has to bring the dons together, focus their differences and provide a forum where agreement can be reached.

Governing Body is a little democracy of dons. There is no other body quite like it. If you were to get a small parliament, a Senate,

say, or House of Lords, and impose on it, without any reduction
in size, the duties of a Cabinet, then you might have something like
a college Governing Body. One of the most savagely satirical
portrayals of a Governing Body at work is in the novel *That
Hideous Strength* by C. S. Lewis, said to be based on his own
experience as a don at Magdalen. It describes how a gang of college
progressives triumph over conservatives by rigging the agenda and
baiting their hooks with tempting inducements. Another picture,
though draped in fantasy, comes in *Lord of the Rings* by Lewis's
friend, J. R. R. Tolkien. There are some strange tree-like creatures
called Ents, who hold Entmoots which are in fact woodland college
meetings: they go on forever, everyone has to have their say and
whenever an object is mentioned its full history has to be rehearsed.

The immediate surface of Governing Body is ceremonial and
formal, almost frigidly so. Gowns are worn, speeches addressed to
the Chair, people referred to by their offices and expressions used
like 'with respect' (when, of course, they mean the exact opposite).
Precise choice of words is crucial. Indeed, the expression 'the
right form of words' often drops from donnish lips. Dons, being
concerned with words – either as objects of study in themselves or
as a means of learned communication – rarely forgive their inexpert
use. An elegant and succinct argument can often win the day while
a verbose and ill-phrased one will certainly lose it.

Who gets listened to in Governing Body? Well, certainly the
college officers, within the ambits of their assigned responsibilities –
but rarely if they stray beyond them. A rich or influential member
who has benefited the college will find his words weighed as carefully as his wealth or power. Yet dons are small respecters of
outside reputation. Anyone who conveys the impression of enjoy-
ing bringing his broader experience to bear in the tiny Lilliput of
the college will find himself rudely and sharply cut down to size.

Maybe a dozen fellows will be regular speakers. Amongst them
will be a number of 'professional backbenchers' who feel their long
and convoluted intimacy with the college entitles them to speak
out on a span of issues. Much more appreciated are the 'court
jesters' – wits and actors who cartwheel in and semi-deliberately
mount amusingly noisy performances for the benefit of their colleagues. These contributions will be signalled by nudges, winks and
grins from the other dons and conclude amidst a chorus of chuckles

and shaking heads. Each college has at least two of these, representing respectively right and left. The one puts on a parody of a deep blue diehard, a one-man academic fortress, furiously fighting change inch by inch; the other, a ruthless Roundhead, slashing at the roots of traditions without mercy. Permanent factions, though, are surprisingly rare, especially in right–left terms. Dons are too individual to belong to parties. *Ad hoc* alliances on particular issues are far more common. If any overriding divide can be detected it is between puritans and epicures – between those who are keen to prune and simplify the college lifestyle and those who seek to defend and preserve its gracious glimmers of luxury.

Many of the issues debated by Governing Body are of almost microscopic importance. The question, say, of the cost of napkins arises: should they switch from linen to paper to save on money and cleaning. The Bursar carefully prepares an erudite paper on the types and colours of napkins, perhaps even their history and manufacture: he concludes with a complex matrix of costed options. The dons deliberate for an hour, then comes the momentous decision: linen on guest nights, paper for the rest.

But there are more serious debates and some issues prove especially contentious. Anything to do with admissions quotas or the relative representation between subjects is generally 'hot'. Emotion will zoom dragon-like from nowhere into the room, a testy asperity descend, necks stiffen and eyes swivel and spluttering speeches are delivered with a sudden, hacking intensity. Oddly, it is often minor matters of an aesthetic nature – the choice of panelling or a college bookplate – that provoke most heat. There is generally one unexploded bomb lurking beneath the smooth surface of the agenda. Similarly, amongst the fellows there is often a 'difficult', emotional don whose explosions – stormings out, threats of resignation, tantrums leading even to tears – are dreaded. The other dons, half guessing, perhaps even sharing the psychic contradictions and constrictions that give rise to these outbursts, endure them with surprising grace and patience until death or retirement finally removes their source.

The one thing guaranteed to provoke irritation and unity amongst the dons is a communication from the outside world. Missives from the University Registry are handled as gingerly as if franked 'IRA' or 'Falls Road'; communications from other colleges can create extreme rancour. There is undoubtedly an implicit world view amongst Governing Bodies. It is rather like medieval cosmology which placed the earth at the centre of the universe: the college is in the middle, the other colleges and the university its outer planets and the world beyond Oxford as distant and unknown as the rest of the galaxy, peopled, if at all, by dangerous little green aliens. It is perhaps for this reason that government communications receive in colleges the same mixed reactions that UFOs do elsewhere – that polarization between jeering disbelief and utter paranoia.

The college-versus-the-world mentality is all the more peculiar if you encounter college fellows in outside capacities. There they are rational, liberal, open-minded. But re-enclose them behind their narrow college gates and a kind of psychic petrification seems to set in; they peer suspiciously out at life like the ancient gargoyles squinting down from their own embrasured walls.

How does business ever get transacted in Governing Body? The key is to understand two things: dons love to pry and meddle and look into questions (it is after all their business), and they like their individual voices to be heard, undrowned in consensus. Therefore, the Head of House must maintain the appearance at least of open discussion. To announce that 'this is not a matter for discussion' is to the don an invitation to discuss it. Instead, the ground must be painstakingly prepared in advance of the meeting, the good seed sown and anyone likely to be touched by an item carefully sounded out. Humour, incidentally, can be an important defuser; this is true of all committees, but especially ones composed of dons. In discussion, consensus should be pursued – but not for too long. It is wiser after a sufficient airing of views to take things to a vote. That way a decision is taken *and* everyone feels they have registered their opinions.

All Governing Bodies have seen changes in recent years. Student representatives, for instance, now generally attend. There was the same sort of apprehension about this beforehand as there was in the House of Commons about televising Parliament, but it has passed off with a similar lack of consequences. Another development has been the increasing deluge of paper – a product of the growth both in complexity of college functions and in outside demands. Some dons make a point of minutely scrutinizing all the papers beforehand, some unashamedly flick through them at the meeting, others totally ignore them. Sometimes a submission will be requested from a particularly expert fellow (on buildings, say, or investments or the wine cellar). When delivered, the protocol of academe comes into play and they are accorded the close attention bestowed on a learned paper at a seminar.

With the proliferation of paper has gone that of sub-committees. All Governing Bodies now have a minimum of three (Tutorial, Financial and General Purposes) and some run to seven or eight (covering such matters as Student Welfare or External Funding). Much labour can be usefully delegated to these committees. As a general rule, the length of Governing Body meetings is inversely proportional to the number of such committees. But a Head of House would be committing a grave mistake simply to treat Governing Body as a rubber stamp of the committees. Their papers must be carefully sifted in advance for potential 'bombs'; these must then be gently excavated and their presence made known in advance of the meeting to any interested parties.

The tone of Governing Body meetings depends largely on the Head of House. The position of Master has undergone tremendous changes in this century. Before the Second World War he was a formidable force before whom the other dons quailed. Thereafter, his power waned; that reduction, coupled with the smaller size of Governing Bodies in those days, produced a brief spring of total, almost Athenian democracy. Now that Governing Bodies have swollen in size, power has been increasingly devolved to college officers and sub-committees. One retired don who had seen the whole process described it as a shift from absolute monarchy to democracy, then to oligarchy. But that is rather extreme. The current situation is perhaps more akin to that for-a-time-forgotten constitutional form – traditional cabinet government under a weak Prime Minister.

But that the Master has been largely stripped of power there is no doubt. Bagehot defined the prerogatives of the constitutional monarch as being to warn, encourage and be informed. A Master can encourage – that is easy enough. But if he warns nowadays, he risks being deeply resented. As for being informed, it is all too easy to keep a Master in the dark. That is not to say the Master has lost an empire and has not yet found a role. Now he wears vulgar new hats: he is a promoter and a publicity man, a ringmaster, a fundraiser and often benefactor in his own right.

As the job has changed, so has the man. Now the trend is to get in outsiders. Colleges look beyond their walls not just to their other traditional recruiting grounds in Whitehall and the Diplomatic Service, but to the media and the arts and (soon, one suspects) to politics and business. Lord Goodman, a recent Master of University College, was a typical example: a fixer, experienced in the ways of government and the City and something of a Maecenas through his combination of chairing the Arts Council and personal munificence.

A classic description of an old-style mastership election, when the candidates were always insiders, is contained in C. P. Snow's *The Masters*. For generations it was the paradigm, almost the textbook on how to appoint a new Master and conduct the necessary stages of preliminary in-fighting. Now it has become a period piece. Currently the form is as follows: the college will advertise. This is largely a protection device, to show the college is open, to guard it subsequently against any charges of discrimination, and facilitate getting a work permit (if they pick a foreign national). The advertisement may bring in a few useful names, but in general to apply is to be at once ruled out. The real action lies in the delicate canvassing and sounding out done by the dons, the sensitive radar beams they emit via a network of contacts in the clubs and Whitehall. Also, there will be shoals of useful letters from Old Members of the type 'Do you realize that X person has recently left Y job, and is most suitable on Z grounds?' The fellows will then draw up a shortlist and pick the one that best conforms with their vision of a Master's duties: someone with the knowledge and personality to promote the college to the outside world but also someone likely to prove sufficiently malleable within the college; someone, too, who might enrich it, either himself or through his friends and contacts.

That is not to say that insiders never get chosen. They do, perhaps more often than not. The insider has the advantage of already knowing the score and not needing to be educated regarding the vacuum of power which he is about to enter. Rachel Trickett, former Principal of St Hugh's, wrote an illuminating essay on the differences between what she terms 'Outsides' and 'Insides'.

'Outsides' often come in with grand ideas but are rapidly dis-
illusioned: stymied and undermined within college, they are also
effectively shut out of the larger arena of university politics (being
debarred from General Board, where, arguably, most of the power
resides nowadays). They usually end up broken men, whining to
whoever will listen to them about their plight. 'Insides', by contrast,
take on the patina of the college, cultivate eccentricity and derive
secret pleasure from observing the fellows' antics.

Such is the fate of the Head of House. Next in rank are the
collegiate barons, the officers, elected by Governing Body from
amongst their own number. These include the Senior Tutor, who
is responsible for the academic policy and progress of the college;
the Dean, a kind of Home Secretary figure, who looks after the
discipline and domestic administration of the college; the Dean of
Graduates; and the Tutor for Admissions. Then there are the
permanent posts: the Chaplain; the Domestic and Estates Bursars
with duties regarding respectively the internal management (catering, rooms, etc.) and the external properties and investments of the
college.

The pattern of the officers' responsibilities exhibits all the delicate
'meshing' so characteristic of the colleges – that subtle overlapping
of leaves on the college plant which over the centuries has grown
so slowly, so organically. Thus, the Senior Tutor is responsible for
the academic standing of the college, and his bailiwick theoretically
includes the other dons and their work. But it would be a bold
Senior Tutor who dared breathe an evaluative or critical comment
on other dons' performances. Organizationally there are many
instances of apparent illogicality and obscurity. The Domestic
Bursar may well come under the Dean but will also attend Governing Body in his or her own right and can independently propose
items for the agenda. I say 'apparent', though, because in practice
points of dispute are reconciled through the continuous seam of
personal contact running through the college, over coffee, in the
SCR, and the endless conferences in the quad.

However, just as change has overtaken the Master, so it is
affecting the college officers. The Senior Tutor now has not only
to mesh sensitively with his colleagues but increasingly with the
university in the endless haggling over whether shared posts should
be filled or frozen. He has become a negotiator, a linkman and

coordinator. The Admissions Tutor's role has undergone a double change. Once he actually had a large say in who was admitted to the college. Then power passed to the tutorial fellows in each subject, and the Admissions Tutor was reduced to a kind of administrative workhorse, fixing up the interviews and ensuring that the whole thing ran smoothly. Now, as the colleges have become increasingly aware of the need to attract high calibre applicants and full fee-bearing foreigners, he has become a kind of PR man, selling the college through glossy brochures and conferences.

Going or gone, also, are the retired admirals and tweedy gentlemen with backgrounds in estate management who used to staff the Bursars' offices. The new occupants of these posts are likely to be keen young men fresh from the City and careers in portfolio management or with degrees in management and experience of catering administration. Many colleges have appointed full-time professional fundraisers, sometimes giving them fancy names like Domus Fellows.

After the Head of House and the officers there are other categories of fellows. The largest, the academic infantry of the college, if you like, are its Tutorial Fellows who shoulder its teaching load in their various subjects. Beyond them are the Emeritus Fellows, floating off into retirement and a slow sea of senescence but still tied, by a long loose line, to port; also the Honorary Fellows, a roster of the Great and the Good connected to the college either through having been there or for some more obscure reason. They will include prominent writers, Nobel prizewinners, a couple of mandarins, and possibly a minor Royal stuck like an artificial cherry into this rich cake of distinction.

Two other categories remain: the Professors and Lecturers 'not on the foundation'. Each college has a number of professorships traditionally attached to it. Magdalen, for instance, has the Wayneflete Professorship of Chemistry and University College Professorship in Jurisprudence. If they are medical men or scientists, they will look to where their real power lies, either the hospitals or labland – that anonymous slab of laboratories and offices north of Parks Road. If they are in the arts, then the professors are in an even more anomalous position. The terms, written and unwritten, of their duties involve giving a certain number of lectures each term and providing leadership in their faculties. But the arts faculties are artificial matrices, shadowy metaphysical entities compared to the colleges. Their professors are like the shades in Homer: they are only given a presence by the living blood of High Table. The colleges give them rooms and treat them with respect. But the professors have to tread with utmost circumspection, careful not to seem to be interfering or giving offence. They are, if you like, admirals on ships run by captains and uncertain whether they have a fleet of their own or not.

The lecturers are also figures caught in limbo. They shoulder much of the college's teaching burden but are not permanent fellows. In these days of frozen fellowships their numbers are on the increase. The 'stipendiary' lecturers are paid a regular salary; the 'non-stipendiaries' simply get the odd fee in return for one-off teaching commitments. Grudging degrees of access to college privileges are permitted them. Some are let in to dine on High Table on certain nights, some not at all. They feel they are the ill-paid irregulars propping up the colleges' triumphs and they smoulder with dark, hidden resentments. But they are careful not to let their irritation blaze into life too visibly: there may always be the chance of a permanent appointment somewhere and they would not wish to spoil it.

Dons have always tempted writers into typologies, and one can attempt a lineage or family tree of them. The first academic to surface in English literature was perhaps Chaucer's Clerk of Oxenford. But he was not really a don, more an earnest postgraduate plodding on his long pilgrimage not only to Canterbury but also a doctorate. The first true don types emerged in the seventeenth century in the then fashionable books of characters. Sir Thomas Overbury isolated a type extant today: 'the Meer Scholler' – 'the antiquity of whose university is his Creed and the excellency of his Colledge (though but for a match at Foot-ball) an Article of his Faith.' A few years later John Earle also described the Mere Scholar in his *Micro-cosmographie* but added two new types – the genuinely learned don, authentic, if unpolished by the standards of the court, and the 'fashionable' don who aped the garb and manners of the capital. In time the fashionable don became the aesthete don, the sensitive collector of plants, pictures and *objets* who made his rooms a bower of decorative beauty.

The aesthete don's opposite, and indeed his enemy, was another type commonly encountered in literature, the hearty don, the 'good coll chap', a large, shaggy, pullovery sort of fellow, tweedy and leathery-footed, with the equivalent of a megaphone permanently lodged in his throat. He could be heard thwacking people on backs in quads, booming from the towpath or bellowing across muddy playing fields on the Abingdon Road. There was something doggy and dependable about him; if there were no successful or handsome athletes to hero-worship, he would turn to the college spirit. He was similar to those bluff padres in World War One or minor public schoolboys who were mown down as they led attacks into no-man's-land kicking footballs before them. Not surprisingly, he is now a dying, if not dead, breed.

These stock types reappear with monotonous regularity in published taxonomies of dons. Rev. W. Tuckwell in 1900 again described the Mere Scholar and the Learned Don, but divided the Fashionable Don into the Cosmopolitan Don ... ('with a home in Oxford, but conversant with select humanity elsewhere') and the Ornamental Don 'a gorgeous butterfly' of arcane learning, who would always be seated next to strangers at college dinners in order to impress.

The survival of traditional don types signalled something deeper, the presence of an underlying don culture. What were its marks? Well, perhaps the most prominent was an extreme individuality, verging on and indeed often toppling over into, utter oddity. The traditional life of dons, so relatively untrammelled by rules and routine, licensed the wilder whorls of eccentricity. Then again, the very geography of colleges, so fortress-like and inward with their cloistered quadrangles, gargoyled walls and labyrinthine warrens of studies, seemed calculated to produce in its inmates strange twists and anfractuosities of the spirit.

Given such traditional extremities of individuality, contacts between dons often sparked friction. One thinks of the story of one don so maddened by another in the room above him that he eventually discharged a pistol through the ceiling. Sometimes differences hardened into permanent hatreds. Lincoln Common Room in the nineteenth century presented a perfect image of this, with young Mark Pattison the reformer sitting next to the Old Guard year after year without ever breaking his steely silence.

The polar opposite of the common room as a bonfire of the enmities was its role as a vanity of mirrors. The need to evoke admiration by the academic equivalent of gorgeous displays of plumage or body paint was another characteristic of the traditional don culture. Off-subject erudition was always one surefire way of compelling applause, be it on Mayan archaeology or the marital customs of Polynesian tribes. Sir Maurice Bowra, Warden of Wadham, was famed for this kind of broad-ranging knowledge, spanning not just the Classical world (his own field) but Persian ceramics and ancient Chinese literature. Travel talk was another way to impress. In the vacations the dons were expected to fly off into the more unusual corners of the outside world and return, magpie-like, with odd bits of local lore between their bony beaks for the entertainment of their colleagues.

Talk lay at the heart of don culture. High Table provided an amphitheatre for gladiatorial contests in conversation. Rev. W. Tuckwell in his *Memoirs* recalled how 'conversation was a fine art, a claim to social distinction. Choice sprouts of the brain, epigram, anecdote, metaphor, now nursed carefully for the printer were joyously lavished on one another.' As he suggested, the energy that went into exuberant contests of wit may have been at the expense of publication: another mark of traditional don culture was a career which left behind only a slim corpus of articles and books. Sometimes, however, the *bon mots* made it into print. After being carefully honed and delivered to applause, they would be relayed throughout the university and endlessly repeated until achieving written immortality in a memoir or anthology.

For wit has always been an essential element in don culture. Don wit is a highly individual form of humour, defined by one Oxford academic in a recent essay as 'the means whereof the language of the tribe is purified'. It is very inward and exclusive, turning on the skilful manipulation of words and often involving swift inversions or subtle changes to a cliché in order to derail it and send it suddenly rolling down the stage of absurdity. An example might be the description by John Sparrow, the Warden of All Souls, of Oxford during the Suez crisis as 'a hotbed of cold feet' or Maurice Bowra's comment on a colleague that 'he was the sort of man to stab you in the front'. The Saturnalian element, the permitted inversion of discipline has already been noted in college culture.

Donnish wit could be said formally to enshrine this subversive tendency, of suddenly sabotaging expectation and yet satisfying it, of simultaneously expressing and containing the impish love of independence and individuality, seeing both sides to any question, and therefore not having to do anything about it. This Saturnalian inversion was perhaps given its most concentrated form in the Spoonerism, whereby letters were transposed for humorous effect (such as 'Which of us has not felt in his heart a half warmed fish?'). William Spooner, a Warden of New College earlier this century, is credited as the source of these but a large proportion are later inventions. They have become a quintessentially Oxford brand of humour, an expression, at the most basic linguistic level, of the reign of the Lord of Misrule.

But words and wit were not the sole means of donnish self display. An important theatre was the don's room or study. The don room is best understood as a three-dimensional or conceptual work of art, carefully constructed to impress, intrigue and intimidate undergraduates and any other visitors who may venture there. Its books, some of them leather-bound antiques and some of them foreign, will testify to a range and depth of erudition, as will the learned journal open on the coffee table and the continental dissertation heavily interleaved with scribbled notes. As evidence of his former youth there will be an indistinct photograph of two figures holding hands under trees or against a distant horizon; testifying to his current if remote married state, a dour don wife stares wistfully out of a frame superciliously supervised by a small school-uniformed child. On his shelves cluster a clutter of collectables – silver snuffboxes, say, or old English pottery. Amongst the artefacts will be evidence of foreign travels – some carved black African horns or Andean figurines. There will also be a small but distinguished collection of stains on chairs and carpets commemorating expensive drinks spilt over the decades. Everything looks shabby and used, from the dull and battered electric kettle to the sagging armchairs. The room must proclaim its antiquity and look as if it has been lived in by its owner from undergraduate days onwards. He is, after all, no vulgar *arriviste* visiting fellow sneaking in lately through the college portals.

The room will also enshrine the Saturnalian principle, that element of subversive donnish humour. Somewhere on the shelves will lurk 'the deliberate piece of bad taste' – a seaside souvenir, or a casino-in-a-snowstorm from Las Vegas – waiting to disturb the visitor's eye. Or there will, astoundingly, be a pop music paper on the table. ('I hold the lyrics of Tanita Tikaram in rather high regard' the don will intone with delight, if questioned. The name incidentally changes: it used to be Bob Dylan.) Another 'talking point', perhaps the latest Booker Prize winner, will indicate the up-to-dateness of his tastes; indicating his popularity and breadth will be a fleet of cards and invitations on the mantelpiece. There will be some drink: college sherry, one dry, one sweet, whisky (the donnish taste for port is by and large a myth) and maybe some bottled beer for handing out occasionally to undergrads. Through a door, hung with caped gown, a sad and rather lonely bedroom can be glimpsed, with a strangely high and spartan bed, a chipped basin, a strip of lino and a threadbare mat.

The don room was however, like its owner, a nest of contradictions. It was a don den – an academic lair and retreat from the world. But it also symbolized a further element in traditional don culture – influence. It was an influence, moreover which was felt to radiate outwards. Oxford was seen as the centre whence instruction was purveyed to the barbarians. It was crammed with objects representing worldly interests, and over the dusty decades generations of undergraduates have trooped through it on their way to positions of real power. The dons cultivated a civilized – almost Chinese – condescension towards the hordes without (whilst acknowledging that their vulgar vitality could be converted into the gold of anecdotes, fellowships and the stuff of research). In return the eyes of the barbarian were felt rightly to be drawn in on Oxford's domestic doings. To a degree this attitude created the state of affairs it enshrined: to this day the media show far more interest in Oxford's affairs than any other university in the world and treat it as the archetype of academe.

Such were once the traditional types of dons and the underlying culture. Today the Fashionable Don is, paradoxically, the Denim Don. They actually do wear denims, fashionably slashed above each kneecap, with tough-looking cherry boots, savagely cropped hair and tiny round gold spectacles. They closely resemble the John Lennon of his final, Yoko-occluded phase. Yes, they are the Spiggy

Topes and Dave Sparts of Oxford SCRs, the ones with ultimate cloister cred. The Denim Dons almost invariably teach in the humanities and bill themselves as Marxists or Poststructuralists or Post-Marxist Structuralists, or ... Whatever it is, it means never having to say you're sorry – or 'please' or 'thank-you'. Society, for them, is so deeply engrained ('and I mean at a most fundamental Freudian level') with repression and injustice that all you can do is lie back – and deconstruct it. It is as if the universities were floating Laputa-like islands from which the Denim Dons can gaze down and identify the deformities in the social and cultural contours as they pass beneath.

They were the last academic generation to be recruited in large numbers. After them, the deluge of cuts came and the drying-up of jobs. This turned out in retrospect to be a blessing in disguise for the Denim Dons. They are still – paunches and wrinkles notwithstanding – the youngest things around. They have had the good luck to be the Younger Generation for almost two generations. Even now their academic colleagues turn a fondly indulgent, almost parental eye on these elderly youths and ageing young men in a hurry.

They have consciously, carefully roughened the smooth surfaces of their manners and their vowels (the expensive products of schools like Shrewsbury and Stowe) so that now they resemble those of the ageing DJ, John Peel, and the actor Bob Hoskins. However, they can snap smartly back into baying prefect or OTC mode, should a sufficient affront to their privileges or patience be offered. This can lead to hilariously sudden, if alarming, changes of verbal gear ('Look, squire, just toss us a couple of bottles of that there reserve port, will you? ... *no, not in five minutes, I mean right now, you bloody little man*'). For this reason the domestics in their colleges hate and fear them and give them as wide a berth as possible.

The Cosmopolitan Don also survives as the Glitterateur – the media don who writes bestsellers or appears regularly on TV. In the 1960s, when they were more of a novelty, they were called 'telly dons' and rather looked down on. Now they are, if anything, admired and envied. In a way they are the descendants of the 'Ornamental Dons' of earlier typologies. They have mastered the arts of lively journalism and entertaining reviewing, of running off general interest as opposed to academic books and of presenting and packaging themselves for consumption on the tube. They are on a parabola which started with an earnest thesis and ends, if they are lucky, hosting a show of zany clips from foreign TV. Generally the Glitterateur still keeps a foothold in the land of don. Of late though they have been tempted more and more to make the break and chance their arm freelancing. But then they think of their monthly pay cheques, their families and the comfortable college common room ... Mostly they stay put. But some hardy spirits do take the plunge. For a time they keep their links with Oxford but, if they are successful, increasingly gravitate towards London with its brilliant cluster of media connections, ditching in the process their high, cold North Oxford houses and their high, cold North Oxford wives.

But nothing stays the same forever, not even in the sheltered land of don-dom. Changes have come, and with them new types of don. One of the most common is the Disappearing Don, the Nine-to-Five Academic. Once dons, even married ones, were expected to stay on in their colleges in the evenings to dine and perhaps participate in college life and activities. The long hours demanded by the college often came as a horrid surprise to out-siders such as visiting professors. In her classic account of American culture shock at Oxford *These Ruins Are Inhabited*, published in the late 1950s, Mrs Muriel Beadle, the wife of the Eastman Professor, concluded that the college was a determined foe to family life.

Now most dons come in in the mornings, immerse themselves in tutorials, lectures or whatever, surface briefly at lunch (which has taken the place of dinner as the main meal in college), plunge back into teaching or research or administrative chores. Then it is back off on bus or bicycle, to Headington or Southmoor Road, to the microwave meal, the playpen and the latest Australian soap. Most evenings in Hall you see a rather pathetic rump of dons clustered round one end of High Table. College life in the evenings is kept ticking over by a tiny handful – the Chaplain, some as-yet unmar-ried research fellows, and the odd confirmed bachelor. These over-night dons are particularly valued by their absentee colleagues for their twenty-four hour service and tend consequently to get wretchedly overloaded with college offices and duties.

With the rise of the Nine-to-Five Academic, the long-stay

inmate – the don who spent all his life within the confines of the college and rarely ventured out – has largely disappeared. A certain sadness clung about such figures, well captured by the Rev. W. Tuckwell in his description of old Senior Fellows in the nineteenth century: 'He mostly lived alone, the other men treated him deferentially and called him Mister ... but no one ever dropped in upon him, smoked with him, walked with him; he was thought to have a history; a suspicion of disappointment hung over him; he lived his own eccentric friendless life, a victim to superannuation and celibacy.' Such dons just lingered until they finally faded away. One college tradition, now mercifully a thing of the past, was the discovered death, the horrified scout backing out of the study, the whispering and clucking in corners, the college flag at half mast and then the funeral and the memorial attended by only a black-clad handful. These were the melancholy dons who would leave all their worldly goods to the college 'because', as one explained, 'I have no one else to leave it to'.

When retirement age was brought in at Oxford, there was a crop of releases. The long-stay dons had been thoroughly institutionalized: they had never had to shop, to cook and clean. Then they were released into their new lives like aged defectors given a new identity in a far, unfamiliar country. You could see them starting all over again, settling into a small but comfortable North Oxford flat and – half frightened, half exhilarated – embarking on a brave new life of supermarkets, launderettes and public transport. 'I have just learned', they would cackle proudly, 'to boil an egg!'

Another new type is the sole woman don in a formerly all-male college. Gradually women are penetrating the Governing Bodies of these colleges, but it is a slow, slow process. In the period of co-education up to 1985, three quarters of these colleges had only one woman don or none at all. Indeed in a way the career chances of woman academics at Oxford could be said to have contracted in that they can no longer count automatically on all the posts at the former women's colleges. Where women are heavily represented is amongst the ranks of the temporary teaching lecturers, the part-time academic mercenaries employed by the colleges. These are often women who, having just completed their doctorates in this era of higher education cuts, are unable to find permanent academic positions. They are sometimes referred to, not without a certain patronizing pity, as the 'new donettes'.

But say a woman succeeds in getting a fellowship in a former men's college. She still finds herself in a delicate position. The tendency of her male colleagues will be to treat her simultaneously as (a) the token woman and (b) an honorary man. She will find herself held up both as an example of college openness and an excuse for thereafter softly shutting the lid on the equality issue. The woman don may well perceive this phenomenon but will be tempted to engage in double-think ('other colleges are prejudiced but this one is undergoing a slow historical process'). In a round-about way the perfectly valid argument of upholding academic standards will salvage her conscience. Positive discrimination is an erosion of excellence, she will stoutly maintain: *We have*, she will say with unconscious irony, *to get the best man for the job.*

Loyalty to the college knots this tangle. To her relief she will quite likely have found not a wall of hostility and prejudice, but its complete opposite. True, the woman don may have to put up with the odd grating bit of male insensitivity (what one called 'the ruggability factor') but in general she is intensely grateful. And herein creeps the insidious temptation. Suffused by the familial atmosphere of the college she will respond by assuming a mother-nanny role towards the difficult don-children in her charge. She will load herself with extra tasks and duties and become a 'college treasure', the solidly reliable, drudging female packhorse who shoulders all burdens uncomplainingly and clears up all the messes left behind by those shaggy, creative beasts, her menfolk.

Yet it is a tribute to the force of the Thatcherite Revolution that any current typology of dons has still to be constructed around its impact. The new typology reflects the Great Divorce between academe and power. In retrospect the postwar period to the late 70s was a golden age. The universities became accepted as a cross between research centre, welfare agency and church – a source of information, an instrument of gradual social change *and* a reposi-tory of élitist mandarin values. The consensus Establishment Don became a leading figure, endlessly catching the Paddington train up to Whitehall, chairing Royal Commissions here, contributing advice there and generally wielding influence behind the scenes. It was all very cosy, well-meaning and good while it lasted. Under Mrs Thatcher, the universities, along with other sizeable chunks of the British Establishment, were sharply uncoupled and sidelined into insignificance, or, worse, backed shrieking on to the bacon slicer of progressive cuts. Gone were the Royal Commissions, the comfortable seats on quangos and the invitations to Whitehall. Divorced, dispossessed, disinherited! Worse, the dons felt they were somewhere up there in the dock, somewhere between the miners and the BBC. No aristocrat walking to a tumbril could ever have felt a ruder flick of fate. They were the dons who were sent out into the cold, their pale clever faces pressed against the pane of power, as the cuts whistled about them and the snow of central directives steadily fell....

Under Thatcher the old-style Tory Oxford dons, the Clubmen, used to hobnobbing in Smith Square and St James's with the old wettish aristos of the party, were practically purple with embarrassment. They resembled the members of a club which has fallen into the hands of some vulgar outsider (with whom they rather regrettably find themselves associated) who has set about knocking the place down about their heads. How to explain things to ones chums? All the Clubmen could do, as the din of academic demolition filled their ears, was to lie low and pray for the return one day of softer, wetter weather.

By contrast, the majority of dons became the Dissident Dons. The Dissident Don was an old consensus liberal who swam somewhere in the left soft centre. He went along uneasily with the privileges of Oxford because he reckoned the place was gradually liberalizing itself and opening up its doors and because he believed in academe. Under Thatcher he felt assaulted, mugged by the very forces who should have been his protectors and providers. But the Dissident Dons fought back. They went on the offensive, they wrote a letter about it, in fact several score letters. They clustered under brave letterheads and founded noble organizations to salvage British science or history or philosophy or academic freedom. With the benefits of their academic training they carefully marshalled arguments and summoned up relevant statistics. They threatened to go down the Brain Drain if they were not listened to. At times, as they pressed their polite academic prose into a semblance of political polemic, their own temerity seemed half to take them aback, as if they had suddenly caught sight of reflections of themselves as donnish replicas of the full-scale dissidents elsewhere. Their flaw, however, was a fatal lack of passion. They were afflicted by an intellectual mildness, a debilitating academic reasonableness, like people trying to hold a seminar with a steamroller as it steadily squashed down on them.

Standing in opposition to the Dissident Don is the Enterprise Convert. The Convert is the new model don. He puts on the clothes and attitudes of the Young Fogey. He believes in the abolition of tenure and in student loans, that all the dying wood of the trendy '60s should be cleared out and the universities become self-sustaining centres of effort and enterprise. He himself works furiously hard, his bony rump fixed for hours on hard library seats as he absorbs books and articles like a kind of academic combine harvester, others' wrong books going in one end and his own right ones coming out at the other. His hopes are pinned on a fellowship at All Souls, that bastion of advanced study and bunker of right thinking.

In reality deep-down he detests Oxford for its indulgent tolerance and privileged variety. He is full of secret bitter impulses and a disappointed desire to belong. His background is, most likely, state school and lower middle-class-provincial, all evidence of which he has of course most carefully eradicated. There is something chill and blank and sterile about him, from the knife-like creases in his clothes to the rigid parting of his hair. The snubs of Whiggish seniors fell heavily upon his young career and now, as the government flail descends repeatedly on the universities, he feels at long last he is getting his own back. Occasionally he ventures into print, placing tortuous pieces in *The Telegraph* or appearing uneasily on TV, but he lacks the slick fluency and glib ease of those to the Union – and *Isis* – born. During the Thatcher years he had a dream, a dream that one day he would awake to find a letter from Number Ten landed on his mat ('read your works with great interest ... clearly One of Us ... so glad if you could lend your efforts to the Cause ... invitation to attend enclosed ...') but it never, never came. Sadness is the final impression that he leaves behind, tempting you to sympathy, were he not so small in spirit.

The new taxonomy of dons could be extended almost indefinitely.

But one thing all the new types of don have in common is that they all to some extent react to external forces or changes in the outside world (whether budget cuts or entrepreneurial opportunism or merely, as in the case of the Denim Dons, changing lifestyles and aspirations). The Oxford Senior Common Room no longer generates its own stereotypes purely from within. Academe is no longer the highly stable and autonomous world it was. It is far more *out there*, in the world, bending in the winds of its threats and challenges. The dons they are a-changing, and that familiar figure, the traditional Oxford don with his dense tweeds and eccentricities is ironically a vanishing breed, examples of which perhaps should be preserved and protected here and there – as a memorial of what was once the general anthropology of academe.

Around

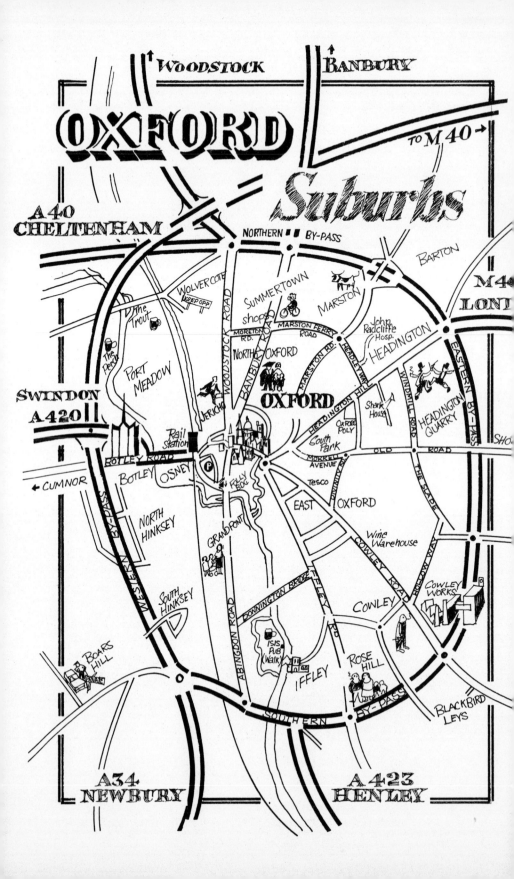

– 10 –

Here be Dragons:
North Oxford

North Oxford is the legendary don-land. It is one of those places so famous that it has entered the language: like Hampstead, North Oxford has become a byword for a particular stratum of society, except that Hampstead's cultural roots lie in the media while North Oxford's are in academe. The inhabitants of both areas have come to represent the intellectually and socially concerned middle class – the Schlegels in E. M. Forster's *Howard's End* as opposed to the brash, mercantile Wilcoxes. Yet there is cash there too: just as the Schlegels were Fabians with family money who kept their principles *and* the property, so North Oxford and its folk are now flourishing as never before.

It is often said that the suburb was built to house the families of dons when they were allowed to marry in the late nineteenth century. This is not entirely true. It has always attracted a broader social mix. North Oxford was a continuation of St Giles, Oxford's first professional suburb, whose eighteenth-century houses were occupied both by members of the university and the leading men of the city. The site of North Oxford, originally known as St Giles or Walton Field and owned by the local abbeys, fell into the hands of royal hangers-on after the Dissolution and was later bought by St John's College. When the college obtained an Act of Parliament in 1855 enabling it to grant ninety-nine year leases, the path was opened up for the development of North Oxford. Park Town was the first part to be built, constructed to the characteristic italianate designs of the architect, Samuel Lipscomb Seckham. Norham Gardens followed in the 1860s. By the time the dons were allowed to marry in the late 1870s, most of the neighbourhood had been built and occupied. Its residents included some university professors (who had always been allowed to marry and live outside college) but mainly consisted of prosperous Oxford tradesmen. The two elements did not at first blend particularly harmoniously. Derisory nicknames were applied to the houses of these tradesmen. The mansion of Mallam the auctioneer, who had earlier been a tobacconist, was dubbed 'Quidville'; that of an ironmaker 'Tinville' and that of the Town Clerk 'Quillville'.

Soon, though, the suburb began to attract a range of people, many of them from outside Oxford – retired civil servants and schoolmasters, clergymen, military officers, doctors and solicitors. A Warden of Merton wrote of the increasing number of 'families of limited incomes but refined tastes' stating that 'it has been discovered that plain living and high thinking can be combined in Oxford more easily than in any other provincial town'. The North Oxford clerisy was in the process of creation.

Prominent in it were its intellectual wives and daughters. They bustled about and organized and agitated. Through them and their creation, the Society for Home Students, the cause of female education was promoted in the university. North Oxford became a kind of extended female collegiate annexe, whose intellectual level often surpassed that of the colleges. A representative figure was Mrs Humphry Ward, the daughter of Thomas Arnold who married a young don and went on to combine raising a family with becoming a prominent novelist and social activist. Before she eventually moved to London she established herself as culture goddess for the whole suburb. 'Everybody writes or lectures here,' she wrote, 'and one must follow the fashion. Besides, it passes the time and the Library is so fine and convenient.' The Bodleian's Spanish Reading Room became for her the equivalent of Virginia Woolf's feminist desideratum, 'a room of one's own'. Staunchly shouldering the burden of bringing up children (with the aid of a small army of servants), she continued to churn out books and articles, even producing a pamphlet on infant feeding after the birth of one child and distributing it to the poor of Jericho. Moreover, in her house in Bradmore Road she invented for the suburb what

today we would call a lifestyle. Woven out of William Morris wallpapers, Liberty print gowns and elegantly plain blue and white vases, it set the North Oxford tone for generations to come.

And so it went on and on. Academics begat academics. North Oxford families passed on their properties to their children who in turn passed them on to their children. But all the time the houses were becoming stranger and shabbier. By the 1950s and 1960s the neighbourhood was slowly spiralling downwards. The ninety-nine year St John's leases were drawing to a close, and multi-occupation gained ground. Externally, cracks and signs of dilapidation and decay were beginning to appear. Yet the North Oxford culture clung on tenaciously until the tide started to turn once more in its favour.

North Oxford's architecture has not always been well regarded. True, for Ruskin, 'the elongating suburb of the married fellows on the cockhorse road to Banbury' was an ideal, but others disliked it heartily. For Rev. W. Tuckwell it was an abomination: writing in 1900 he complained of 'the leafy thoroughfares of the bewildering New Jerusalem' with its 'interminable streets of villadom, converging insatiably protuberant upon distant Wolvercot and Summertown'. Similarly Thomas Sharp in his postwar report *Oxford Replanned* thought nothing of sacrificing the 'gloomy severity' of the suburb to new spine roads. If any one figure was responsible for moving public taste towards North Oxford's Victorianism it was John Betjeman. In his poems and other writings he celebrated its buildings and its culture. It was to Betjeman that local councillor Ann Spokes turned in 1962 when North Oxford fell under the threat of various university development schemes. Between them they set in motion a campaign, leading to the neighbourhood being declared a Conservation Area in 1968.

The tide had turned. Several factors came together in this – the growing popularity of the architecture, the Leasehold Reform Act of 1967 which enabled lessees to get their hands on their properties and the increasing middle-class demand for the good schools in which the neighbourhood is strong. Today Seckham's Park Town villas and Wilkinson's spacious Gothic mansions command close to half a million pounds each. Only very successful professionals or dons with serious private money can afford to live here now. Though some of the larger houses are still being converted into flats, there has been an astonishing swing back to the original Victorian pattern of single family dwellings. Residents boast of the number of gas meters they had taken out when they re-consolidated, and the only flats retained are a floor for granny or one let out as a nice little earner to visiting scholars from the States.

As the neighbourhood's desirability has shot up so it has once again sucked in people from outside, from the villages and beyond. A fair number of London commuters have settled in North Oxford – professionals and business and media people – drawn by its relatively low property prices, sedate lifestyle and its excellent schools. Such is the grip of the traditional North Oxford culture, however, that the incomers have had little effect upon it. Instead it has worked its powerful alchemy upon them, converting the pinstripes and producers into don-clones, squeezing them into its tweeds, making them learn its vowels and observe its calendar and rituals.

The heartland of North Oxford is the original Victorian suburb stretching from St Giles to Summertown. Within it Seckham's regency villas in Park Town remain a distinct sub-culture, a tiny top drawer containing senior surgeons and consultants, the ramrod-backed daughters of retired generals and noted *emigrés* and intellectual refugees. In the 1930s it became something of an international academe in exile, a little St Antony's College before that cosmopolitan institution came into being nearby. Around its oval there is fastened a firm bond of community spirit. It shone forth in the Second World War. When the residents were refused permission to set up their own municipal restaurant on the grounds that no workers lived there, they went ahead and set one up anyway, eating there themselves and converting ration coupons into tickets, using an ingenious formula designed, characteristically, by a resident mathematician, one Dr Prag.

Going beyond the heartland there are nevertheless plenty of people in adjacent areas, in fact right up to the ring road and beyond, who also claim to live in North Oxford, although these claims would probably be disputed by the heartlanders. To the west lies the *rive gauche* of North Oxford: Southmoor Road and its environs. Once an interestingly louche area, home of burglars and scene of drugs busts, it has now had its thunder largely stolen by East Oxford and has gone straight, displaying all the overzealous respectability of the newly reformed. It has filled itself with puritan, socialist dons and yoga-and-yoghurt radicals transplanted from East Oxford or percolating upwards from Jericho. The transplants bring with them their spray-on sense of community. They are *so* proud of their road and in 1985 celebrated its hundredth birthday with a street party. The children's bedrooms are walled with black-boards or white gloss sheets for crayoning in order to give the fullest possible opportunity for educational self-expression. In the words of Betjeman's 'May Day Song for North Oxford' it has replaced Belbroughton Road as the place where:

> Emancipated children swing on old apple boughs
> And pastel-shaded book rooms bring New Ideas to birth.

But in terms of moves on the property board game, the *rive gauche* represents an excellent *entrée* to North Oxford. Let us say you first-time-buy in Iffley Fields in East Oxford, then you sell and with the proceeds trade up to a house in Southmoor Road. Or, if you have done a little better and also inherited a little money from Mummy you can get a house in the Chalfont Road area (a small large house as opposed to a large small house in Southmoor Road – the distinction lying in the number of bathrooms). Once you are on the North Oxford property board the advice thereafter is always 'Go east, old man' and the winner is the one who gets nearest to the Dragon School in the least number of moves.

Another distinctive area outside the North Oxford heartland is Summertown, originally settled in the 1820s as a healthy outpost from the city and its diseases, a colourful mixed community of artisans' cottages and substantial residential villas. Its varied nature continues to this day in its mix of shopping parade, offices, early nineteenth-century rows, turn-of-the-century estates and brand-new blocks of flats and sheltered housing. House prices range correspondingly from Harpes Road (the only area in North Oxford in which average first-time buyers could hope to get a property) to the more central Summertown district. Its inhabitants are also rather a mixed bunch: young professional couples; foreigners; widows and divorced single parents. The latter pass their married phase north of the shops but soon emerge to the splendour of single parenthood and migrate south of the shops where they live, self-absorbed and self-sustaining, each with two children of pre-school age and a drone-like lover buzzing on the periphery.

The fourth and final area is the ring road suburb to the north of Summertown where the houses are ... well ... suburban: largish twentieth-century villas with small drives, tile roofs, rendered walls and lawns that look as if they have been trimmed with nail scissors, which would not look out of place in Weybridge or Guildford. People here are financial professionals, accountants, bank managers, solicitors, administrators and inspectors of police. Here live many who catch the 7 o'clock to desks in the City or Whitehall and return when day is done. Here the property board game moves are different – these people have come in from Headington, Wheatley, or even London; if they prosper their next move will be out of Oxford, possibly to Boar's Hill. The ring road itself forms a kind of *cordon sanitaire*. Beyond it, the houses are even more suburban and less expensive; people who live there claim to like it because it is near to the country and the golf club: one suspects it is because they cannot afford to live closer in.

'Only connect', that famous E. M. Forster phrase, could well be North Oxford's motto. Drill anywhere into the durable social tundra of North Oxford and you reveal a dense, rich rootwork of relationships and contacts: X will turn out to be the daughter of a famous composer and widow of a prominent figure in the Foreign Office; her son Y is a professor who is married to the sister of Z, a well known publisher; all of which is invaluable for gaining access to key people, information or skills. Not only do the North Oxford *nomenclatura* know all the right people, they also know the wrong people, or rather the right kind of wrong people in the shape of wonderful little men who mend their Saabs for next to nothing or 'helps' from Cutteslowe or Blackbird Leys who come and clean their houses. The role of these 'helps' is of course an acute embarrassment to the liberal conscience of their employers, and their visits tend to be passed off as a sort of socio-cultural exchange whereby through a process of osmosis they gradually absorb civilizing values and quite incidentally scrub the floors.

Ernest Gellner in his critique of linguistic philosophy *Words and Things* referred to the 'simple but strong' folk culture of what he called the 'Narodniks' of North Oxford after the *narodniki,* the nineteenth-century Russian bourgeois liberals who sought to defend national culture against foreign contamination. Linguistic philosophy was, he maintained, an ideal weapon to defend this culture in that it enabled you to invalidate by verbal analysis any arguments against the status quo. 'It provides a powerful rationale for anyone wishing to have nothing or as little as possible to do with one or more of the following things: (1) science and technicality (2) power and responsibility (3) ideas.' An overstatement perhaps, but one with much truth in it. Take power: actually obtaining power, getting elected, wielding authority, and being answerable, is to the North Oxford mind unspeakably vulgar. Influence, however, is quite another matter ('Professor, the Minister wondered if you would care to comment on these drafts' – 'Ah, delighted, delighted'). Or, again, technology: North Oxford people certainly do not warm to technology – or to industry and commerce generally – though they are glad enough to have its products in the Summertown shops. They especially do not want the clanking, smelly, smoking thing anywhere near them and protest vociferously about radiator factories and proposed science parks in the neighbourhood.

What are the external marks of the folk culture of North Oxford? One of the most noticeable is a distinctive verbal style, an over-fastidious exactitude, a habit of *italicizing* certain words by stress and also a love of vehement contradiction and confrontation (I *absolutely* disagree with you there ...', 'you're *quite* wrong on that'). These features almost certainly derive from the university tutorial system with its adversarial emphasis, and contrast strongly with, say, East Oxford where people like to play conversational games of 'Snap' with their opinions, and where verbal styles tend to be consensual and confirmatory ('That's right man ...', 'I know what you mean ...') deriving from the polytechnic seminar, the consciousness-raising session, and the protest meeting.

The personal appearance of the North Oxford tribe is also distinctive, marked by a heavy use of natural fibres. The males wear tweeds, corduroys, Barbours, grey flannels, wool scarves and thick-soled shoes from Duckers that last a lifetime. Heavy pullovers are also favoured but if there is one garment above all others which distinguishes the tribe and all its various sexes it is the navy blue Guernsey. The women folk have a choice of two looks: 'Matron' with polo neck or artists' jackets that fasten up the back; Puffas, (which have ousted the once ubiquitous Huskies), with cord trousers tucked into boots; or 'Dragon lady', of which more later.

Natural materials also play an important part in North Oxford interiors. But unlike East Oxford pinestrippers who go for bare wood, matt white walls and plain paper lampshades, all in North Oxford is Victorian or greenery-yallery, full of antiques, brass, velvet, and wood polished to a deep rosy-red darkness. Moreover everything has a heavily used, lived-in look. In part this is because the owners have had to rely on family heirlooms to furnish their houses but also because they want to make several important statements about themselves: we have been here a very long time; even though our possessions are of fine quality we are not at all materialistic and do not allow such concerns to stunt our children's intellectual development in any way. If these infant dons – their children – wish to calibrate the flow rates of raspberry as opposed to, say, strawberry yogurt down the velvet curtains, given their differing indices of adhesion, who are their parents to stop them? The ideal North Oxford house also contains an Aga oven in its kitchen. Their owners feel at ease with these cumbrous objects because they are rather like themselves: large, solid, durable and frugal. Moreover, Agas also appeal to the neighbourhood's intellectual snobbery. Based on a simple but ingenious Swedish design, they are the kitchen appliance equivalent of the many famous foreign academics and émigré intellectuals who throng the neighbourhood.

North Oxford folk have large families and to accommodate them have to drive around in cars almost as big as their living-rooms. If the Guernsey is the archetypal garment, then the archetypal car is the Volvo estate, preferably painted an ecologically acceptable shade of green. However, big old Daimlers will do at a pinch as will old Saabs which again rather resemble the dons who own them, being heavy, round-shouldered, slow but powerful, and going on forever. The sportier will run around in a Saab Turbo, but again always painted a traditional Oxford Dark Blue to tone down any suggestion of raciness. Generally it is the women who drive, with their menfolk huddled nervously next to them. The males do not like to drive and often have never even learned to do so.

Above all, in clothes, in houses and interiors the great thing is to avoid flashiness: flaunting wealth is the greatest sin in North Oxford and a recipe for social disaster.

The rituals of North Oxford folk, their social calendar, follow a clear pattern which has its daily, weekly and longer cycles. The day begins with what has been called the 'morning prayer meeting': the delivery of children to school ('O Lord, deliver us from Volvos as we deliver others'). Every morning fleets of estate cars fill Bardwell Road like long sleek lines of *wagons-lits* waiting patiently to disgorge their cargoes of infants before surging away smoothly up Charlbury Road. Sunday brings services at the Anglican St Andrews ('St C. S. Lewis's Church' – Betjeman) with capacity congregations. This is usually followed by a vinous lunch and maybe a walk in the University Parks where you nod to acquaintances and sometimes run shrieking down the paths with your children – a valuable learning experience for the whole family.

The most characteristic social event in North Oxford is not, say, the drinks party as in London or the street party as in East Oxford but the dinner party, which is small enough to be socially controllable and to permit conversation (or that attenuated blend of disputation and allusion which passes for it in North Oxford) to flourish. These occasions are mini-High Tables, two- or three-a-side High Tables, training sessions for the bigger affairs in the colleges.

Seasonally come ballet school examinations in St Gregory and Augustine's Church Hall, scenes of mothers with infants in tulle dresses, in forests of brushes and hairgrips, frantically preparing their charges and complimenting one another's daughters in the hope of reciprocation; also, visits by opera companies when North Oxford empties and flows in furs to the Apollo to see and be seen, and then streams back again.

Annual events include Walters' winter sale, when North Oxford matrons battle to buy *themselves* men's gloves, scarves and other accessories, and the autumnal evening-class enrolments at Frideswide's or Cherwell School where (with serious scrubbed faces and grey or beige overcoats) they stand in long queues to sign up for introductory metalwork, intermediate Russian or basic artistic appreciation, and generally get, as the middle classes do, the best out of the goodies on offer from the educational system.

The major annual events are the holidays. In spring the folk flock to Cornwall, particularly to the Fowey Estuary, a kind of Summertown-on-Sea where they invite one another in for drinks and round for dinner and generally do what they did back home. Summer brings a migration to the Dordogne which they like because it is that part of France which most closely resembles the Cotswolds. There they have what they call cottages, really sheds and outhouses sold to them by wily French peasants, and there they invite one another in for drinks and round for dinner, etc. . . . However, there is one way in which they do go deeply native: they consume the local food and drink in large quantities. North Oxford is very Elizabeth David and anything smacking of French cuisine highly acceptable. It was not by chance that Britain's premier French restaurant, the Quat' Saisons, was formerly in Summertown (ironically next door to Oxfam headquarters).

North Oxford is studded with a constellation of distinguished schools. They act as seed cultures, crystallizing and transmitting the larger host culture. They include the 'High' – the Oxford High School for Girls – whose pupils, often the daughters of dons, are the intellectual *crème de la crème*. Reputed to be a ferocious academic hothouse, it is renowned for its university and especially Oxbridge entrances (at the 'High' it is said to matter not *if* you go to university but *where*) and of late its success in fund-raising and extending its own facilities.

Another microculture is the Dragon School: a boarding school with some day boys which also takes girl pupils (interestingly known at first to the boys as 'hags'). It is athletic, extrovert and geared to achievement – the pupils' marks and form places together with their *full addresses* used to be published annually in the school magazine the *Draconian*, not a thing you would find, I daresay, in a Haringey comprehensive. By all accounts its approach is unusually individual, informal and stimulating. Individuality is prized, one senses, even to the degree of eccentricity. Attitudes towards dress are relaxed and staff known by their nicknames – a clever device which acknowledges and absorbs the pupils' own counterculture. Yet you cannot help being struck by what a private world it all is, with its own language, rituals and lore, and how very inaccessible it remains to the outsider.

Certainly education and children's success at school preoccupy the neighbourhood's adults, as anyone who has attended a dinner party there can testify. In North Oxford inheritance is of great importance – of money of course but also of brains. The area is full of donnish dynasties; if a child is doing badly there, that is a serious matter not only for its own prospects but also for the blot it casts on its intellectual pedigree. It is an area not so much of the selfish as of the self-conscious gene.

Another burning educational issue there is the choice between state and private education. All over North Oxford a very English, very civil war is being fought between opposing factions. But it is a war being fought not by two but by three armies, for there are those who are committed socialists or social democrats who despite their principles still cannot bring themselves to deny their children the benefits and opportunities of private schools. This third army is in a parlous state: uneasy in their own consciences, its members are forced within the articulate arena of North Oxford to defend their position at every turn and come under shot and shell from all sides. For a time they put off the evil day when they must commit themselves, they get their children into Church of England primary schools like St Barnabas in Jericho and 'Phil and Jim' in Leckford Road, but sooner or later the choice has to be made and it is a torment to their soft, liberal consciences.

Yes, North Oxford's children are definitely amongst its most notable features. Even their names are distinctive: none of your affected Tamsins or Damians here. Instead the names are traditional, strong – often Scottish – big-boned, high protein names like Jonathan, Rupert and Alexander or, for girls, Penelope, Rebecca, Victoria and Rosalind. These are the names with extra inches, and the owners of these names are themselves amazingly advanced, knowledgeable and sophisticated – presumably from years of absorbing conversations over North Oxford dinner tables. In my day the undergraduate newspapers prattled on about the 'lovely Lolitas of the High School' with their mini-skirts and long Pre-Raphaelite locks down their backs. Had the undergraduates actually met any of these formidable young ladies they would probably have run a mile. The same is, I am sure, still true today. Apparently during school breaks at the 'High' you can still hear the daughters of consultant surgeons analysing the cultural (as opposed to the philosophical) importance of existentialism and dissecting the inadequacies of each other's postgraduate lovers. Sophistication sets in early in North Oxford. There is a story, possibly apocryphal but which deserves to be true, of an excursion from Greycotes School (the preparatory school on Bardwell Road) being shown around Oxford's Covered Market in the course of which one of the infants was heard to yawn 'I'm simply dying for a sherry.'

North Oxford children are also past masters at patronizing their elders – I dare not say betters – and in administering indirect social pinpricks, often by means of a disingenuous quotation of their parents' words. (At the door: 'Is Mummy in?' – 'No, my mother has gone out. She said someone boring might be coming round.' Ouch! The brat here has achieved a triple score: administered the pinprick, made trouble for Mummy, and left itself completely in the clear.) Sometimes North Oxford children rebel in adolescence against their middle-class culture: half the girls hanging on to the punks in Oxford's Bonn Square are said to be North Oxford girls *getting their own back on Daddy*. But their rebellions are usually short-lived and they are easily re-absorbed into the comfortable folk culture, so accommodating is it to eccentricity and individual self-expression.

Pity the wretched males of the neighbourhood, exposed on the open board game of North Oxford, surrounded by such threatening pieces – the superbrats to one side and the neighbourhood's formidable women to the other. North Oxford women come in three basic shapes: Matrons, Divorcees and Dragon Ladies. Matrons are the successful family models, spinning at peak efficiency, operating the merry-go-round of their children's lives and generally deciding on the exact detail of family ritual and costume. Sometimes, though, they keep in a stripped pine kitchen drawer an unfinished novel (about North Oxford, naturally) which they will pull out from time to time and work on. As their children grow up they return to work. There they capitalize upon their prodigious organizational skills, either as school secretaries (bossing around their children's friends) or university departmental administrators (bossing around their husbands' colleagues).

Although superficially there is a certain studied simplicity to the surface of the Matrons' lives and tastes, beneath it considerable covert competition gnaws away. This mainly centres, naturally, on their children's progress at school but also on such matters as how many people of note you can attract to your dinner table, whether you have an autonomous career, how well your last book did and of course the Great High Table Contest (keeping tally of how many High Tables you have been invited to during your time in Oxford). But mainly the rivalry has to do with the game of Getting it Right, how closely in cuisine, clothes and lifestyle you can approximate to the right North Oxford note of understated quality and good taste.

Sometimes, however, the fall of the dice decides that the Matrons have to become Divorcees. Their marriages cave in under the enormous bathyspheric pressure of the North Oxford lifestyle, or – less frequently – collapse because of an affair. Amongst all the other games going on in North Oxford is a bookish minor adultery game. But it is of a watery, cerebral nature, rather like a discreet swap of conversational partners or a game of musical chairs with identical partners, which leaves you wondering why they bother at all. However, such affairs can lead to marital hiccups, and if the Matrons do become Divorcees, a strict set of rules comes into operation. They will be permitted under their settlements to keep their children in their present schools but they are not allowed to pass Go and have a second chance at being Matrons: they must advance at once either to the Oakthorpe Road area of Summertown or to Chalfont Road or to open an arty shop in North Parade. Increasingly, however, these spaces are becoming too expensive for the Divorcees and they drop off the board altogether and end up in places like Jericho or East or South Oxford, thus ceasing to exist in North Oxford terms.

However, if the North Oxford Matrons manage to stay on the board long enough they end up by winning extra status and power, rather like a draught that has made it to the other side and been crowned. Then they can become Dragon Ladies. These are easily identifiable, with pale, scrubbed faces behind perspex-framed spectacles, matt hair, usually well coiffed or swept back into a bun, tweeds, Huskies, thick socks, and sensible shoes. Whereas the women of East Oxford tend towards benign earthmotherish rotundity, the Dragon Ladies of North Oxford are all sharp angry profiles and sudden piercing glances of interrogation or intimidation. There is also something masculine about their appearance, a certain solidity and strength that is muscular rather than motherly.

Imperious rebukes, hectoring challenges and ceaseless admonition flow from their sharp lips: 'you must'; 'you should'; 'come come'; 'pray'; 'if you please'; 'don't you *see*'; the intensified imperative is one of their favourite verbal forms, as in '*Do* check your references'. They make great use of selective stress and rising and falling patterns of intonation: these 'tunes' often more terrifying to their listeners than the tellings-off they are actually receiving.

They rather resemble brainier versions of Barbara Woodhouse and like her they love to own, walk and command pedigree dogs. You see them out in the parks with these dogs and their menfolk, holding one leash around the dog's neck and another, invisible but far tighter, round the necks of their wretched emasculate males. For they easily dominate the males in their families, usually outliving them and producing introvert irresolute sons of unresolved tendencies who take up careers as water-colourists, writers of children's books, or printers of fine, limited editions. You feel that in some of North Oxford's Gothic mansions there are metaphorical closets out of which one or more hapless males are vainly trying to come, only to be checked by the stern Woodhousian command, 'Stay!'

Being Fabians and *Guardian* readers the matrons used to despise Mrs Thatcher (with whom they nevertheless share many characteristics) and spoke of her as if she were a headmistress of opposed, disastrous tendencies ('Have you read her latest pronouncement?'). They love to do battle with minor officials and with teachers at the 'High', never hesitating to pull rank, and *always* winning. Tireless in their organization of committees and of other people's good works and in their championship of their husbands' literary estates (of which they are the executors) they are the Red Queens of North Oxford, perpetually running to stay in the same spot.

As they get older and less formidable, they beat a scaly retreat to the many culs-de-sac and closes of sheltered housing in and around Summertown to lead quieter, sadder lives. There the loudest sound is the discreet purring of the Paternoster Dairy van making its deliveries of eggs and cream and natural yoghurt. Around mid-morning, a mysterious metallic tapping begins. It is the tentative music of the Zimmer frames as they head towards the Summertown Public Library in search of reading matter and the chance perhaps to correct, in slow, spidery handwriting, any mistakes in the catalogue description of their late husbands' works.

For Time tames even Dragons. There is a whole army of the elderly in North Oxford, leading proud, lonely lives behind their dense velvet curtains. Some find a lifeline in the Ferry Centre and the North Oxford Association which cleverly involves them by giving them one last chance to organize other people's lives for them. Being staunchly independent the Old Dragons at first approach the Centre rather stiffly and sniffily, claiming to be far too busy to get involved. But soon loneliness drives them back again, and you can see them in an Indian summer of efficiency taking it in turns to organize lunch clubs, discussion groups or yoga classes. Next door, in the baths, carefree young Dragons leap and splash in the water as lucent as dolphins, cavorting in the clear spring of their North Oxford lives.

North Oxford has been justly reflected and celebrated in literature – notably by Betjeman but also by many other writers. Lewis Carroll can hardly be cited as a commentator as the suburb was still being built when he was writing but his work nevertheless provides a superb handbook to the area. It is all still there; the sharp little Alices, the Tweedledum and Tweedledee arguments, the dominating Duchesses and Queens, and the hapless terrified males – the White Rabbits, gardeners and Knaves.

Another writer of fantasy, and one interested in dragons, lived for a time at 20 and 22 Northmoor Road: J. R. R. Tolkien. There have been various interpretations of *Lord of the Rings* – as an allegory of the threat of nuclear war or the struggle against Fascism, or a brilliant philological *jeu* – but its rootedness in Oxford and specifically in North Oxford seems to have been overlooked. The hobbit heroes are clearly North Oxford children: they have the bodies of children but the minds of adults; they speak with all the distinctive spry confidence of Dragon School pupils; they are good marksmen (Ouch!); they become extremely distinguished in the outside world: 'Frodo (O.D. 1929) has done outstandingly well in Mordor ...'. There is also a range of other peculiar races and creatures in the novel, odd little particularizations of the British class system: the orcs are miniaturized Cowley yobs and the wizards are of course superdons, with added magical powers.

It is also deeply charged with the anti-industrial ethos of North Oxford. Whilst Tolkien was gestating his fantasies in the 1920s and '30s, the real city was undergoing massive industrial expansion under Morris and correspondingly altering its social and political complexion. Many immigrants (especially unemployed South Welsh) were attracted to the city. A chapter towards the end of the book clearly reveals Tolkien's view on all this. While the hobbits have been away, their homeland the Shire has been devastated by some rotters who have introduced an early form of industrialization and set about thieving under the guise of socialism. Tolkien makes much of the 'small swarthy men' who have come in from outside. The returning heroes soon put a stop to all this by rousing the populace and kicking out the ruffians ('those that surrendered were shown the borders'). In real life Tolkien (who had come to loathe the motor car) would certainly have been only too delighted if the same had happened to Morris and all his works. 'On your bike, Lord Nuffield' is really what the message amounts to.

But what of the matrons of North Oxford – are they also represented in the novel? Well, possibly: the only vivid female character is a terrifying monstrous spider who gives one of the heroes a sting from which he never fully recovers and tries to squash another by lowering her bulk on to him. But the doughty little fellow whips out his blade and, holding it resolutely erect, drives off the crushing female. It is an intensely revealing, deeply Freudian scene, shot through with *l'horreur feminine* and full of jubilation at a tiny phallic triumph.

More generally it is striking just how many writers of fantasy and children's literature the place has produced, and one cannot but speculate on the reasons for this. Is it due to the large don families and the importance of children in Oxford culture? Or the numbers of adults who spend their days mentally playing in their own private intellectual constructs? Or simply the curious dreamy atmosphere of the place? If so, North Oxford with its fantastic mock-medieval architecture and its broad, secluded gardens plays a potent part.

– 11 –

Rural Rides

Once the countryside came right up to Oxford's door. 'The approach to Oxford by the Henley Road,' wrote the Reverend William Tuckwell about the 1830s, 'was the most beautiful in the world. Soon after passing Littlemore you came in sight of, and did not lose again, the sweet city with its dreaming spires, driven along a road now crowded and obscured with dwellings, open then to cornfields.' Oxford's towers rose straight out of fields and meadows, and between its stones and spires the green broke through at every turn. 'A towery city and branchy between towers', Gerard Manley Hopkins called it. 'Cuckoo-echoing, bell-swarmed, lark-charmed, rook-racked and river rounded.'

The city's markets sucked the country into its streets, while, in return, rural pastimes drew undergraduates out to the land. Some Oxford street names still enshrine these excursions: Pullen's Lane, which led to a Headington elm to which Josiah Pullen of Magdalen Hall walked 'every Day, sometimes twice a day, if tolerable Weather'; and Five Mile Drive, the loop of a circuit tramped by athletic undergraduates.

Villages – little clumps of cottages clustered round a church or inn – dotted the countryside around Oxford every two or three miles – Binsey, the Hinkseys, Marston, Wolvercote, Headington, Cowley and Iffley. Their names preserve their marshy, meadowy Saxon origins: Binsey – Bynna's river island; or Cowley – the cattle clearing in the wood.

Oxford spread and swallowed the villages in three great gulps.

The first came in the nineteenth century. Until then the city remained the core of streets that had once lain within its walls, and a small outer ring of medieval parishes – St Clement's, St Ebbe's, St Thomas's and St Giles's. After 1830 it spread north adding Jericho and then Park Town in the 1850s and eventually the rest of North Oxford; after 1850 similar growth took place to the east, south and west. In the 1920s and 1930s the expansion resumed and accelerated to accommodate the workforce of Morris's new car factories. An outer range of suburbs was thrown up, often building on the cores of ancient villages, absorbing and transforming them. After the Second World War, this growth continued unabated but, checked by the green belt, assumed a different form, bubbling up at a distance in spillovers, dormitory settlements and nearby county towns.

Interspersed among all these developments are the remains of the older villages. Even now some of the villages – such as Binsey with its irregular line of thatched cottages and its green surround – still retain their original character. Ancient memories seem to cluster in these corners. Walk along the chestnut-shaded lane to the tiny church of St Margaret's, Binsey, with its sunken holy well behind, and you feel very close indeed to the original shrine, as old as Oxford itself. Yet there is often a fragility, a sense of precarious hemmed-in survival about these villages. You feel it most, perhaps, in the Hinkseys perched on Oxford's rim, lassoed by the roaring ring road and overshadowed by a broad stride of pylons. The same fragility is present in Iffley: with its walled closes and discreet infill there is something peculiarly enclosed and atrophied about its atmosphere, that sense of blooms preserved under a belljar.

Some villages have been almost utterly swamped, a fate most typified by Headington. With its endless rows of semis, its fuming traffic jams, its long High Street straggle of estate agents, video rentals and fast food outlets it resembles nothing so much as a part of London – an outer borough that has somehow detached itself and floated some 50 miles to affix itself to the city of Oxford. It is a curiously muffled, insulated sort of place. Its residents say they live in Headington, not Oxford and turn their backs on the rest of the city. Yet it cannot be said to have a character of its own. It is, said one resident, the 'ultimate double-glazed suburb' – although as in all such places one can often glimpse the intense vibrations of an inner life: a violent abstract on a sitting room easel here or a Texan ranch-style interior there. So it is altogether fitting that stuck into the dull and lumpy porridge of Headington's suburban streets is a wild surreal sprig of garnishing – the giant polystyrene shark's tail which local cinema-owner and radio personality, Bill Heine, has stuck perpendicularly on to his roof.

At its centre still lies the village of Old Headington. In the course of this century it has suffered a curious double fate. Surrounded by the proliferating suburban cells of New Headington, it has been both destroyed and reborn, emerging burnished and fresh-minted, a little rural icon with its village atmosphere lovingly re-manufactured. Now it is exclusively middle class, but in living memory it was the home of college scouts, laundresses, gardeners and the like. From the 1930s onwards an academic influx took place, a daring North Oxford diaspora to the healthy climes of Headington Hill. Famous figures settled there, such as Sir Isaiah Berlin, the historian A. B. Emden, Lord Elton, John Johnson (the University Printer), J. R. R. Tolkien, and, out of the Kilns, C. S. Lewis.

Old Headington became a little intellectual Athens on the hill. Its beacons were a flourishing literary society, vigorously chaired by the novelist, Elizabeth Bowen, the Headington Labour Party, and a new and revolutionary Women's Institute which let in men and fostered radical debate (sadly, remarked one member, the jam-making element has since won out).

Prominent amongst its organs is the local preservation society, the Friends of Old Headington, formed initially to combat an unwelcome development proposal from a firm of speculative builders. Since then it has been most active, publishing booklets, commissioning reports and advising on planning applications. Deep down one senses that they would rather be involved with the gardeners and laundresses. But if you don't have a person an amenity will do, and the Athenians instead turned their high powered faculties to the composition of paving slabs and the correct colour for lamp standards (black). Indeed, such is the darkly taste-ful profusion of the lamps that the neighbourhood now resembles some strange Stygian tulip field.

Elsewhere Headington is a sprawling mishmash of a place. It

mixes up medics (many in 'Lakeland', so called because of street names such as Coniston or Bowness); house-sharing polytechnic students or similar groups of nurses, teachers and academics; and London commuters who daily catch the M40 coaches down to town. There are famous schools; a football ground; hospitals galore and Harberton Mead Catholic workers' college; and, next door, Robert Maxwell's stately pile. Further out, you find the honest working-class estate of Wood Farm and the aspiring gentility of Risinghurst with its trim rose bushes and weekly ritual of waxing the Rover.

Barton, over the ring road, presents a grimmer spectacle. Only reachable on foot by a dank underpass, on a ledge-like site slanting down to a brook choked with old prams, bottles and other rubbish, it is a scene of dreary prefabs, apartment blocks in anaemic brick and row after row of pebbledashed houses that look as if they have been constructed of identical squares of emery paper. All the tell-tale signs of council-built estate are there: the modernist pillbox of a church, the central defile of shops, grilled and shuttered, the menacing dogs (following the rule of the smaller the yard the huger the Rottweiler), the motorbikes and old bangers full of litter, stranded in pools of oil and a perpetual state of semi-repair.

Originally a hamlet of half a dozen houses (some of which are still detectable by their Headington stone walls at the top of the estate), the council expanded it rapidly after the Second World War to rehouse people from the city's central slums. Many were 'problem' families whose high index of deprivation pushed them to the head of the housing queue ('You have to be special to get a house here', said one early resident, showing the perverse pride people will take in almost anything).

As such, it always had a rough reputation – perhaps justifiably. According to one social worker who knows the estate, it was dominated in its early days by a matriarch of crime, a female Fagin, who sat at the centre of her extended clan, fencing goods here, plotting a job there. Even today it can easily erupt into the wild lawlessness of a frontier town, as this description of a Barton Karnival, taken from the local Newsletter in 1987, shows: 'Though the patrolling Alsatians, Dobermanns and other Very Large Dogs made it look at times like the Police Dogs' convention, everyone

was having a good time till soon after five, when fists and bodies
started flying around the beer tent ... Bystanders were treated to
the unusual sight of bodies flying through the air over trestle tables
laden with geraniums in full bloom...'

But Barton has always made an effort. This 'can-do' spirit
showed itself early on in the Saga of the Community Centre, an
episode which had it occurred in Soviet Russia would have made
a fine uplifting film propagandizing proletarian effort. Shortly after
the first families trickled on to Barton's barren steppe, a mass
meeting was held at which it was decided to build a community
centre. The council promised the land and materials if the residents
would provide the labour. It all began in a blaze of enthusiasm but
then keenness cooled and faction fomented. Eventually only a
handful of volunteers were plodding on, forgotten. Then one day,
they finished, and the new centre stood forth in all its glory...

Recently replaced, the centre provided a focus for a noble suc-
cession of individuals – local councillors and residents – who strove
to make a go of things on the estate and build its communal
life. That same spirit of self-help, of pulling yourself up by the
bootstraps, is evident throughout Barton in proudly kept gardens
or laboriously constructed extensions and annexes. The great god
of the locality is DIY, and every evening and weekend he spreads his
invisible rule and Black and Decker drill over the estate. Recently,
Bartonian self-improvement has taken another upward twist as
residents, benefitting from government encouragement, have
bought their own houses. A further fillip has come from young
middle-class couples unable to break into the Oxford housing
market anywhere else. Down these mean streets a gentrifier must
go, and by ironical consequence the Magnet Joinery Georgian door
and the carriage lamp are now taking their place even in Barton,
alongside the Alsatians, Dobermanns and old bangers.

No, Barton is by no means Oxford's worst council estate. That
dubious accolade must go to Blackbird Leys, a few miles to the
east, just below the Cowley car factory. Physically, Blackbird Leys
is not all that bad a place. It is spacious and green, has two pubs
and two churches, and the council has gone to the pains of plugging
in a range of amenities (such as a library, community centre and
youth clubs). The local MP, Andrew Smith, who lives on the estate,
says that when he shows round visitors and tells them it is Oxford's

most deprived area, their reaction, thinking of Toxteth or wherever, is to laugh in his face.

But in Oxford terms at least, 'the Leys' is the pits. A formidable pile of statistics indexes its social problems: with less than 10 per cent of the city's population, it is responsible for nearly a third of its crime; a quarter of its residents are terrified to walk the streets at night; one in five of its boys aged 10–16 have been apprehended by the police. The study from which these figures are taken, conducted under the auspices of the university's Department of Socio-Legal Studies, was so afraid of adding to the estate's bad name that it referred to it throughout, dolefully and anonymously, as 'Omega'.

Residents have other names for it: 'the Black Hole', 'the Ghetto', 'Botany Bay', 'the Place for Forgotten People'. A third of them would like to escape it altogether. By contrast, those born to Blackbird Leys – the teenagers – love it. Young 'Leysers' have built a street-centred life all of their own, based on biking and speeding, chatting up the local talent, fighting and sparring with the law. They delight in the estate's tough reputation, venturing out to 'best' groups from other parts of the city, often in semi-ritualistic, pre-arranged bouts. Of late there has been an explosion of joyriding, especially in races around the estate's circular road system (which, unintentionally on the part of its planners, provides the perfect racetrack). With their daring displays of skill, these draw large crowds of spectators which the police have difficulty in dispersing.

All this has given the estate a terrible name ('Unless I punish these men', said one local judge sentencing some Leysers, 'everyone else on the estate will be tempted to have a go, won't they?'). This image is, of course, massively unfair. In law-and-order terms the population of the estate breaks down into a large 'respectable' or 'decent' majority who live there because they cannot live anywhere else and simply want to get on with their lives and their jobs; a 'rough' minority, not really criminal but irresponsible, kicking against rules because they do not like rules; and, finally, a very small hard core of utter sociopaths, devoted to wrecking the well-being of those around them.

Socially, Blackbird Leys is a place at odds not just with the rest of the city but with itself. With unusually high proportions of single parent families, ethnic minorities, isolated elderly and of young people (over a quarter are teenagers) it is heavily unbalanced in demographic terms. Even physically it is deeply split. East Blackbird Leys, being squeezed in later on, is much less spacious, thus creating divisions of envy and resentment between the two halves of the estate. Surveys have shown not only more crime on this estate than elsewhere but more willingness to report crimes and complain as well as intolerance and dislike of neighbours.

In one way Blackbird Leys is on a par with an earlier marginal community on the edges of Oxford – the 'Quarry Hogs' of nineteenth-century Headington, whose lawlessness became a local byword. But people at least chose to go and live in the Quarry. It had its own rough and ready internal laws, was held together by a vigorous local patois and a folk culture of music and sports. Blackbird Leys, by contrast, in its size, anonymity and fragmentation, is a monument to the kind of bad planning that crams people together like cans in a supermarket. It is a place where all bonds of community, tolerance and restraint have been weakened, where your neighbour is potentially your enemy, and where the young, seeking to break the cycle of boredom, divert themselves with displays of 'creative delinquency' and try vainly to impose their own twisted versions of territoriality. And although never visited by the tourists or mentioned in the guidebooks, it is but a few miles from the cloisters and the quadrangles.

Boars Hill is in many ways the polar opposite of Blackbird Leys: wealthy, spacious and at ease with itself and its country setting. But in fact it is just as artificial a creation. Unlike Headington it did not grow out of any existing village. What fed the formation of Boars Hill was the nostalgic rural dream of the English middle classes – the desire, having made your pile, to flee the city and adopt a simpler, landed lifestyle nestling on a comfortable carpet of green. Significantly, it was on the very slopes of Boars Hill, just as Oxford's brickish expansion was beginning, that Matthew Arnold wove a golden Oxford pastoral out of the stuff of undergraduate outings and a rejection of the 'sick hurry' of modern life.

Its house names are a delight. What essence of English rural idyll breathes there – Inglewood, Deepdene, Orchardlea, Greenaways! Some chase butterflies on Boars Hill, but you can collect house names with equal pleasure, and minutely classify them. There is

the Sylvan–Substantial genus – Gorselands, Pinecroft and Brack-
enhurst – which have a robustness and heathery toughness and
would make excellent names for furniture ranges or household
deodorizers. Then you encounter the Rustic–Romantic family
which dwindles to the twee and dimity world of faery, the sub-
Tolkien underworld of the country garden gnome – the Rustlings,
Windswept and Tinkerbell. Enough nonsense! barks a third class.
As clipped as colonels, these bristle with briskness – Grainings,
Downings, Haltings and Sprivers. Finally, after the 'animal house'
category (a whole warren of badgers' holts and foxes' combes)
come the Exotics, named for idiosyncratic or sentimental reasons.
These often sound like racehorses ('And at the line it's 'Lamorna'
neck and neck with 'Craigellachie', with 'The Sheiling' in third
place and 'By the Way' trailing badly in fourth!').

   You have to know the names because there is not a single street
number on the Hill. Indeed, if you do not want to get lost it is as
well to obtain the house location guide put out by the Boars Hill
Association. What do you find when you finally track down the
houses behind their dense hedges? Well, let it be said, in architectural terms nothing tremendously distinguished. There is a
handful of Voysey-style houses with their distinctive large low
eaves and Quakerish charm. Otherwise five types prevail: upright
Victorian and Edwardian monsters, red brick and Queen Anne in
style; super-suburban villas of the 1920s, white rendered and half-
timbered; outsize Cotswold cottages; a clutch of smaller converted
cottages in Old Boars Hill; and a scattering of Bauhaus boxes. But
the houses of Boars Hill, if not outstanding to look at, are nearly
always good to live in, substantial, unpretentious and comfortable.

   Their true claim to distinction is less their architectural style than
their green setting, that manicured wilderness blending three very
English ideals – the garden, the greenwood and the seashore.
Because the neighbourhood was developed piecemeal as plots were
sold off by farmers and family trusts, there is a remarkable lack of
uniformity and a low density – only 350 houses in the whole
neighbourhood. You search in vain for a central focus, a parade
of shops, a church or village hall. Instead there is a long winding
involvement of lane and close, flanked by broad verges and boxy
beech hedges permitting discreet glimpses of lawn and drive and
garden outhouse. And there are trees, everywhere trees, thickly

clustered with ivies and flourishing in the light upland soil – firs, Scots pines, hollies, horse-chestnuts, oaks and cherries, and bank upon bank of gleaming rhododendrons.

But the seashore? Yes, for while Oxford dozes in its low bowl of air, the Hill is braced by south westerlies whistling across from Cornwall and the Channel. After night gales residents often wake to windows lightly misted with sea salt. And after all, what is the Hill fundamentally but an island of sand and coral deposited over the ages by sea and glacier? Walking on Boars Hill you sometimes feel as if you are stepping on a beach under a fringe of pine or, as when approaching the coast, sense some unexpected expanse just beyond the skyline. Yet once step off the Hill to the south and you are in a different world. As the tree screen closes behind you, the tide that rises up is of brown fields, a broad clay vale stretching to the horizon with only the funnels of Didcot smoking bluely in the distance.

So deeply rooted seem the houses and trees of Boars Hill that you might think they had been there forever. In fact, before being enclosed at the end of the eighteenth century, Boars Hill was largely a bleak and treeless heath. Thereafter, parts were intensively cultivated as small farms and nurseries, one of which was Jarn (probably a corruption of *jardin*). The only dwellings were on Old Boars Hill, a wretched cluster of labourers' cottages forming the outlying hamlet of Wootton.

It was a pocket of grim rural poverty. To eke out their husbands' meagre wages, women took in corduroy finishing, and each family also kept an allotment and a pig. Into this harsh world the first middle-class families arrived in the 1880s, including the Mathews family who were in trade in Oxford. Emma Mathews, a woman besotted with rural life, badgered her husband to move out of the city. They moved into a vacant cottage on the Hill – which promptly fell down. Undeterred, Mr Mathews built a larger house, Broome Close, which still stands today. Once established, Emma, a redoubtable figure – non-conformist, teetotaller, and early feminist – set about trying to remedy the living conditions of the labourers' families on the Hill.

Hard on the heels of these first families came a second wave of settlers, many of them eminent people. If the eighteenth century had missed Boars Hill the first time round, it arrived with a vengeance in the 1890s with a number of figures firmly in that earlier century's tradition of gentleman-savants and aristocrat-builders. Lord Berkeley constructed a mock castle with a laboratory in its grounds in which he conducted a series of celebrated experiments. Sir Arthur Evans, in between digging up Mycenae and Knossos, gradually pieced together the enormous rambling fantasy of Youlbury.

This house was the Boars Hill equivalent of San Simeon, William Randolph Hearst's notorious castle in California. It contained twenty-eight bedrooms; nine baths; three staircases; a library as big as a ballroom; and an octagonal breakfast room with a solar room above it. There was a marble-floored hall laid out in maze pattern flanked by Minoan pillars and thrones, and the whole pile was topped off with a 150-foot wooden spy-tower from which one old gentleman actually claimed to have seen the Bristol Channel. Sadly, when the house passed into other hands after Evans's death, its upkeep proved too expensive and it was demolished.

After the savants came the poets. Of course Boars Hill (or rather Hinksey Hill) had long enjoyed poetic associations through Matthew Arnold's 'Scholar Gypsy' and 'Thyrsis', but these were intensified when Robert Bridges settled on the Hill in 1907 and Masefield in 1917. Both became Laureates ('If Boars Hill gets it three times does it get to keep it?' joked Housman) and both produced out of their Boars Hill seclusions a series of poetic bestsellers, most notably Bridges' *Testament of Beauty*.

Poets in turn bring in younger poets, and Masefield invited Robert Graves and his wife to stay in a cottage in his grounds after the First World War. Yet Graves was too Bohemian and unbuttoned for the Hill. He tried to inject some life by opening a shop which he ran on Robin Hood principles, overcharging Boars Hill residents in order to undercharge those of Wootton. Then prices dropped, the shop went bust and Graves was left saddled with a sizeable debt. But by then Boars Hill had become stifling to him ('Too many poets' he grumbled in *Goodbye to All That*), and he cleared out to Islip.

The final element in the social evolvement of Boars Hill was the influx of dons and professional people who settled on the Hill mainly in the course of the first three decades of this century. The most prominent of these, Gilbert Murray, moved into Yatscomb with his wife, the wealthy and formidable Lady Mary, in 1919, and remained on the Hill, a benign tutelary presence, until his death in 1957.

From his Youlbury fastness Evans saw the invasion of the professional classes and the depredations of 'speculative builders' (a term he used with the venom reserved today for football hooligans) and vowed to fight back. With his encouragement, the recently formed Oxford Preservation Trust acquired Lord Berkeley's golf course with its classic view of the dreaming spires.

Then he backed a successful attempt to buy Jarn, creating there a wild garden and erecting a mound with a panoramic view of the surrounding countryside. Jarn Mound is also something of a monument to Evans himself – if you like, his pyramid. Pharaoh-like, he himself directed the vast earthworks. Twenty men toiled for thirty-four months, then – disaster! The local clay out of which it was built slipped and the whole thing collapsed. A lesser man would have been broken, but Evans pressed on and finally completed it: fifty feet high, surmounted by a pedestal and a plate explaining the view.

Today you can still climb the Mound but it is all rather sad. The Mound seems low and unimpressive, the stairs are tilted and cracked and the pedestal vandalized. Even the view, once panoramic, is now blocked – perhaps appropriately – by a vigorously growing screen of trees.

One could view the sequence of settlers on the Hill rather in terms of waves of invading tribes whose remains Sir Arthur Evans might have disclosed on one of his digs. First was the original rustic population, revealingly still called the 'Hill Folk'. These were dislodged and absorbed by the incomers, becoming their cooks, maids, gardeners, etc.

The incomers in their turn displayed a great craving for rootedness, for identification with the land and an idealized version of the past. An almost Tolstoyan reverence for the simple life of rural community inspired Mrs Mathews and her daughters, one of whom, Mary Rix, wrote in *Boars Hill Sixty Years Ago* (1941): 'the very isolation of these small cottages in the midst of so wide a heath strengthened the feeling that each was responsible for all ... There are deep spiritual experiences which bind a community together, and they are being threatened by the superficial urban habits of a machine-made age'.

Alongside this feeling ran rival claims on the part of the incomers to greater originality and, thus, social precedence. Mrs Mathews, one feels, was in no doubt of her own position. 'As the years went by,' her daughter wrote, 'many eminent residents built houses on Boars Hill, but Emma's eyes were on the village and not the Oxford dignitaries ... *they made the first advances*' (my italics). The 'eminences' and poets in turn looked down their noses at the dons who were turning the place into a North-Oxford-on-the-Hill. Bridges deplored the new developments on the Foxcombe Road, refusing to walk into Oxford that way and preferring instead a direct descent down the Hill to Ferry Hinksey. There, if the ferry was on the opposite side, he would wade across unabashed, his trousers held aloft in his hand. By the early 1930s Masefield too was declaring it 'no longer pleasant country here but thrusting suburb', and abandoned the Hill for Pinsbury Park in the Cotswolds.

Perhaps the social contest was felt all the more keenly because no formal structure had been inherited from the past. Never having been a village, Boars Hill had no squire or mayor. Instead a series of surrogates were thrown up, Sir Arthur becoming perhaps the first 'squire' and Mrs Mathews 'mayor'. Subsequently her dynasty of strong-minded daughters inherited this role, and, in the words of one contemporary resident, 'told us all what to do'. This surrogate tradition, incidentally, continues to this day with leading families acting as mayoral equivalents.

A related and very powerful cultural strand on Boars Hill was that of highminded liberal benevolence. Both Mrs Mathews and Sir Arthur busied themselves in local good works of various kinds. With Masefield this impulse took the form of cultural missionary work, and he set about organizing local theatricals. 'The simple souls will accept everywhere the great work', he enthused in a letter. But where to hold them, given the lack of a hall on Boars Hill? Wootton, came the answer, and its inhabitants were duly enrolled in the proceedings. As one might have foreseen, the resulting productions had their moments of farce and disappointment. Later he wrote somewhat ruefully to a friend: 'There is a lot of class feeling. The poor are shy of the rich and the rich shy of the poor.' Eventually he withdrew the plays from Wootton altogether and took to putting them on in an outhouse in his own grounds.

The liberal benevolence of Boars Hill, as well as dropping like the gentle dew on the immediate countryside, was also directed – one might say, beamed – at the outside world. From Yatscomb Gilbert Murray carried out important work on behalf of the League of Nations and welcomed a long line of European refugees to his house. Evans too brought Serbian evacuees to Youlbury. Somehow this rural internationalism is all symbolized in Evans' spy-tower. During the First World War he apparently had a hot line in Whitehall that he could telephone for the latest military news, and would hoist flags on the tower to show the state of the Front, hours before it was known through the Press on the streets of Oxford.

But there was always a battle on Boars Hill between the Beacon and the Burrow, between involvement in, and influence over, the larger world on the one hand and solipsistic seclusion on the other. Without Murray working away in Yatscomb the United Nations and perhaps the world would not be as we know it. Yet many residents retreated, and still do, into private lives of prodigious eccentricity. One resident spoke to me of 'the weird people who embed themselves, bunkerlike, in the sides of the Hill'.

Overall, it is remarkable just how many cultural features of its past are preserved in Boars Hill (a persistence in itself peculiarly English). 'The population is somewhat monotonous and vulnerable and is now predominantly aged', P. J. Steward wrote in the 1950s of Boars Hill. He was referring to its trees, but the comment could well be applied to its academic residents, the Fogies. Most moved there about thirty years ago, when house prices were lower. Now they are far beyond the reach of most dons, whose numbers are in constant decline. It is all rather reminiscent of North Oxford's genteel descent into flats and dilapidation in the 1960s, except that multi-occupation has yet to gain a toe-hold on the Hill. 'I have an impression that a lot of people here are quite broke', says the writer Brian Aldiss, who moved to the Hill a few years ago.

A faint air of decay hangs over many Fogy dwellings. Lichen and moss are starting to penetrate the rendering or creep up the brickwork. Elsewhere, in the grounds of Youlbury, the Greenwood is beginning to win back what once it lost. Deep in the undergrowth you stumble over crumbling walls and doorless cottages, lost in an English jungle. Aldiss finds his imagination responding to this: 'There is a feeling of Nature coming back into its own – one of the

obsessive themes of my books. It is *Greybeard* personified' (referring to his novel of a future Oxford, a childless city slowly sinking
into the wilderness).

The Fogies are being dislodged in their turn by a fresh wave of
newcomers, the 'Veneerings'. These are younger, yuppie-ish, and
make their money in business, industry or the City. The Veneerings
differ both in attitude and style. The Fogies tend to be liberal and
Fabian and rest securely on their position and investments. They
are, in the words of Brian Aldiss, 'people for whom the battle of
life is largely over' – if indeed it ever began. The Veneerings on the
other hand are still fighting away in the world of 'telegrams and
anger' piling up pelf. The Fogies condemn them as pushy but then
add with scrupulous academic honesty that they probably envy the
Veneerings their money. 'Thatcherite' is a term often applied to
the Veneerings by the Fogies, but that is not quite right. They are
nouveau and brash certainly but smoothly alloy rather than harshly
ferric. 'Heseltinian' might be a better word.

Yet it is in domestic style that the differences most stand out.
The Fogies' houses are North Oxfordy, comfortable, tasteful but
slightly shabby in that English tradition of *Do Not Flaunt It*. There
will be some decent paintings, velvet curtains and Persian rugs, the
odd small chandelier lurking in the background, a nice bit of
polished maple and lots of one-off easy chairs with handmade
covers. On the shelves you glimpse a lifetime of memorabilia (small
gilt framed photograph of Nicholas and Sarah) and, on a side
table, a decanter with a thick old half-inch of sherry . . .

The Veneerings, on the other hand, flaunt it as if there were no
tomorrow. Their houses and possessions are all brand new and
glistening, immaculately painted and pointed, as if some high pressure jet of money had turned its nozzle on everything in sight,
sandblasting, scouring, burnishing to a brilliant perfection. Their
furniture is the best that expensive department store can offer and
their windows hidden behind festoons of blinds. Everywhere are
cordless phones and huge flatscreen TVs and videos like giant black
monoliths. *Flaunt it!* And the more bathrooms and bedrooms the
better, especially bedrooms with en suite baths. *Flaunt it!* Whereas
Fogies' kitchens are old-fashioned 1950s jobs ('modern' cupboards
with large plastic handles), the Veneerings have designer-built ones
in expensive wood, with built-in hobs, fridge-freezers and micro-

waves, all in any colour except white. *Flaunt it!* Fogies' gardens
might have a croquet lawn or a lily pond, but the Veneerings have
put in tennis courts, heated swimming pools, parterres, con-
servatories, artificial lakes with tiny artificial islands which you
reach via delicate little lacquered Japanese bridges. *Flaunt it!* Fogies
drive around in any old battered thing. On the deep new gravel of
the Veneerings' drive you will find a Jag, a Merc, a BMW, and,
for the wife, a Peugeot 205 GTI. *Flaunt it! Flaunt it!*

What is more, the domestic servant, that endangered species, is
making a comeback in the house of the Veneerings. The Fogies
might stretch to a cleaning lady or an *au pair*, the Veneerings have
full-time 'housemen' and gardeners. You can see them beavering
away near the artificial lake or revving across the gleaming parterre
on gleaming minitractors.

There has always been an American tinge to Boars Hill. Those
house names would not look out of place in the shore suburbs of
southern Connecticut. With the advent of the Veneerings this has
increased. Check out the security systems at the gates or glimpse
Mrs Veneering jogging in her apricot velour designer running suit
with two large white floppy dogs gambolling behind her, and you
might be in Beverly Hills, not Boars Hill. Indeed, weekend walkers
and joggers apart, it is becoming as suspicious to be out on foot
as in LA: sorties are made increasingly by car.

There is also with the Veneerings a quasi-American cultural void:
they have the money but not the taste and knowledge how to spend
it. At the back of it all there is still a small and strangled English
reticence about going the whole hog. 'Boars Hill could have been
the Burbank of Oxford,' chuckles Aldiss, 'complete with haciendas
and similar fantasies, but it has never been as adventurous as it
could have been', and, Evans's Youlbury apart, one tends to agree.

In odd nooks and corners you can still find a few 'oldtimers'
descended from the original Hill Folk, providing a link back to the
1880s described by Mary Rix. One such is Old Smith the Gardener,
or, to give him his full name, Sidney Shirley Smith, who lives in a
bungalow at the bottom of Orchard Lane. Eighty-one years old,
'born and bred on Boars Hill', he started work at fourteen as a
gardener for Sir Arthur Evans. He still speaks bitterly of the poverty
of those days, of servant-girls having to pick up soldiers on 'Money
Alley' (Cornmarket), and of the new free-spending ways of Morris's

car workers in the 1920s. He is an old man around whom the social
and financial landscape has changed utterly beyond recognition.
With his long white hair and abstracted manner, he reminded me
of Ben Gunn, the castaway in *Treasure Island*, except that it is time
and a long life that have marooned him on the treasure island of
Boars Hill, in the midst of a community that to him is now completely unreal.

Change usually creates casualties, and one small victim of the
new Sainsbury superstore at Heyford Hill was the Boars Hill shop.
So now, as in Graves's time, there is again no shop on the Hill, no
central focus of facilities. Nevertheless the Boars Hill Association
does its best to draw the community together, publishing a newsletter and fostering such activities as playreadings. There are apparently enthusiastic performances ranging from Coward to Rattigan
and Barrie to Priestley, with the occasional Shakespeare and Ibsen
for good measure.

It may all seem a far cry from Mary Rix's community bound
together by 'deep spiritual forces', but the fact is that most people
on the Hill do not want to be *bound* at all. If you ask them what
they like most about the place, they will reply 'the green, the
quiet...' and then after a pause, 'the people'. The great thing is in
fact the ability to close the door and be, as Aldiss says, 'non-joiner'.
For the moment on Boars Hill the Burrow is certainly triumphant
over the Beacon.

Of course fear drives people back together, and in particular fear
about crime. There is a steady trickle of burglaries on the Hill;
indeed rumour has it that crack teams of London thieves periodically tackle the place. Recently a Neighbourhood Watch Scheme
was started, although one resident joked that the grounds are so
large on Boars Hill that you would need a telescope to spot
intruders on your neighbour's property.

The future, too, worries residents. A sinister triad of threats has
been identified: increasing traffic, rat-running through the neighbourhood; encroachments on the Vale of the White Horse by the
city, bringing in its Labour-dominated, expansionist train such
amenities as gypsy camps and science parks; and, most threatening
of all, invasion by institutions. Although Boars Hill is a conservation area within the Green Belt, a statutory loophole allows
for the presence of institutions 'standing in their own grounds'.

Boars Hill already has two colleges (Warnborough College and the Open University), a language school, a monastery and a nursing home, and residents fear the forging of a solid 'institutional ring' at the heart of the community.

Yet, if one possible future for Boars Hill is to become a select area of country clubs, tutorial colleges and old folks' homes, there are others, and perhaps the clue to one of them can be found, not on the Hill itself, but at its foot in Wootton. In its exposed straggle of ribbon development – so long regarded by Hill residents as a place where you found, if lucky, a servant, if unlucky, a burglar – stands incongruously a large business equipment centre. It bulges with electronic gadgetry – modems and micros, software and fax machines. There is everything for the office, and everything too for the office at home. Already many work from home on the Hill – people in financial services, information technology or the media. Few are as yet 'wired' but it is bound to come.

Other straws are in the wind. There are several extended family or clan communes on the Hill, housing the several branches or generations of a family in a group of houses within a kind of compound. Might one be seeing the first signs of a new branch of rural society? If present trends of rising affluence and urban diffusion continue, could something evolve similar to the villa society of the Ancient World but with each centre also a node within some larger electronic network? If so, communities like Boars Hill might well be in the van of such developments.

This vision of the future is reminiscent of the Eloi in *The Time Machine*, protected and looked after by their technological palaces. But then you also recall Wells's Morlocks, those creatures of the night that fed upon the Eloi. Below every Boars Hill lie the shadows of the deprived and alienated, and you ponder just what will in future prey upon this bright new dream of the Electronic Garden.

In some places, however, the old village life of Oxford clings on. This is especially true of Wolvercote. It is surprising because Wolvercote has long been a sprawling patchwork of a parish. The coming of the canal and then of the railways, laid down along the edge of Port Meadow, effectively sliced it into two villages, Upper and Lower Wolvercote. Divide people and they will fight, and fight they did. There are still stories in the village of the battles between the 'Upstreeters' and the 'Downstreeters'.

At the core of Wolvercote are still the original village families – the Colletts, Tollets, Warmingtons and Parsons, many of whom originally worked at the paper mill which remains an important feature of the village (having ground corn and swords in the Civil War and made paper for the University Press, it is now owned by a Finnish combine). Between the wars a new Wolvercote arrived – the lower middle-class immigrants who moved into the area around Rosamond Road. Nowadays they – or their children – are the predominant force in the village.

In the 1960s a third Wolvercote rolled up – the middle-class commuters, called by the other villagers the 'Out and Abouters'. One block of houses overlooking Port Meadow, Rowland Close, has become a particularly rich concentration of Wolvercote Three. Clasping their Pimms and G and Ts, its residents (dons, psychiatrists, lawyers and writers) hold Close parties, bay to one another between its balconies and – being middle class and Green – drop their empties into a Rowland Close recycling depot. (Unfortunately, the local dustmen, not being so ecologically aware, frequently empty it.)

Miraculously all the Wolvercote fragments somehow gell to produce a living village. The agency largely responsible for this is the Wolvercote Commoners. Formed in 1929 when, like Headington and Iffley, the village was absorbed into the city, they jealously guard its greens and, like the Freemen of Oxford, exercise grazing rights on Port Meadow. 'Redeem the Time' reads the faded sundial on Wolvercote Parish Church, and the Commoners redeem it endlessly. They have helped resume the horse races which ran for hundreds of years on Port Meadow. They organize fairs and fêtes and tend allotments. (These incidentally are a very important part of Wolvercote. Even the middle classes dallied with them for a time in the 1970s until their backs gave out.)

The Commoners have a powerful sense of purpose and antiquity, tracing their lineage back to the Abbess of Godstow and looking down on Oxford's Freemen with all the sturdy contempt of practising yeomen for absentees and sell-outs. Yet in reality the Commoners are largely drawn from the ranks of Wolvercote Two, lower middle-class suburbanites who have garbed themselves in

Wolvercote Green. In fact the organization suits all three Wolvercotes: it pleases Wolvercote One by perpetuating their ways; it gives Wolvercote Two identity and something to do; and Wolvercote Three can, from its balconies, share the delicious vicarious frisson of belonging to an organic rural community.

Above all, the Commoners are a tenacious knot of resistance to the city. For centuries Wolvercote has fought a bitter battle against Oxford – both the Town and the Gown. As late as 1892 the ceremonial beating of the bounds of the city – along Wolvercote ditch by the Mayor and Corporation – led to a bloody battle into which Wolvercote's vicar and curate – muscular Christians if ever there were – pitched with great gusto. Wolvercote's takeover in 1929 is still resented, and the Commoners form a sort of parish council in exile, concerning themselves with a wide range of business. They even have a press officer who solemnly pronounces in the local papers. One summer's day a local junta closed the borders of Wolvercote and as in the Ealing comedy *Passport To Pimlico* issued their own passports. It was by all accounts a hugely enjoyable prank, but one, I suspect, with a small hard grain of seriousness at its centre.

If what focuses Wolvercote is the Commoners, what inspires them is the presence of Port Meadow. It is to Wolvercote what the sea is to a tiny seaport, a broad horizon encompassing and dominating the community at every turn. Common land for over a thousand years, and washed by an ancient stillness, it is also full of change and movement – thundering charges of horses, veerings and massings of cattle, sudden sweeps and swoops of birds, under a constantly changing sky-scape of scudding cloud. Through the year it shifts from a summer prairie of grass and thistle to a fenland of flood and pool; in a good year it freezes to an apparently endless rink of ice on which it seems possible to skate forever. Port Meadow pulls people to it – to skate, to walk, run or ride, to fish or boat or swim. It beckons them into the air in balloons or, vicariously, in kites and model planes.

Port Meadow with its vast flatness and unending cycle of seasons absorbs and transcends all. Under its enormous skies human affairs are dwarfed. One thinks of King Charles's army, as it abandoned the siege of Oxford, trooping away across Port Meadow into a line or two in the history books, while its green remains around us.

Port Meadow deserves a bard, and of recent years has found one in the Wolvercote poet, Roger Green. He writes eloquently of the Meadow and also of Wolvercote with its shared life of Common, allotments, church and pubs, a place 'on the edge of things', a place –

> Neither city, nor country nor suburb
> A no-man's land nourishing uncertainty and hope
> Where exhausted asphalt yields to earth.

– 12 –

A Bridge Too Far: East Oxford

'Come to a street party!' read the invitation dropped through my letter box shortly after I moved to the neighbourhood. *A street party in December?* A joke surely – but a quick 'phone call brought confirmation and also reassurance: at least it would be held indoors. 'But we wanted to call it a street party anyway. Everyone's invited. Do come and meet people.'

So a few nights later I stepped, ice crunching underfoot, through the streets, on the lookout for social clues. They were not far to seek. The area was heavily parked with 2CVs, and Beetles, many of them painted in bright primary colours – banana yellow, fire-engine red and jungle green – as if their owners, uneasy at owning such expensive, adult pieces of machinery, had tried to make them as toylike and unserious as possible. Paper lampshades bobbed like barrage balloons behind windows lined with posters: 'Nuclear Power – No Thanks'; or 'Hands off Nicaragua'.

I reached the party and knocked on the door. It swung open on a smiling host and a large well-lit room – or rather two rooms now knocked into one and painted a severe white. Surfaces of stripped wood rose forbiddingly on every side. There did not seem to be a square inch of wood which had not been sanded, scoured and lightly varnished. A message was being transmitted, not so much in code as in a shout: here the bourgeois veneer has been stripped away and with a vengeance. A scatter of artefacts and rugs – Third Worldiana – relieved the bareness but that was all. On a long low table large bowls of food leered uninvitingly, earthenware mangers of brown rice and lentils, wooden vats of bulky, bowel-scouring nutrition.

A drink was thrust into my hand, and the instruction given 'to circulate'. It was then that I realized that I had already made an irretrievable social gaffe: I had put on *a suit,* opted for the constraining rigidities of line, the repression of a collar, the phallocentricity of a tie. Everyone else had gone for the loose democracy of texture. A mobile collage moved before me of corduroy, denim, leather, beards, peasant frocks and fibrous pullovers that looked as if they had been woven from the stuff in the foodbowls. Feeling intense culture shock I sank my nose deeply into my glass.

The conversation, when I resurfaced and tuned in, was very Channel Four. Keywords like 'consciousness' and 'participation' were batted about above the drinks.

'I've got a job timesharing with Jocasta so I usually leave Cyprian in the crèche. Alaric's a real problem, though, because he's hyperactive ...'

'For me the Cuban cinema reached its highest point ...'

'The entire group is still agitating to get the street made closed access ...'

'Of course that's what *she* really wants – totally efficient toilet training at the level of economic functioning.'

Everyone was precisely $36\frac{3}{4}$ years old and had gone to universities in the late 1960s or early '70s. They either worked for the university or, more usually, the poly, teaching subjects like geography, communications studies or sociology, or in bookshops, publishing, art galleries, schools or hospitals. Not a businessman, banker or lawyer to be found amongst them. These were the Mueslimen (or persons) surrounded by their Habitat. It was wrong to sneer: they were good, as good for me as natural yoghourt: kind, wholesome, liberal – but very, very similar.

If the room proclaimed high thinking and plain living, there was nevertheless considerable affluence discreetly hidden behind the stripped pine and ethnic rugs. The wine was of high quality, and round the corner from the wholefoods lurked a real give-away: a table groaning with gourmet puddings straight from the pages of Robert Carrier, drenched with brandy and cholesterol – the soft centre of the radical life style. Overheard conversations supported this impression; holidays had been taken in Tuscany and the

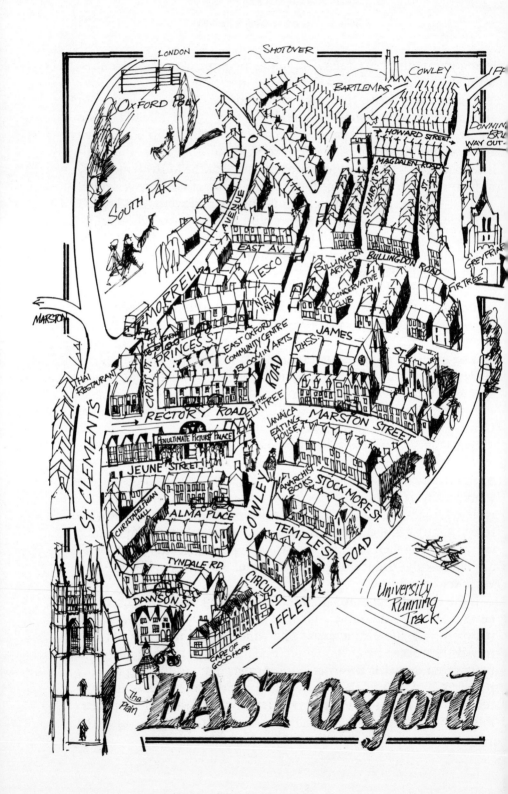

Dordogne. Many of the guests were working couples whose joint annual incomes, I computed, could not have fallen short of £40,000. Yet they were still true to their principles. Others might have transferred to North Oxford, Saabs and the SLD: these had stayed put, were still paid-up members of the Labour Party and ran about in tiny Renaults.

On leaving, I congratulated the hostess on her 'streetparty'; she shyly confessed that *not everyone* on the street had been invited, only those 'who might be interested in meeting one another' – an exquisite piece of code this, meaning that only the middle classes had been invited, and that poor, boring old Mr and Mrs Allotment who had lived in number fifteen all their lives had been left out, abandoned in their scullery to their bottles of milk stout. I was not surprised, a bit disappointed and, curiously, slightly relieved. It was perversely reassuring to know that in spite of the stripping and re-varnishing all the old British prejudices and hypocrisies were still firmly in place.

Where was I? Where else but East Oxford, a state of mind to some but in fact a real place that can be delimited geographically with some precision. It consists, in the main, of the triangle of housing between the Cowley and the Iffley roads, whose apex is formed by the Cape of Good Hope on the Plain and whose southeasterly baseline, though more difficult to fix, is possibly Howard Street. Disputably, three adjacent areas might be included: St Clement's up to Cherwell Street; the neighbourhood lying south of the Iffley Road next to the river, known (only) to estate agents as Iffley Fields; and finally, the streets rising from the northern side of the Cowley Road. Great caution, however, must be exercised in defining this latter area, for as the ground rises it merges into the 'White Highlands', where the conservatism of the inhabitants rises in direct correlation to the contours.

How best to sum up East Oxford? Years ago when I was a student, wits dubbed it 'a bridge too far', referring to its position on the wrong side of Magdalen Bridge, branding it as a remote region of student digs, some of whose streets were under sentence from a proposed spine road. Revised plans, spiralling property prices and an influx of gentrifiers have changed all that. Nowadays the wits play upon its left wing image, calling it the People's Republic of East Oxford, the Delta of Dissent, Oxford's Red

Wedge, or the Radical Triangle where countless middle-class adolescents have mysteriously sunk without trace into the counter-culture.

East Oxford is similar to Jericho but at the same time quite different. Its flavour is much more international and multiracial, its pace more commercial. It is Greener, more 'eco' and 'bio' and the needle of its politics further to the left on the band of the alternative and radical. With its shifting population it is even more diverse and transient than Jericho. Indeed it is East Oxford's differences that make it so interesting and, in the eyes of many living there, the most vibrant part of the city. It is a tremendous mixture, and its streets a fascinating blend of the drab and the bizarre, of decay and renewal. To me, it is also something of a microcosm and rather an encouraging one.

East Oxford has always had an alternative, beyond-the-pale, Sherwood Forest character to it. For many years part of it was known as 'Robin Hood' on account of the lawless types who congregated there. Just as soon as the Normans had flung their wall around the city, St Clement's sprang up in its shadow, quickly earning an unsavoury reputation for its violent brothels and streets. Later, when the neighbourhood began to be developed after the 1850s by an army of speculative builders, a contemporary still described its residents as 'a residuum of the thriftless, careless, lazy, ne'er-do-well sort whose nomadic instincts prevent them settling down to anything'. Some of the builders saw a chance of tempting the middle classes then settling in North Oxford into buying the tall houses that lift their noses southwards over Iffley Road. But the neighbourhood's tone told against it, and it is only in the last two decades that the middle class have moved in in any numbers.

Yet the place has always seethed with commercial vitality. From the fifteenth century tradesmen flocked to St Clement's to feed on the university's custom whilst breathing free of its rules and regulations. As a plaque records, William Morris, founder of the car factories, set up his first workshop in his parents' parlour in a house in James Street. Today, East Oxford still bubbles with the dreams of small businessmen and hopeful one-man-bands.

The curious atmosphere of East Oxford is perhaps best sampled through a walk from its easterly end to its apex on the Plain, the tip where its essence is most concentrated. You begin drably enough in an area of two-storey terrace houses interspersed with traditional small businesses, hardware and cycle shops, and builders' yards. The roof line is almost oppressively low. But as you progress down Cowley Road interest quickens: in amongst the hairdressers and newsagents are dotted an increasing variety of strange and specialist enterprises. Divinity Stores stocks odd beers from round the world – everything from the dour brews of Trappist monasteries to light lagers from Thailand. Nearby, Rainbow's End falls to earth with its bins of comics and lurid science fiction magazines in which customers can rummage for hours. Over Sweet Charity, the used clothes shop, dinner jackets dangle like the bodies of plutocrats swaying in the after-breeze of a revolution. The peculiarity of many of these shops is equalled by the love of wordplay and allusion shown in their names – Earth n' Ware, The Gameskeeper (board games), World Wise (Third World books) and Bead Games (jewellery, but cf. Hermann Hesse).

The Asian and West Indian presence is amply reflected, not only in the Indian restaurants and Asian grocers – which sell everything and never seem to close, so that you can buy typewriter ribbons or malt whisky from morning to night – but also in restaurants like the Jamaican Eating House with its red, green and yellow frontage, or SK Fashion unveiling a gorgeous profusion of Indian fabrics. Even in otherwise ordinary shops an alien note often obtrudes: some of the slogans which race in red across a signboard in G. K. Chemists would seem more suited to Bombay than Oxford. 'Do you require freedom from flying insects?' it asks. 'If so, try . . .'

What certain shops are exactly selling is often something of a mystery. In one nondescript emporium frothy female underwear nestles next to pairs of Dr Martin's boots and sets of precision machine tools. Many businesses have a decaying dinginess about them, and the frequency of boarded-up premises points to a high commercial casualty rate. And yet they do not seem to stay boarded up for long, soon re-emerging having undergone a metamorphosis and new management. After failing several times, they can then become Indian restaurants, in which role they appear to achieve a final ecological stability, however few customers they may attract. The general impression, though, is one of pullulating commercial vigour. The pattern of death and renewal, decay and growth is as rich as on the floor of a tropical forest. It is a paradox that East

Oxford, an area so widely seen as socialist, should be a seedbed of commercial enterprise, but it is so.

Diversity is the keynote. East Oxford is so miscellaneous that it defies generalization. Describe it as an area of terraces and you ignore the vast Victorian mansions on the Iffley Road; characterize it as a hive of commerce and you overlook the numerous churches and mosques. Like everything in East Oxford, its religious life has always flowed counter to the mainstream. Branches of esoteric cults cluster amongst its houses, and it was fertile ground for the free and non-conformist chapels. When Catholicism edged back into Oxford, it did so via St Clement's and St Ignatius' Chapel. Tucked away in East Oxford's terraced streets is a rookery of missions and religious houses, founded by far-sighted and perhaps wild-eyed clerics. These included the self-styled Bishop of Mercia and Middlesex, U. V. Herford, who set up the Church of Divine Love in Percy Street, and Rev. R. M. Benson – 'Benson of Cowley' – who established the Order of Cowley Fathers, now a dwindling handful of old men in an Iffley Road hostel.

Perhaps significantly, there has also always been something peculiar about East Oxford's church buildings. When St Clement's was rebuilt in the Norman style in the 1830s, it was reviled as 'a boiled rabbit'. For a time there was even an iron church until the clanging stones hurled by local lads made its services unendurable. Today Greyfriars stands proud in its curious Norman flint, while the Methodist Church floats up in an unexpected Art Nouveau whirl on the Cowley Road.

Nowadays change and renewal add to the diverse detail of the neighbourhood. Pass the straggle of run-down shops at the end of Cowley Road, turn a corner, and you find yourself in the yuppie heaven of St Clement's where everything is as sharply bright as a new coin. It is full of places selling expensive jogging suits and glitzy wine bars and brasseries defined by their pastel strip neon and curtains of hanging ferns. The marks of the restorer can be seen elsewhere throughout East Oxford's terraced streets, in smart new shingles and fittings and in snug junction boxes for the meters on the outside walls. Some of the restoration is of the hideous stone cladding variety which makes houses look like Disneyland models, but mostly it displays the more subdued tastes of the middle-class gentrifier.

Also, throughout the neighbourhood can be found institutions showing the humanitarian and communitarian concerns of the neighbourhood. There has long been a tradition of institutional benevolence in East Oxford. Almshouses such as Stone's or Boulter's were amongst its earliest buildings. The local Dawson Charity still owns large parts of St Clement's. Today on Leopold Street is the recently established Helen House, a small hospice which cares for gravely ill children and supports their families. And there is a network of social and community centres – the East Oxford Community Centre (which embraces both the Claimants' Union and Bloomin Arts) and the Oxford Asian Centre and the Oxford Women's Centre on whose doors a notice of engaging comradely frankness can be read: 'There will be no lunch to-day as no one has volunteered to cook or serve it.' Such, one assumes, is the occasional price of non-authoritarian feminist collectivism.

East Oxford leans undeniably to the left, and this is reflected in its posters. On Cowley Road a boarded window is plastered with them. Space is of course at a premium in such an agitprop environment and there has been considerable overpasting. A thick wodge has fallen away from the board and peeled off in parts, providing a kind of laboratory section through the radical mind: 'Nicaragua support ... Greenham womyn ... no to Maggie's cuts ... protest against racism ... troops out now ... AIDS benefit gig ...'. Some of the posters startle you with their social viciousness. One issued by the organization Class War reads 'Anarchist health warning. Smack the rich. Leave heroin to the rich bastards'.

However, it is EOA Books that holds up the mirror most closely to East Oxford's radical concerns. This is a bookshop of the 'isms': socialism, anarchism, feminism, pacifism, vegetarianism, of the Third World, the environment, and the anti-nuclear movement, and, increasingly, of more private and subjective matters such as meditation, parapsychology and spiritualism. A poster in the window proclaims the teaching of 'a spirit stalker' called Nomad. Nomad is, you learn, 'a Metis Apache Medicine Man ... a Road Chief and a Pipe Carrier who teaches the Sundance Way in the traditions of the Ancient Ones ... to relearn our proper relationship with the Earth Mother'. Wandering about the streets near to the Plain many likely candidates can indeed be spotted for both Nomad and his Earth Mother: wispy ageing hippies and globular women swathed in flapping belltents and clacking wooden beads.

Being Oxford it is also typical that a kind of antiquarianism should cling about this district, preserving the authentic flavour of the 1960s. You half expect to see Vietnam protest gigs advertised, and it was with some accuracy that an American once commented to me that East Oxford 'surely is like Berkeley was', wistfully recalling the heady heyday of the Free Speech Movement. Yes, if Oxford is the home of lost causes, then the more radical of them have certainly flocked across Magdalen Bridge.

Not that all the street people are veterans. Outside the bookshop a group of the young stand determinedly across the pavement holding a vigorous seminar on the state of their lives. Fragments drift across and then suddenly it all falls into place: they are trying out their parts, learning their lines, rehearsing. Some they will retain, others discard. Eventually, after they have tried enough roles, some may end up as computer programmers, librarians or teachers. But for the moment you feel how very appropriate it is that on the Cowley Road there are theatrical costumiers, boutiques selling yesterday's fashions, and even a place offering stage lights. You are in a place where, in the words of the old '60s cliché, the theatre, man, is on the streets.

To round out your picture of East Oxford you must walk through it by night: then the crowds have dissipated and it seems a sadder, seedier place. Two figures loll on a bench, oblivious to everything except the bottles of cheap sherry and cider between them – possibly tramps, possibly just unemployed. Many of the large houses on the Iffley Road, apparently guesthouses, are in fact thinly disguised social security lodgings offering claimants an address through which benefits can be claimed in return for a share of them. Elsewhere people are going out and having fun. In a side street a taxi controller crouches over his radio and sends out clicks and messages into the night air. And on the Cowley Road the fast-food joints are doing brisk business dishing out styrofoam boxes of fried chicken, burgers, kebabs and fries to the residents of bedsit land. In a West Indian pub where a sound system throbs in the background a gang of tarts strides in. These are no delicate *filles de joie,* these are heavy-duty pieces of sexual machinery, large and powerfully robust. Like workers clocking on for a shift they take up their positions and are almost instantly crowded around with prospective clients.

The pace is picking up too down on the Plain. The wine bars are filling up and so is the discotheque; its owner stands outside, a cross between a theatrical manager and a headmaster, backed up by his bouncer, an enormous man with an absurdly cherubic face. If you do manage to get in, you will find that it is not typical – naturally, being in East Oxford; it is not full of the usual young swingers but of people well into their thirties or even forties. Many of the women here are either separated or divorced, or quite often married – moonlighting housewives from Cowley out for a night's excitement.

In the surrounding streets the suggestion of unreality sensed by day is heightened by night, perhaps enhanced by the topsy-turvy open-all-hours commercial rhythms of the place. On a dull terraced street an enormous illuminated pair of hands and grinning mouth reach out above you: the Penultimate Picture Palace. What, you wonder, is the ultimate picture palace – the afterlife? or life itself? Turn another corner and you expect to find the Magic Theatre from Herman Hesse's *Steppenwolf,* proclaiming 'Madmen only enter here', enticing you on a perilous journey into the inner mind.

Groups of the young, punks and Rastas, drift on the Cowley Road. On a large elevated shelf outside a shop a tall Rasta, dread-locks dangling, seems to be keeping watch. But despite the edge of threat there is little or no trouble on the streets. What violence there is seems deflected, turned in on itself. A skinhead marches down St Clement's sucking in solvent fumes from a bag as hard as he can, inflicting the maximum of self-damage. Abruptly, aware of scrutiny, he veers aside into, of all places, Angel Meadow.

A few years ago there was a spate of rapes in East Oxford, and for a time the tabloids called it 'Oxford's Triangle of Terror'. One fine morning the middle-class residents of Iffley Fields woke to find the tyres of their Golfs and 2CVs had been systematically slashed. But in general there is little overt tension – social, racial or sexual. There are few muggings and, despite the large number of women living on their own, it now seems relatively safe. This is not Brixton or Handsworth – although it is not impossible to imagine a similar breakdown if the social controls were given a more adverse adjust-ment. The diverse groups and classes co-existing in East Oxford –

Asians, West Indians, gentrifiers, white working class, single women, gay couples – may not blend into a single community as some of them might hope, but for the time being at least they live happily side-by-side – which is after all a type of triumph and a considerable one.

– 13 –

The Walls of Jericho

Every year in early summer a Saturday of special significance circles round on the Jericho calendar – the annual street fair.

They close off Canal Street and line its length with stalls: rows of yesterday's books, of chunky, handmade jewellery, and of clothes, all woolly and jumbly and arty and crafty. A bloated ogre pounds the Holistic Massage Bed, while the Pagan Table spreads its snaps of Stonehenge and Glastonbury and postcards bearing mysterious mottos ('Life flows and the future knows ...'). Pause before another stall, and a pallid young man, like some sun-starved mushroom from a cellar, will mumble out your fate from Tarot cards, fed with truffles of dubious content by a twin-like girl, as he feeds you what you want to hear.

Life flows ... and so does the warm beer in the plastic beakers from the Jericho Institute. Outside a pop group belts out oldies at top volume. To cheers, a middle-aged couple, he with beard and paunch, she buxom in cheesecloth, find their limbs twitch them to the centre of the street where, faces warmly lit with grins, they waddle to the beat. At their rear tight ranks of punks, all tropical cockatoo hairstyles, studs and straps and baking leather, squint into the sun. One, clad in Union Jack underpants, idly flicks a jester's bladder. There are all sorts: vampiric goths, old punks and even older hippies, workers and pensioners, gay clones and be-sandalled alternatives, smart singles and yuppie couples. Through it all flutters a twist of messages: an unbuttoned, day-out-by-the-sea feeling, with deep down something medieval and Albionic, perhaps even a touch of Tyburn mob. But in the noonday sun the Canal Street crowd is a happy one, presenting in all its variety and easygoing tolerance a miniature of Jericho itself.

Geographically as well as socially Jericho is a kind of island nation within Oxford, a surviving small density of streets between the canal and Walton Street, bounded to the north by Lucy's Eagle Ironworks and to the south by Worcester College. Two further outcrops form part of the neighbourhood – the grimy terraces of Walton Well Road and Upper Fisher Row, dangling like an appendix at the end of the long tape of land over the canal and known to generations of Jericho children who played there as Snake's Island.

It is a defined neighbourhood, but also a diverse one. Even its nineteenth-century artisans' houses come in several shapes and sizes: chequerboard-fronted cottages; italianate-style houses, elaborately patterned in polychromatic bricks; attenuated Gothic residences with minuscule mullioned windows and pencil-thin columns; the bay-windowed solidities of Juxon Street. Around Richmond Road you find an area of larger houses in a sort of castrate North Oxford style, pallid in brick and pruned of all ornament. Then there is the long straggle of commerce on Walton Street, the scatter of street corner pubs and tiny shops, and finally the blocks of new flats, ranging from the meekly unassertive to the boxily obtrusive .

Jericho has both large and small, high as well as low. The lofty candle of St Barnabas towers above its terraces, its campanile as high as its ritual, answered by the distant globe of the Observatory, the pair like two tall ships overlooking a harbour of smaller craft. Walton Street's façade of restaurants, tobacconists and chemists suddenly breaks into the crumbling ionic splendour of St Paul's and the proscenium solidity of the University Press. There is an ambiguity about these grander buildings – as there is about Jericho generally. Enter St Paul's and you find a bistro; the Press seems unable to make up its mind whether it is a factory, a college or a country house; St Barnabas, so striking at a distance, seems gimcrack closer to, bleak in its thin coat of yellowish cement. The clash of elements is at its most violent in St Sepulchre's Cemetery, where gloomy cypresses and the tombs of Oxford eminences such as Jowett are encompassed by the metallic screeches and acetylene flickers of Lucy's ironworks. It is as if the souls of the Jericho dead were suffering some last industrial purgatory, howling as they are beaten and burnt into a final state of perfection.

The atmosphere of Jericho is shot through with contradiction. Through its factories and the thumping and hooting of the railway's diesels it gazes out to Port Meadow and the hills of Wytham beyond. Even the chequerboard pattern of its narrow terraces recalls the rural wicker and wattle of a village. And there is always that pervasive sense of island and lagoon. On certain days in certain lights, when the setting sun levels its rays past the boatyards and the St Barnabas basilica (itself modelled on the cathedral on the Venetian island of Torcello) towards the pillars of St Paul's, you feel you are indeed in some little Venice. Jericho is a strange, across-the-tracks, in-between sort of place, neither one thing nor the other, a debateable land, a splintered mirror which gives you back in pieces a new picture of yourself. It is full of people running away from, but also seeking, something – authenticity, community or simply a fresh beginning. Significantly, quite a few mystery novels and thrillers have been set in Jericho – by P. D. James and by Colin Dexter, in one of whose novels *The Dead of Jericho* his hero Inspector Morse gets entangled with an enigmatic Jericho divorcee. It was in Jericho that the transsexual writer Jan Morris, as she tells in her autobiography *Conundrum*, first came to terms with skirts and cosmetics, safely ensconced between an Indian family and some college servants.

Jericho's streets in shape and name preserve its past. Nelson and Wellington, Cardigan and Combe, Clarendon and Hart – with what squared-away neatness do they salute British victors and the early grandees of the Press! Wits trace the name 'Jericho' itself to the suburb's jerry-built origins, joking that when the trains blew their whistles, its walls fell down, but in fact for many centuries the name simply signified an outlying area. Its first mention came in 1688 when the Oxford antiquary, Anthony Wood, recorded spending 6d in a Jericho tavern. Following the arrival of the canal in 1790 and the establishment there in the 1820s of the ironworks and the Press, Jericho, during a spasmodic period of growth stretching over half a century, became Oxford's first industrial quarter.

Even then social diversity was its keynote. Its narrow rows housed compositors and ironfounders, tailors and masons, and labourers from the canal wharf and railway yards, while on Walton Street and the streets by Worcester a slightly higher class of tradesmen and college servants were to be found. From Jericho's landlords – from the big ones such as colleges and factories down to a mass of minor figures with only a handful of houses each – dangled a parasitic chain of letting and subletting. It was famous for its transients and temporaries. In Thomas Hardy's *Jude the Obscure*, Jude, on coming to Oxford, settles in 'Beersheba', a suburb based on Jericho, known, says the novel, for 'its number of lodgers'.

Although not the worst neighbourhood in Oxford, Jericho had its notorious pockets of squalor, notably Jericho Gardens near the site of the present school, an inner sump of poverty, prostitution and cholera. By the university and middle-class Oxford Jericho came to be dreaded as a potential 'fever belt'. When its sewage seeped into the moat of Worcester College, its Provost complained to the local Guardians, and only then were Jericho's open street drains closed.

Yet as well as fear, Jericho also inspired benevolence of the best Victorian paternalistic kind. Thomas Combe, the Superintendent of the Press's new premises – who came to be nicknamed 'the Squire' – acted towards Jericho as a kindly lord of the manor towards his industrial village, teaching in its Sunday schools and setting up evening classes so his workmen could better themselves in proper Smilesian manner. Concerned also for the spiritual welfare of his workers, Comb paid out of his own pocket for a new church, St Barnabas, stipulating that 'not a penny' should be wasted on external decoration. Nor had it been when the church was completed in 1869 at a cost of £6,492. St Barnabas became a vessel of the High Church Oxford Movement, indeed almost its flagship. At first the locals viewed the ritual with respectful bemusement but 'Barney's' also became a source of immense pride and a focus for the neighbourhood. When Comb died, his funeral was a great affair in Jericho. After a full choral requiem and Eucharist in St Barnabas, his coffin was censed, followed in procession through the neighbourhood, and interred with great pomp in St Sepulchre's Cemetery.

During this century Jericho kept its distinctive character for over fifty years. The neighbourhood was largely self-sustaining, almost inward-looking. With its dozens of pubs and off-licences, its butchers and bakers, with Cape's the drapers and the Scala cinema on Walton Street, there was hardly any need to venture beyond its borders. The men still mostly worked at the Press, the ironworks or the colleges, the girls in service or shops or offices. For entertainment there were the 6d hops at the parish hall on Nelson Street, the plays and concerts put on by the Scouts and, for the men, the pubs. Jericho even felt it had its own hospital: if 'Barney's' was its church, then the Radcliffe Infirmary was its hospital. Local women would volunteer to scrub or take flowers there.

Jericho was poor and seen by some as insalubrious, both physically and morally. But for most of its families the key note was a tautly sustained respectability. 'You might have been living on bread and scrape', said one old lady who still lives there, 'but you kept the front of your house tidy and your children clean. You despised anyone who let the side down.' A tight net of neighbourliness knotted Jericho together. Everybody knew everybody, and doors were left unlocked. 'People helped out. If you were sick, people thought nothing of shopping or cleaning for you.' In that time of restricted educational opportunity, the neighbourhood generated its own natural aristocrats, able individuals who lived out their lives in the area and served as local founts of knowledge and guidance. In this no doubt Jericho was much the same as the parishes of St Ebbe's and St Thomas's but distinguished perhaps by an additional literacy, some inky rub-off from the presence of the Press's many printers and proofreaders.

By the late 1950s, however, Jericho was physically sinking fast. The small landlords lacked the resources to maintain their ageing properties. At that time Oxford, like the rest of the country, was in the first fine flush of urban demolition and redevelopment. St Ebbe's was in process of being knocked down and its inhabitants banished to far-flung fringe estates like Barton and Blackbird Leys, and many residents feared a similar fate would soon descend on Jericho's walls.

So began the Battle of Jericho. A doughty resistance campaign was mounted by vocal locals, and a local councillor, Olive Gibbs. The Council resorted to a survey which in due course revealed a long, firmly settled community. Many had lived in Jericho for more than thirty years, and the vast majority did not wish to be uprooted.

So the Council caved in and opted instead for a strategy of gradual neighbourhood renewal.

This volte-face by the Council was hailed as a bold new experiment in community architecture and lavishly praised by professional journals and official bodies. In fact the extent of demolition was far greater than sometimes represented. Nearly a third of Jericho's houses were in fact knocked down to make way for new development. Socially too the experiment was only a qualified success. The Jericho community soon began to be eroded, either by death (residents tended to be elderly) or by the new middle-class influx, drawn by Jericho's proximity to the city centre, its now renovated housing stock and still relatively low prices. Paradoxically one upshot of the neighbourhood renewal scheme was the massive fillip it gave to the inner-city-gentrifying housing market.

For the Oxford middle classes were on the move once more. In the 1950s and '60s the taste for rural living had swept them out to the villages. Then when the petrol price rises turned that sour, they switched back to the city and – no longer able to afford the former middle-class strongholds – turned instead to the old working-class neighbourhoods. Lips which once entranced had proclaimed 'thatched roofs' and 'genuine beams' now mouthed words like 'original community' and 'authentic street culture'. When an article appeared in the *Sunday Times* citing Jericho as *the* place in which to live in Oxford, the trickle into what was being called 'Oxford's Little Chelsea' turned to a deluge.

The settlers, the new urban frontiersmen, were a mix of academics, often retired yet wanting to stay close to the centre, and young professionals, many of whom commuted to London. There was also a sprinkling of child-laden divorcees in flight from North Oxford and failed marriages, who soon set up little support networks amongst themselves. Where once the inhabitants of Jericho had taken in one another's washing, now they took in toddlers, freeing one another to run antique shops and picture-framing businesses or copy-edit Clarendon Press textbooks. But, divorcees apart, the general pattern was two adults per house – an ironic contrast to the dozen or more who had filled them when first built a century earlier.

If, for the middle-class commuters, Jericho was a kind of dormitory-land, a series of living modules dropped down into a working-class landscape, for others it represented an opportunity to *belong*. What cherishing of the neighbourhood's features, what preening of its pubs, what assiduous attendance at local residents' meetings! There were no doughtier defenders of the architectural status quo ante. Significantly, the most vocal opponents of the Council's demolition plans were the new middle-class residents. However, they were not always alone. When the Council, swept away on the wave of its urban renewal success (and perhaps needing to find further work for its planners) proposed blocking off whole streets and turning back gardens into ghettoes of garages, Jericho was united in its opposition. The middle-class residents, seeing their freedom to park their Renaults outside their toytown houses under threat, were horrified; the older residents, with the funereal preoccupation of the working class, dreaded that when at last the Grim Reaper called, he would not be able to back up the hearse to the front door.

Yet in general the demarcation between the old and new residents was marked and nowhere clearer than in their interiors. The houses of the old working-class residents had been full of *things*: a dense clutter of ornaments, and calendars (Oriental girl, sea-scene or sunset), horses' heads, toby jugs, colour photos of Royals, souvenirs from Torquay or Weston-super-Mare, encapsulated spires-in-snowstorms and whole families of strange objects hammered out from livid orange copper. Everything was patterned and bold and floral. Every surface had its cover and most covers had a second cover.

Such houses reproduced within their contents a miniature version of the class system. There was a whole category of things reserved for 'best' or 'show', such as wedding presents, cakestands or 'best' china, guarded behind the gleaming glass doors of cabinets. The parlour – a memorial reflecting that working-class Jericho preoccupation with keeping up respectable appearances – was preserved as a kind of highly polished museum, often containing such trophies as a stopped clock, and reserved for high days or funerals. Living was largely restricted to the back rooms. When fridges began to appear in these houses it was a mark of the superstitious awe in which these objects were held that they were often placed in the parlour.

As the gentrifiers moved in, out went all the clutter and in moved the toilets. Rooms were mercilessly knocked through, staircases gutted and rotated. In came the light, the white and the gently patterned – the chill white walls, the stripped pine, the Berber carpets, the Japanese lampshades and the Sanderson and Laura Ashley curtains. Later, in the 1980s, that harder decade of money values, there was something of a shift in taste. Interiors moved, as it were, to the right. Carpets became deeper and richer, walls became more ambiguous, full of hues and hints and stipples. Polished wood and brass suddenly surfaced, fitted kitchens and bathrooms became more expensive. Moreover, as conservation consciousness mounted, original features were increasingly cherished. Bits of glass and plasterwork, banisters and arches were all painstakingly restored, almost labelled and put under glass. It stopped being the fashion to knock through walls and open up staircases. Indeed some walls were carefully put back. Look at our cornices, was the message, now indeed we belong.

If there is one place that captures the quintessence of the gentrifier it is Oxford Architectural Antiques, a business fittingly based in Jericho although it operates nationwide. Its yard at the bottom of Nelson Street is an amazing sight, a Victorian pawnshop on a Brobdingnagian scale: a garden of chimneys, with stacks of stained glass, doors, iron fireplaces and heaps of stair rails like piled muskets. They sell almost everything – mirrors, washstands and old baths with claw feet, even some Victorian dogcarts pressed into service as garden ornaments. It is like a giant DIY kit for assembling the house of a hundred years ago – if not the House Beautiful then the House Authentic. Roll up, roll up, make your house a Victorian theme park!

Other Jericho businesses attest to the tastes of the gentrifier. In corner shops where once you bought your packet of Woodbines or your jar of pickles, you now find delicately gluttonous delicatessens tempting you with stuffed vine leaves and fine sherry vinegars. Start counting the home improvements shops on upper Walton Street and you will soon run out of fingers. Jericho had always been full of little backstreet workshops – printers, garages and repair yards. Now these have been converted to gleaming ateliers and high tech studios for printmakers, furniture designers and typography consultants. The gentrifiers who protested bitterly about the noise of the old repair shops and the pollution from Lucy's (which they assiduously collect and measure in bags), extend to the ateliers a tepid approval.

If the gentrifiers, as it were, parachuted into Jericho from more affluent parts, then different detachments have infiltrated it from below. It was the rehabilitation of the neighbourhood, which left many houses temporarily unoccupied, that first opened the door to them. Squatters moved in during the 1960s and '70s, and this led inevitably to friction, and even on occasion pitched battles with the residents.

Today such drop-outs form a small but distinct part of the Jericho community, congregating particularly around the Walton Well Road area. You can tell the 'Waltons' by their vaguely post-punk or Gothic appearance. They struggle along on odd jobs in nearby shops or pubs or working, say, as despatch riders. Many are middle class, for the 'Waltons' operate a late entry scheme for the children of North Oxford academics in their rebellious phase. A surprising number are musicians. There is a continuous flux of abortive musical alliances, oddly named bands, which do not favour contemporary pop but older bluesy or acid sounds and, like doomed mushrooms, rise and are re-absorbed almost overnight.

The 'Waltons'' scene is loose and shifting, gathering and unravelling, as they move in and out of pads and jobs, as they shack up, split and then just as mysteriously re-materialize. Over much of it eddies the smoke of hash – but usually nothing stronger. This prohibition may be due to the continued existence amongst the 'Waltons' of a soft core of mellowed-out hippies who have lived in Jericho since the 1970s and have emerged from addiction with their benevolence, if not their synapses, relatively intact. These hippy oldsters warn off the younger members from hard drugs and are listened to with respect, for, with typical Jericho tolerance, the 'Waltons' are not all 'ageist'. The 'Waltons' also mirror Jericho's larger community instinct, organizing outings on the canal and to the country and sometimes prolonged exchange visits to similar groups in other cities – only marred, they will tell you, by the local constabulary 'hassling' them when 'nobody was out of order'.

Accepting the 'Waltons', Jericho has also forged alliances with other fringe tribes, most notably the Boat People. The tale of the neighbourhood's first encounter with the Boat People is lovingly preserved in Jericho. A handpicked body of boatmen clumped one day into a residents' meeting, where, wrapped in sturdy silence, they seated themselves at the back. As the proceedings were drawing to a close, their leader rose dramatically and pointed to his people's plight. Might they not, he boomed, be considered part of Jericho? Consternation to the gentrifiers! But then the residents rallied, and with due Jericho openness, protractedly argued the question to and fro. After much lengthy debate finally came the answer 'yes', and ever since the Jerichoites have seen the Boat People as a dependable presence guarding their western marches and have welcomed them to their meetings.

The Boat People are semi-attached. They often have regular jobs on land and send their children to local schools. They are constantly hitching a temporary harness to society, fixing up boxes by their barges or arguing the Post Office into regularly delivering their mail. They are quite diverse: some are water gypsies, preferring to wander on water; others (rather looked down on by the rest for having a 'house mentality') have taken to boats because they are hard pressed to find Oxford accommodation on dry land. A further group have chosen the water-borne life as more ecologically acceptable (one of these is famous for having erected on his barge a fifteen foot windmill). Nevertheless, there is a strong bond between them, and indeed the query 'How full is your El-san?' has acquired the status of a tribal greeting.

Latterly their presence has given rise to a new Battle of Jericho. Since the mid-1980s British Water has been trying to move them on. But the Boat People are an articulate lot, well prepared to defend every inch of their moorings. A media campaign was mobilized, which even led to a Soviet TV crew coming to film the plight of the Jericho Boatmen. The battle is still unresolved. The authority is now making available a limited number of moorings with facilities for which a fee is levied. Some of the Boat People have paid up; others have moved off north of the two mile 'exclusion zone' and periodically renew their protests by blocking the canal. Meanwhile the land Jerichoites are furious, seeing their dependable allies replaced by a troop of littering, overnight floaters.

Another tribe of outsiders with which Jericho has links, albeit much more tenuous ones, is the Bus People, who periodically park their convoys on Port Meadow. But these are seen as a much more anarchic and menacing lot than the Boat People. Even the

'Waltons', whilst dimly acknowledging some distant kind of kinship with the Bus People, think they are 'well out of order'. The Bus People bring down too much heat from the police and so, as the summer solstice nears and they roll their wagons towards Stonehenge or wherever the ley lines cross, both Jerichoites and 'Waltons' breathe a profound sigh of relief.

As well as its working-class residents, its gentrifiers and fringe tribes, Jericho has also amassed a whole curio shop of cranks or – to take a more sympathetic view – the New Age or 'alternative'. There are legions of artists, aura-detectors, writers, sculptors, cartoonists, photographers, jewellery-makers, mediums and masseurs, acupuncturists, astrologers and teachers of yoga or the Alexander Technique. Most are charming and interesting – if a little odd. Some are very odd indeed. I met one gentleman who had lived in Jericho with his mother since the 1950s and who was, he told me, a part-time cabinet-maker and spiritualist. He had outdone the gentrifiers: whereas they restored the earlier features of their houses, he summoned up the previous occupants of his – including a little girl who made her presence known by the scent of violets and scattering the cutlery. When he told me the chair in which I was sitting was usually occupied by the disgruntled spirit of a Victorian printer, detectable by the noxious reek of his tobacco, a strange chill crept over me and, having blurted my excuses, I made a quick exit.

So Jericho is a mixed bag. It is the sort of place where you can find a labourer living next door to a premier mathematician. But does the old community spirit still survive? Ask Jericho residents, and generally they will say, yes – but only just. There are still substantial pockets of working-class and older residents, but spiralling property prices are irresistibly driving it beyond the reach of ordinary buyers. After the Second World War Jericho houses were being sold for £150 or so, and even in the late 1960s you could pick one up for under £1,000: at the height of the late-'80s property boom they might have cost a hundred times that. Many fear it will end up as a middle-class mono-culture. And it is not just the gentrifiers who are pressuring the old community. Increasingly houses are being snapped up by outside buyers and then profitably let out to students.

There are strenuous efforts to keep the old community going.

The Community Centre organizes playgroups and lunch clubs and publishes a vigorous neighbourhood news-sheet, *The Jericho Echo*. But the Centre is really more of a facility than a centre, renting out rooms for the life-drawing classes, meditation circles and creative voice workshops with which Jericho abounds. Indeed much of its income comes from a regular let to d'Overbroeck's, the top-drawer Oxford crammer.

Particular battles can still mobilize the community, such as the use of the nearby station site for science park purposes. The survival of St Barnabas School is another rallying point, threatened as it is by competition from 'Phil and Jim' in nearby North Oxford. 'Phil and Jim' is resented as a kind of para-prep school, poaching the already rare children of the Jericho gentrifier. 'No Poll Tax Here' and 'This Council Home Not For Sale' chant other posters in Jericho windows. The neighbourhood's concentration of council tenants and of the temporaries and transients who still find lodging there make it a natural centre of resistance for both these campaigns.

However, these protest mobilizations are more sectional than general. The Council Tenants' Association, set up in 1988, typifies this tendency. It has, under formidably competent leadership, become a thrusting force in Jericho life, organizing home visits and regular parties. In a way it has become the voice not just of Jericho's less well off but also its marginalized original population. But its rise is viewed with dismay in some quarters. There is dark talk of 'divisiveness' and of 'council tenants believing they are the only righteous in the land'. Jericho has long been known for its absorbent tolerance but may be emitting the first faint fumings of faction and partisan mood.

Even Jericho's pubs, for which the neighbourhood has so long been noted, reflect the evaporation of the old community spirit. In the nineteenth century there were twenty-seven taphouses here and Jericho still tempts outsiders with its lure of an evening's compact pub crawling. But as the old neighbourhood life has contracted so have the numbers of its pubs. Some residents still remember eleven or more. Now there are five and one of these is temporarily closed and may never re-open. True, the surviving pubs retain something of their old distinctive character, and the Bookbinders (the 'Bookies') is still deservedly *the* neighbourhood pub, warm, bright and cheerful, attracting a broad cross-section of Jericho. But the lifestyle culture of the young and affluent does not flow towards sawdust and warm pints of bitter. On evenings when Jericho's pubs are as vacant as a country railway waiting room, the Walton Street wine bars bulge with bodies, splashing their pools of light and noise on to the pavements. It is odd to think that among the snazzily-suited braying for piña coladas and tequila sunrises there are descendants of compositors who once hunched over their porter in The Printers' Arms or sat, straight-faced and stiff-collared, in Mr Comb's evening classes.

Cocktails are also taken amid the gold and purple of Freud's behind the crumbling Ionic columns of St Paul's, a place that rather resembles the modernist setting of a Greek tragedy (where Oedipus, say, might drop in for drinks on the way to Colonnus). It is a source of some local bitterness. St Paul's was Jericho's first church, founded in 1836. When it closed in 1967 there was much local support for its becoming an arts centre. It did so, but only briefly, before being taken over by a businessman and turned into a restaurant-cum-art gallery. It draws a young and varied crowd from round the city, but is felt by many residents to do little for Jericho itself.

The essence of old Jericho, for me, still survives if anywhere in St Barnabas, preserved and concentrated, beneath its mock Byzantine frescoes, its hanging ironwork cross (made specially by Lucy's) and the smoked golden glow of its sanctuary and canopied altar. 'St Barnabas, all change for Rome!' read the caption of one nineteenth-century cartoon, and it still resembles some kind of holy, Victorian railway station. Bells sound, announcements are made, congregations pull in and out, swathed in clouds not of steam but of incense. The schedule of ritual slides undeviatingly forward. Its congregations too have a solid core of 'Barneyites', young Jericho mums with kids and old men and women who have lived out their lives in the neighbourhood. The prayers for the sick and dying are a passing bell for a disappearing community.

But Jericho's children, even if they have drifted away, still regard it as their church and return to celebrate their weddings, christenings and funerals – all the symbolic crossing points of their lives. I dropped in late one autumn afternoon and came across a young couple in the nave, little more than teenagers, being coached for their wedding ceremony, surrounded by a small smiling circle of family and friends. It was an intimate neighbourhood tableau. Watching it, I felt years peel back and that I could well have been watching a scene from a century ago: some young Jericho workman and his bride-to-be about to pass the threshold of their future lives within the narrow walls of Jericho.

– 14 –

Good Vibrations

Nam Myoho Renge Kyo! Nam Myoho Renge Kyo! The rhythmic chanting flows in a low, droning hum down the East Oxford street. As you get closer to its source, an ordinary terraced house, the chanting gets not only louder but more frantic, urged on by the clangorous beating of a gong. *Nam Myoho Renge Kyo! Nam Myoho Renge Kyo!* It is all most bizarre, like a mixture of the patter of a Texan cattle auctioneer and the beehive hum of a Tibetan monastery. Faster and faster, louder and louder drives the chanting. Then, suddenly, silence falls, followed by the last solemn bangings of the gong. But around you, the battered air seems to go on twanging and throbbing in ever-wider circles of vibration.

Step inside the house and you find some twenty people crouched, kneeling and shoeless, in front of a large stripped-pine cupboard of a type common in this neighbourhood. But instead of the usual wholemeal loaves, lentils and homemade wine of East Oxford there is a *Gohonzon,* a shrine complete with candles and burning incense sticks and a dangling scroll of Japanese calligraphy. The kneelers are mostly young, mostly women. One by one, hesitant and somewhat clumsily, they start to talk about the way the practice of chanting has sustained their lives.

They are followers of Nichiren Shoshu Buddhism, a non-traditional sect, inspired by a thirteenth-century Japanese, Nichiren Daishonin, who they believe to be the incarnation of Buddha for the present age. Believing, like other Buddhists, that all creation is interrelated by Karma, they differ by substituting mechanical chanting for traditional Buddhist meditational practices. This chanting, they believe, brings the Larger Forces into harmonious alignment. As you get into chanting, they tell you, you start to notice strange patterns of coincidences. You find yourself obtaining the material rewards for which you pray (a phenomenon which they call 'conspicuous benefits') as well as spiritual enrichment and elevation to a higher level of awareness.

They also differ from other Buddhists in that they actively proselytize. With some 20 million Japanese followers, the movement is also strong worldwide, particularly in South America (where there are many Japanese immigrants). In Britain numbers though small are growing at 30 per cent a year, and it has gained a reputation as 'the showbiz religion' from figures such as the singer Sandy Shaw and the designer Jeff Banks, who practise it. In Oxford there are several groups, one in East Oxford, two (perhaps not surprisingly) in Jericho, one in North Oxford and several outside the city. Each group has about twenty members: as it gets larger, it will split and multiply like a cell.

Its spread in the backstreets of Oxford may seem odd, but there are a surprising number of orient-influenced cults in and around the city. Another movement is Beshara (Aramaic for 'Good News') whose followers have just bought a country house in Frilford, a village near Oxford. Founded in 1969, Beshara claims to have some 300 members and has two other houses, one in Gloucestershire and another in Scotland, the Chisholm School of Intensive, Esoteric Education where for £2,500 acolytes can undergo a six-month advanced course.

For anyone interested, weekend introductions are laid on at Frilford. Polite, intent and somewhat humourless young men in beards display photographs of the earth at various orders of magnification and diffuse a fog of words like 'ipseity', 'immanence' and 'transcendence'. Should any sharp little jet of scepticism flare up amongst the attenders, the extinguisher of nebulosities is immediately turned on it, and it is foamed into non-existence. Beshara, although it claims to focus on the spiritual aspects of life generally, is, when you look closer, a watered-down version of Islam and, specifically, Sufism. One of its leading lights is a Middle Eastern businessman, Bulent Rauf, and followers are encouraged to learn Arabic. About what goes on at Chisholm the acolytes are pretty coy but it would appear to revolve around a practice called 'Zakir', a ritual of rhythmic movement – the ecstatic whirling, no less, of the Sufi mystic.

Attenders at these weekends seem to fall into two groups – the New Seekers and the Old Seekers: either prosperous couples with a large house, a large Volvo and a hollow life, or others in their fifties and sixties, benign silver-haired creatures, freed of their mortgages and their children, and looking, nostalgically and retro-spectively, for a share of those spiritual excitements which others revelled in during the 1960s.

A longer-established cult near Oxford is the New School of Economics which has a centre at Waterperry near Wheatley. It does not like to be called a cult, preferring to be known as a 'school'. (Avoiding terms with religious overtones, incidentally, seems to be a feature of these cults: Beshara similarly bills itself simply as an 'organization'.) Waterperry House is an odd place. In one way it is a typical country manor house, open to the public, with a garden centre and a teashop. It runs a popular arts and crafts festival each summer, *Art in Action,* which attracts over 20,000 visitors. But if you wander around you notice hints of a further dimension. Inside the house there are large rather badly executed murals of Renaissance luminaries such as Marcellus Ficinus and, in the gardens, ladies can be glimpsed floating in old fashioned long dresses – garments favoured by the School's founder, Leonardo Da Vinci McLaren.

Originally the School focused on economics (hence its name) and the search for its fundamental laws. Now it has increasingly turned its attention to philosophy in which it offers advanced classes in the major cities, again attempting to isolate what it sees as philosophy's fundamental laws. These consist, it teaches, of a series of Absolutes: by a mix of discipline (involving set tasks and extended periods of sleeplessness) and meditation, the self can be expanded and freed and so approach these Absolutes. Just as behind Beshara there is Islam, so behind the New School of Economics there is the presence of Hinduism, of Krishna and texts such as the *Bhagavad Gita* and the *Upanishads,* oriental influences laundered via Platonic idealism and the Renaissance (hence Marcellus Ficinus). Run rather like an Oxford college by a self-perpetuating fellowship of about a hundred, it now has several thousand members nationally and about fifty in Oxford itself.

The New School of Economics has been dubbed 'the secret cult' and criticized for inducing breakdowns and divorces amongst its members. But in fact such damage seems limited to a small fringe of unstable individuals who are attracted to the School. In general it is the blandness and innocuousness of these movements which is their most striking feature. They represent a successful bottling of esoteric, Eastern tradition for middle-class Western consumers. They are the designer religions with the dogma and the priestly middlemen taken out, psychotherapy in philosophical clothing, helping their followers surmount the obstacles and stresses of modern life. One student of the New School of Economics spoke eloquently to me of its value to her as an 'anxiety distancer'. And all three movements, it is claimed, not only enlighten you but make you more industrious and, presumably therefore, better at your job – 'aware, awake and in service' as one Beshara member put it. They are the Perrier cults, containing a lot of fizz and generally nothing harmful, and there will be more of them.

Oxford brews a whole mishmash of beliefs. Alongside the Perrier cults there are other more sinister sects, either modern ones such as the Moonies who are quietly active in Oxford, or older, darker beliefs such as witchcraft. Then there are what you might call the behavioural religions, embracing anything from yoga, the Alexander Technique, aromatherapy and colour therapy to vegetarianism, zen jogging, acupuncture and macrobiotic cooking. Oxford – and particularly East Oxford and Jericho – is full of practitioners of these 'faiths'. The Jericho Institute and the Alternative Bookshop on Cowley Road are their powerful transmission centres. Indeed one local publication, *The Green Guide to Oxford*, is a kind of Oxford cranks' *Crockford's*.

Why do so many beliefs and cults cluster around Oxford? In part it reflects the numbers here of both New Seekers and Old Seekers – the rootless, transient young people passing through the city (and not just its students) and the well-off leisured retirees. Moreover Oxford, by virtue of its very history and academic image, attracts the seeker. It is a city traditionally felt to revolve around higher things, to be a place where deep questions are pondered and perhaps answered. The seekers are like latter-day Judes the Obscure hoping in some unclear way to catch some insight glimmering from

Oxford's halls and towers, emitted from the hive of thought at its heart.

Vibrations! Down the ages Oxford and religion have always gone hand in hand. From the heats and tremors of its religious disputes, movements have radiated out to the world. Lollardy, which aimed at the purification of the medieval church and the transmission of the Gospels in the vernacular, sprang out of Wyclif's teachings in Oxford's pulpits, and is said to have involved the 'flower of Oxford' before it was suppressed. Methodism was invented here in the 1720s by John Wesley (then a don at Lincoln), and his brother Charles, an undergraduate at Christ Church. Other university members viewed them with contempt, calling them the 'Holy Club', the 'Bible Moths' and even 'Methodists', from the rigorous detail of their devotions. The name stuck. They were seen almost as the Moonies or Jesus Army of the day, consorting with disreputable characters (they made a point of visiting the poor and sick and those imprisoned in the city's jails) and inducing breakdowns in students through excessive enthusiasm. Eventually Wesley turned his attention from Oxford to look, as he put it, 'upon the world as my parish'. After an episode when six Methodist undergraduates were expelled in 1768, Methodism withered in the university, to return only slowly via the city in the next century.

With the Oxford Movement of the nineteenth century, another religious wave spread out to the world. It was a movement at once radical and reactionary, seeking a return to the pristine simplicities of the Early Church and liberation from meddling in church matters by the state. Its leading lights were John Keble, a devotional poet and the Professor of Poetry; Edward Pusey, the Professor of Hebrew; and John Henry Newman, vicar of the University Church of St Mary's. Their views were propounded in a series of *Tracts for the Times* which earned them the name Tractarians. 'Newmanism' swept the city: 'Who could resist', wrote Matthew Arnold, 'the charm of that spirited apparition, gliding in the dim afternoon light down the aisles of St Mary's, rising into the pulpit and then in the most entrancing of voices breaking the silence with words and thoughts which were a religious movement, subtle, sweet and mournful.'

Many detected the hand of Rome in the Oxford Movement. An

inquisition atmosphere enveloped the city, complete with denunci-
ations and defections. Tensions mounted. Finally, when in 1837
Newman published *Tract XC,* in which he argued that Catholicism
was no bar to adherence to the Thirty-Nine Articles, the storm
broke, and in the ensuing furore Newman decamped to the tiny
church at Littlemore, where he eventually fulfilled the expectations
of his critics by being accepted into the Roman Catholic Church
six years later. The Oxford Movement was in a way the religious
twin of the Romantic Movement and, as such, it left a deep aesthetic
imprint – on everything from devotional poetry to railway station
architecture – as well as giving rise to an Anglo-Catholic tradition
within the Church of England which continues to this day.

In our own century, Oxford has continued to emit a steady
stream of religious impulses. It was here that Frank Buchman
created the movement that came to be known as the Oxford Group
and, later, Moral Re-Armament. He was first invited to Oxford
by a number of Rhodes Scholars from Princeton, and his first
encounters with Oxford undergraduates were somewhat improb-
able collisions of style – on the one side the pudgy American
pastor with his combination of the prosaic with high pressure
salesmanship ('PRAY! – Powerful Radiograms Are Yours' was
one of his favourite slogans) and, on the other, various hearty,
pipe-smoking undergrads. However Buchman, scenting the value
of the Oxford name and its nexus of important connections, pressed
on indefatigably and soon attracted a substantial following through
lunchtime meetings and vacation house parties. The Groupers in
each college were instructed to select the most difficult person to
turn and then bend all their efforts on that individual. It apparently
became a minor Oxford pastime to try to spot who would come
out next as a Buchmanite. However, Buchman himself eventually
outgrew the university. As he moved to a larger arena, he set up
headquarters in London and Switzerland and America, launching
into a campaign against Communism and even going to the lengths
of a brief flirtation with Fascism.

If Buchman was a thoroughly twentieth-century figure, an
opportunistic bird of passage who found in Oxford a useful but
temporary platform, another Christian impulse which came shortly
after him was much more intrinsic to the place and set its face
firmly against the modern age. Its source was the circle of dons

and hangers-on which included C. S. Lewis, Charles Williams, J. R. R. Tolkien and the Inklings Society. Inklingism was a kind of literary Christian compound, which turned away from psycho-analysis and sociology and looked instead to the myth, the worlds of the imagination and the intense simplicities enclosed within the pages of children's books. It was above all a quintessentially Oxford phenomenon, deeply imbued with the philological and classical strength of the university and the fictional traditions of earlier writers such as Carroll.

Oddly, this movement – one hesitates to call it such, rather a congeries of Christianity and donnish tastes, hobby-horses and whimsies – went on to have an enormous impact. Certainly its progenitors influenced an entire generation of undergraduates. In his autobiography *Sprightly Running,* John Wain wrote 'It was impossible at that time to take in "Oxford" without taking in, if not exactly the Christian faith, at least a very considerable respect for Christianity ... Everybody to whom an imaginative and bookish youth naturally looked up, every figure who radiated intellectual glamour of any kind, was in the Christian camp'.

The ripples from this donnish circle spread far and wide beyond the university, reaching eventually all the way across the Atlantic. There, Lewis and Tolkien societies now produce a deluge of fan-zines and newsletters, and Midwestern theological colleges zeal-ously hoard their memorabilia and manuscripts, and send pilgrims to Oxford to tread the suburban streets of Headington in search of authors' homes, and to gaze with awe, in the glass cases of the Bodleian, on C. S. Lewis's very own hand-drawn map of Narnia.

Vibrations! Oxford Sundays still fairly resonate with worship. Tolling out from Christ Church, tinkling in from Marston, chiming from college chapels and a score of city churches, the bells proclaim the continuing presence of religion in Oxford. The range of worship in the city is staggering – from the coped and choired magnificence of the Cathedral down to the humblest Baptist chapel in the suburbs. In St Andrew's sturdy sandstone, North Oxford parents and children thank the Creator for their blessings, while in the bleak estates of Blackbird Leys, congregations join hands in the ecumenical Church of the Holy Family. A liberation theologian expounds from a pulpit in Blackfriars; Methodists, all neat white buns of hair and well buttoned-up coats, cram the Wesley Memorial Church in New Inn Hall Street; a handful of Russian Orthodox huddle in Canterbury Road; Punjabi services are held in the churches of East Oxford; black Pentecostalists sway and moan, American-style, in the New Testament Church of God off the Cowley Road. And a faith healer, risen up in Jericho, lays on healing hands in the spiritualist church of Middle Way, Summertown, and feels the current flow. Vibrations, vibrations!

St Giles, dominated by the spire of the Protestant Martyrs' Memorial, is a kind of thoroughfare of religion. On it are the Dominicans at Blackfriars, St Benet's, two Anglican churches (St Mary Magdalen and St Giles), a college chapel (St John's), Pusey House, the Christian Scientists and the Quaker Meeting House. The Meeting House is a strangely testing place: no choreography of ritual, just a bare, white-painted room full of people on wooden benches who rise between intense intervals of silence to share their perceptions with painstaking honesty. It is like a spiritual radar station, a field of human listening posts, each straining to catch and unscramble messages and then press them into the service of practical benevolence.

Going beyond the Christian faith are a range of places of worship catering for Oxford's varied communities. In Jericho, oddly opposite a Lebanese restaurant, stands the Jewish synagogue. For the city's Moslems there are three mosques – one in Bath Street, one in Stanley Road and a small one on Cowley Road catering for Ahmadiyyas, a nineteenth-century sect regarded by other Moslems as a more westernized version of their beliefs. Islam, like Christianity, has its schisms and divisions. The city's original mosque in Bath Street was riven in the early 1980s by a furious dispute which at times broke out into violence requiring intervention by the police. Eventually a splinter group broke off and a mini Oxford Movement of the Moslem faith set up a second mosque in Stanley Road.

Yet it is with Christianity, and specifically Anglicanism, that Oxford's links are strongest. The Church of England in Oxford still remains marked by the Oxford Movement. It was like a nuclear explosion, a melt-down within the core of Anglicanism. The modern contours of Oxford Christianity, 150 years later, still testify to its impact. It irradiated the Anglo-Catholic churches of the city, enveloping them in an intense devotional afterglow, particularly at St Mary Magdalen's and St Barnabas, which was built as a rallying place for the movement. Generations of undergraduates and holy aesthetes have gone to it in Jericho to get some of that old-time religion amidst its incense and mock-Byzantine frescoes, and today it still maintains its High traditions.

Also springing from the Oxford Movement were a number of new religious orders set up in the city, such as the Society of St John the Evangelist, commonly known as the Cowley Fathers, founded by R. M. Benson, the vicar of Cowley. Now they have dwindled sadly to a few old men cared for in a hostel in the Iffley Road, and their house on Marston Street has been taken over by a theological college. But their sisters at the Convent of the Incarnation continue to thrive.

It is a tenacious little community. Its first sisters were well-bred Anglican ladies set on re-creating an Anglo-Catholic version of the medieval orders of contemplative nuns. What a struggle those refined Victorian ladies must have had in the early days, despite the substantial dowries they brought with them into the order, scrubbing and gardening and doing all the chores that previously servants had done for them! However, the Convent still survives with some forty members, in age ranging from twenty to ninety. They lead an inward life of silence and prayer and observe a routine revolving around their chapel and gardens and printing press, but are also keenly alert to their neighbourhood and the outside world generally. It is an unexpected little island of calm green order a stone's throw from the washeterias and kebab houses of East Oxford.

The current High Church temple is St Mary Magdalen's – 'St Mary Mags' or, as it is more vulgarly known, 'Smells and Bells'. From a portrait in a side chapel, the martyr-King, Charles I, looks mournfully down at a statue of Mary, swathed in white lace. In the liturgy you catch more than the odd 'Hail Mary'. Several members of the congregation are, you feel, always teetering on the brink: one more step would take them to Rome. Indeed, on the Sunday I attended the congregation was in some disarray. The vicar, like his retired predecessor, had 'gone over' to Roman Catholicism.

At the opposite pole, the 'Low' churches, you are still treading on ground indirectly thrown up by the Oxford Movement. The livings of St Clement's, St Ebbe's and St Aldate's were all acquired by evangelical bodies and set up as alternatives to the temples of ritual. The amazing popularity of St Aldate's is a striking phenomenon of Oxford church life. Every Sunday it is packed to the sills. With its families, students and young people, the initial impression is of a sea of T-shirts and jeans, of cheesecloth and gurgling infants. Then guitars twang, and the congregation launches into a peppy, up-beat hymn. Not for nothing are worshippers there known as the 'Happy Clappers'. You will be made to jump up and down and wave your arms, clap and perhaps embrace your neighbour. On the morning I went, a stiff sermon was delivered by the visiting vicar of St Ebbe's on the intermittent Christians, those who 'only swan in and out of church at Christmas and Easter'. 'Oxford', he stated, 'is littered with churches, some empty, some turned into libraries, some just vacant plots of land. Who goes to Oxford's churches any more?' Perhaps they all go to St Aldate's. I counted over 500 in the congregation.

But many of the most engaged Christians bypass the organized churches altogether. Often they find a home in the fundamentalist 'house church' movement of the Oxford Community Churches. Their members, shunning what they see as the hollow shells of traditional denominations, practise a highly ecstatic and charismatic form of Christianity, meeting in groups of ten or twelve in one another's houses, dancing, singing and speaking in tongues. Evolving out of the West Oxfordshire Baptist Churches, the Community Churches are, as they see it, the growth sector and cutting edge of Christianity. Strong in suburbs such as Botley, Eynsham, Kidlington and Witney, the movement has spawned ten groups in Oxford since 1985 and also draws followers from Westminster College, the polytechnic and the university. 'More and more students', says the Rev. Ian Paton, until recently Chaplain of Wadham, 'are coming from a background of the free churches and look for something similar when they arrive here.'

Every Sunday hundreds of Community Church members gather in the Cannon Cinema, George Street. It is an amazing sight: throngs of respectable primary school teachers, Inland Revenue clerks and computer programmers rocking in the aisles, eyes closed in rapture, swaying and erupting into bursts of dancing and glossolalia. ('Do not', said one elder, 'all dance at once. The floor may give way.') To the backing of electric guitars and synthesizers, the 'presenter' croons over the congregation like a DJ, orchestrating the ecstasy and inciting individuals to testify (which they do, quavering out the formula, 'God says ... God says ...'). The message is total commitment to Christ, total renunciation of all else ('God', said one elder, 'hates mixtures'), and it is easy to see the appeal of such absolute certainty, such utter security of position, to anxious young couples cut off in the new housing estates of West Oxfordshire, struggling with children, mortgages and demanding but unsatisfying jobs. 'We desire', says their Pastor, Stephen Thomas, 'some absolutes, something that will bring values and backbone back into society.' They take hard-line positions on divorce and abortion and, politically, are well to the right.

The Community Churches stress their concern with the under-privileged, but to me they seemed a largely middle-class or, more precisely, lower middle-class group. By contrast, the Jesus Army, clad in paramilitary uniforms, scours the gutters of society, the street people, the addicts and the prostitutes, in its search for converts. Northampton-based, they are active in Oxford (their double-decker bus, emblazoned with slogans, could recently be seen incongruously parked outside Balliol) and are rumoured to be seeking a permanent base here.

Whether you take the High road or the Low or sidestep the conventional churches altogether, every shade of belief is rep-resented at Oxford. You can generally find what you want, if you are prepared to shop around – and many are. Mobility has long been a characteristic of Oxford churchgoers. In 1829 the local bishop denounced the universal custom in the city of 'running from one church to another'. Today the truly committed Oxford Christian turns his or her back to the city's middle-class con-gregations, heading out to Blackbird Leys, to show *solidarity* and breathe the *authentic,* almost Third World liberation theology air of the working-class churches.

This mobility results in a series of highly eclectic congregations, united only by a predilection for a particular brand of worship. Conversely, ecumenism is correspondingly weak in Oxford. There is some collaboration between the Anglican St Peter's Church and the United Reformed Church in Summertown, but mostly the

various denominations have little to do with one another. It is as
if in Oxford religious tradition is too vital a force to be diluted by
association or cooperation. Even out in Blackbird Leys where
a modernist church like a solved problem in spatial geometry
brings together Baptist, Methodist and Anglican, the Roman
Catholics keep themselves aloof in their own Church of the Sacred
Heart.

Rome, so long banished from Oxford, is now a powerful element
here. The story of its return is in itself interesting. Excluded from
the university by the Religious Tests until 1854, Catholics thereafter
preserved a further self-imposed ban for another fifty years. While
Newman remained keen for a Catholic college to be established at
Oxford, Cardinal Manning vetoed any Catholic involvement on
account of the threat posed by Oxford to unhardened Catholic
faith ('a youth', stated the Church, 'can scarcely go to Oxford
without throwing himself into a proximate occasion of mortal sin').
However, with Manning's death, the door to Oxford opened up.
In 1896 a Catholic chaplaincy was set up for members of the
university and the Jesuits established a hall, the present Campion
Hall, followed by the Benedictines' St Benet's in 1891 and the
Franciscan Greyfriars in 1910.

In that era of English romantic Catholicism – of Chesterton
and Belloc – an intense emotional glow surrounded the return to
Oxford. The return was seen as a homecoming, a re-joining after
many centuries with those Catholic roots out of which the university itself had sprung – feelings not entirely dissipated today. As
that glow faded, Oxford Catholicism went on – in the decades of
Ronnie Knox's chaplaincy and of the famous Catholic don 'Sligger'
Urquhart at Balliol – to develop its own distinctive character: a
world both precious and tweedy, a world in some ways more
Oxford than Oxford, where the scions of Catholic county families
(long regressions of Recusant pride!) would drift across St Aldate's
from the House to the Chaplaincy for 'Marss' or a session with
their 'confessor'. In a paradoxical way the pride of belonging
to an ancient, exclusive club was blended with the satisfaction,
particularly for the convert, of making a highly public gesture of
commitment. It was, perhaps, the equivalent then of declaring
oneself a Communist or, today, of 'coming out'.

This phase of Oxford Catholicism is preserved, if anywhere, in the Amplefordian air of St Benet's where, alongside grizzled, black-cassocked monks, fresh-faced young men in cavalry twills attend Mass and afterwards, if taking dinner in the Refectory above, bray at one another over their plates of solid school pudding. In general, however, the character of Oxford Catholicism has nowadays changed completely, becoming far less exclusive and self-conscious and far more a matter of personal, private belief. In part this reflects the more representative social complexion of the university and, possibly through that, its increasing number of Catholics: in Ronnie Knox's time there were 170 Catholic undergraduates; now the Chaplaincy caters for 1,500 students, and there are over 200 Catholic senior members of the university, present or retired, including three Heads of Houses.

Today, as a glance at the *Catholic Directory* shows, there is an immense variety of Catholic institutions, ranging from the private halls and the nunneries sprinkled around North Oxford to Plater College, the Catholic workers' college. Amongst the Catholic churches there is – with one notable exception – something of a Town–Gown divide. While university members go to the Chaplaincy, a church like Greyfriars (St Edmund and St Frideswide) out on Iffley Road is very much a local parish church, catering for instance for the Irish immigrants of East Oxford and St Clements. St Aloysius, a portly building on the Woodstock Road, is also a Town church although it does attract rather more Gowns than Greyfriars. Recently it has passed through somewhat troubled times. Originally a Jesuit foundation it found itself cast adrift and passing through a period of declining congregations and of incumbents not always appropriate to the parish. Now it has been taken over by the Birmingham Oratorians who promise to set on it their firmer and more traditional stamp.

Just as Oxford Anglicanism runs from High to Low so its Catholicism ranges from right to left. The halls and suburban churches, with the exception of the Sacred Heart, tend towards the conservative. At the other extreme is Blackfriars – radical, intellectual, modern and socially concerned – 'a place', in the words of a member, 'as liberal as you can be whilst still staying Catholic'. In the engaged, post-Vatican II days of the 1960s it lived in the land where theology merges into Marxism (an influence once especially strong in, but now purged from, its journal *New Blackfriars*) and it still bristles with commitment and causes, everything from AIDS to the environment. Blackfriars pulls in all sorts, both Town and Gown and, going further afield, many radical refugees from other parishes, in flight from current Vatican hard-line rulings on such matters as birth control. Anything new or controversial gets a look in. When local Catholic ultras were looking for a place to celebrate Tridentine Mass they gravitated to, of course, Blackfriars.

Yet 'family' perhaps remains the keynote. For all its plungings into controversy Blackfriars preaches underneath it all no heresy but solid Catholic doctrine. When the ultimate crunch comes Catholics fall into line. In this they contrast with the primed fragmentation bomb of Anglicanism, whose members under pressure shoot out in one direction to Catholicism or in the other to the militant free churches. If Catholics are overwhelmed by doubt, they tend to move out altogether, becoming renegade rationalists or Marxists, and quite a number do at Oxford.

The lapsed Catholic remains a recognizable figure on the local landscape. Although places like Blackfriars seem deeply imbued with liberalism, the harsh rays of Oxford rationalism can erode belief. Anthony Kenny, Warden of Rhodes House and former Master of Balliol, has recorded in his autobiography *A Path From Rome* how a doctorate in philosophy at the university delivered the *coup de grace* to a shaking faith. Perhaps Cardinal Manning was right after all, and there is something intrinsically inimical in Oxford to the Catholic faith.

This in turn raises the larger question of Christianity's current status in this once so Christian university. There is an amazing range of religious institutions. Like the city churches, university Anglicanism also runs the gamut from High to Low. Thus, amongst the university-associated theological colleges, you find at the Low end Wycliffe Hall, Ripon College Cuddesdon in the middle and on the High wing, St Stephen's House – an institution of reputedly overheated greenhouse atmosphere in which many an exotic velvety flower is said to bloom, and in whose student rooms, beneath the golden Marian icons and photographs of friends hand-in-hand in St Peter's Square, the aroma of eau de cologne blends with that of incense. Also on the High Church wing is Pusey House, founded in 1884 as a memorial to Edward Pusey. Intended to be a 'house of sacred learning' it took in Pusey's books and now contains a fine library (its members are known as priest-librarians). Today it also guards the Anglo-Catholic flame, and is noted for what its Principal, Father Philip Ursell, calls 'strong sacramental nourishment'. Once it had a somewhat hearty reputation – of strong public school voices baying out hymns – but now is said to be more defensive and cliquey.

On the Low side there is OICCU, the Oxford Intercollegiate Christian Union, founded in 1879, 'to present the claims of Christ in the University'. Currently it has 480 members and is particularly strong in St Edmund Hall, Jesus, Lady Margaret Hall, St Catherine's and Wadham. As OICCU has no place of worship of its own, its members often patronize city churches like St Aldates. OICCU also proselytizes actively in a one-to-one way; one of its secretaries estimated that 90 per cent of its contacts are made through personal acquaintanceships, especially in 'conversations over late night cups of coffee', a Christian-in-chum's-clothing approach which many students resent. A novel and somewhat yuppie-ish development in OICCU has been the hiring of restaurants for meals followed by after dinner speeches, half religion, half entertainment.

In the liberal centre are the college chapels and the University Church. Once attendance at chapel was compulsory and in fact continued so as late as the 1950s in Keble, Pembroke and Worcester. Now the college chapels present a scene which, if varied, is somewhat precarious and anomalous. St John's, University, Worcester, Pembroke and Wadham are relatively well attended. New College, Magdalen, Exeter and Worcester Colleges are sustained by their fine choral traditions. Keble, once a red-brick Anglican pillar of strength, is now poorly attended. The University Church, however, though never as strong as at Cambridge, has experienced a minor rally of late, its friendly and middle-of-the-road approach attracting those repelled by the Happy Clappers or the mysteries of Anglo-Catholicism. One of its odder features, though, is the University Sermon – really a guest sermon, a hymn and a prayer, preceded by a panoply of university officers and bowler-hatted beadles bearing maces. Held at 10 o'clock each Sunday morning it attracts exiguous congregations and is widely felt to have lost its way.

Towering above the other Anglican churches and chapels – and indeed standing somewhat apart theologically – is the Cathedral in Christ Church, which maintains its 'High and Dry' traditions of conservative liturgy, fine music and meaty, intellectual sermons from its Canons, some of whom are also Theology Faculty Professors. It has a striking atmosphere ('I am conscious', said one agnostic worshipper, 'of communicating if not with Christ then with the whole of English history and tradition') and attracts many visitors, especially Americans, and also a sad fringe of what Archdeacon Weston calls 'lonely people from student bed-sitter land', drawn by its colour and warmth.

To describe university Anglicanism on a spectrum from High to Low is, however, to make it seem a harmonious gradation. In fact it is increasingly marked by polarization and fragmentation – a thrusting Low tendency, an uncertain liberal centre and a jittery and introspective High wing. OICCU has become much more militant. The Oxford High wing for its part is increasingly restive and intolerant of what it sees as the fudges of mainstream Anglicanism. Its preoccupations recently fell under the Fleet Street spotlight when Gareth Bennett, a Fellow of New College, attacked the Archbishop of Canterbury in the anonymous preface to *Crockford's Directory* in 1988. With donnish savagery he lambasted Runcie for 'nailing his flag to both sides of the fence simultaneously'. Eventually, hounded by the tabloids who had accurately pinpointed him as the preface's author, he took his own life in the garage of his Oxford suburban home.

If the Anglo-Catholics are often in a pitiable plight, one should also feel sorry for those left in the centre – the theological liberals, found mainly amongst the dons and the college chaplains. They are attractive, if somewhat limp, figures – witty and urbane, learned and humane, tolerantly able to see all sides of a question. They hark back to the glory, glory days of the 1950s and '60s – those Observer-influential, Ban-the-Bomb-marching days before the Fall. Just as there were once liberal consensus dons, these were liberal consensus churchmen. They occupy the theological equivalent of the wettish middle ground of the Liberal Democrats. Now they feel they have entered the wilderness: bypassed and isolated in a harsher climate; secretly appalled by the vulgarity of the evangelicals (whom the liberals, again like political wets, criticize in code) and exhausted by the struggle to jolly along their increasingly jumpy Anglo-Catholic brethren. But one day, they hope, the pendulum will swing back and they will be led back into the land, overflowing with state milk and honey, of liberal consensus.

There is undoubtedly a connection between changes within the Church – the inroads into the centre of a narrower evangelicalism and the secessions of the ritualists – and the larger shift to the right in society in the 1980s. The connection was underlined in a sermon I heard in St Mary Mag's: 'We all remember the heady days of the sixties', said the preacher, 'when we looked for *relevance* and sought to drag the Church into the World.' That, he felt, was mistaken: Christianity was a 'mystery' only to be approached by commanded forms of worship, after which one could return, recharged, to the world. Edwin Barnes of St Stephen's, endorsing this view, welcomed the waning of 'social' Christianity: 'Liberalism went out with Mrs Thatcher – it is only now going out in the Church.'

'Undergraduates nowadays are a conservative body', says Archdeacon Weston: 'Just as they have become more conservative politically, so they have become more conservative theologically.' It is hard to imagine the university now producing a figure like Tony Williamson who in the late 1950s became a worker priest at Cowley. Williamson, a Trinity graduate who trained for the ministry at Cuddesdon College, chose to go into the car factory in order to build up the sort of pastoral relationship with the men which he would not have done as a normal parish priest.

At first, as permission was refused by the management, he got a job incognito, manhandling huge sheets of steel. His immediate impressions were of the overwhelming noise and smell, but the factory also gave him a chance to straighten out his basic religious and secular positions. Williamson became a kind of factory-floor Trappist: 'The noise made talking difficult. It was a kind of seclusion in the midst of other people. I kept my mouth shut so as to get to know people and not get labelled. My whole way was to work with the men, just be useful and take seriously the circumstances in which they were living and working.' In return he experienced little hostility and indeed felt sustained by the instinctive camaraderie of the shopfloor. After a time he declared himself. He was offered an office job by management which he refused: 'Just as a priest who teaches physics in a school has to be a good physicist as well as a good priest, so there was a need for me to be a good forklift truck operator.' He stayed nineteen years at the factory becoming a shop steward, a Labour councillor and Lord Mayor of the city.

'For a lot of undergraduates today,' lamented one cleric, 'religious matters scarcely impinge.' Yet the picture is not all black. At the last University Mission (organized every three years by college chaplains in the Sheldonian) there was standing room only. One college chaplain estimated that only 12 per cent of students attended chapel, and about a third were 'open to faith'. Generalizing from these (admittedly limited) data and taking into account that this was a college of higher than usual attendance figures, it is perhaps fair to say that, including all denominations, of 13,600 undergraduates, some 2,000 are open to religion.

At University College, Bill Sykes has taken a quantum leap in another direction. A Christian Jungian, who stresses the need for 'excellent whole people as well as excellently qualified people', he has gone on the offensive and organized a series of 'reflection groups'. Astonishingly, these are attended by over a third of the College. The Rev. Sykes ascribes this to the tensions and uncertainties of modern students' lives and the fractured family backgrounds from which they frequently come. The groups consist of four or five members, usually centred around a college chapelgoer but also including those of a less specific spiritual hunger. Each one-hour session moves from silent meditation on a text to talking about it together. But they are not mere discussion groups: the atmosphere is intensely personal, eclectic and cathartic. It is as if whole Californian congeries of encounter groups and therapies had been successfully absorbed into Christian pastoral practice.

This phenomenon of assimilation or mirroring alien elements may account for the recent Oxford enthusiasm for Taizé worship. Taizé is a village in Burgundy, the centre of a highly successful new monastic community which has evolved an interdenominational liturgy of great simplicity and accessibility. Based upon a pattern of refrain and antiphon, it is capable of building up through repetition structures of surprising complexity and beauty, reminding me somewhat of the music of Philip Glass. Its appeal is enormous. Each summer thousands camp out at Taizé, singing and dancing in an atmosphere resembling (if the thought is not too horrendous) a religious Woodstock. The movement's internationalism is enhanced by its use of Latin as a means of communication (a striking modern revival of its medieval function). 'Taizé is the very opposite of the Tower of Babel,' said one worshipper. Another student, put off by the 'holy pantomime' of the High Churches and distractions of the Low, spoke of discovering in it 'a meditational depth'.

Two Taizé brothers introduced their liturgy at the University Mission of 1988. Now, early each Tuesday morning in the University Church, about fifty students, kneeling on prayer mats, perform in the grey light an exquisitely moving Taizé service. Listening to it, the secret of its appeal suddenly dawned on me: Taizé is a Christian mantra, inducing a holy, trance-like state. Which brings us back to Beshara, Nichiren Shoshu Buddhism, the New School of Economics and the other modern cults. Christianity, in a climate in which oriental traditions now flourish in the West, has evolved equivalents to Buddhist or Hindu forms.

Wyclif called Oxford 'the Vineyard of the Lord'. Such has been the sheer devotional intensity and critical mass of the city that as religion and society have simmered and interacted, throwing up new forms, those forms have often been glimpsed here first. Today, as our culture splinters into solipsism and uncertainty, religion in Oxford seems to be shifting once more, sending its followers after new grails, voyaging deep into the inner self or seeking that self's dissolution in ecstatic pursuit of Oneness. The Bishop of Oxford comments: 'There are many parallels between our time and late antiquity. Christianity itself sprang out of a proliferation of religious and mystery cults. Today again desire for religious experience is finding new forms.'

Support for this view came from another quarter in Oxford. I visited the Alister Hardy Research Centre in George Street. There, above the roar of Oxford traffic, volunteers toil in a cramped office, coding for computerization thousands of reports of mystical experiences – visions, dreams, out-of-body experiences. There is something absurd about reducing these cosmic moments to byte-sized fields, but one staggering statistic emerged: nearly 40 per cent of the British population will have a profound religious or spiritual experience at some time in their lives. This being so, religions – in Oxford and elsewhere – seem set to thrive.

– 15 –

A Last Glance

'*The Towne of Oxford lyes out of the road ... It serves only for the entertainment of Scholars.*' So, as already quoted, the university characterized the city to the Crown in the seventeenth century. It is interesting to speculate just what would have been the fate of Town if there had never been a Gown. Oxford would doubtless have passed serenely down the centuries, a quietly busy market town, topped off by its cathedral – a place, say, not unlike Lichfield or Salisbury. Probably it would not have escaped industrialization – its centrality is just too tempting. Light industry would have brought an overlay of Slough or Swindon between the wars. Probably, too, it would eventually have had a university – a shining plate-glass institution of the sixties, a technological university on the model of Surrey, locked closely in to the local light industries.

But what a rich cultural and historical density would have been lost! And the city of Oxford would never have been torn by the duality that makes it so interesting a place. Certainly it might have been less fraught, less the victim of conflicting pressures, and its future easier to predict and manage. For the question inevitably occurs, what will Oxford's future be?

Behind it lies a further question, how shall the conflicting aspects of the city – Fort and Ford – be reconciled. Should the ancient centre, as bodies such as the Oxford Preservation Trust seem to want, be slotted under a planning belljar? Should Oxford simply become a pastiche of the past, at worst a historical theme park Disneyland, at best a museum tastefully stocked with repro antiques and safely disinfected from the rich clutter and all those happy accidents of juxtaposition that go to make a living city? On the other hand if the Ford prevails, the result can only be a choking confluence of conflicting impulses, resulting in a nightmarish mish-mash in which the colleges, the crowds, the offices, shops and businesses implode to form a veritable Black Hole of Oxford.

And inextricably bound up with the future of the city is that of the university. Less dominant than in the past, Gown still remains firmly knotted with Town. Will it coil up the city in its own further spirals of expansion? The university is currently shuttling between a weaver's loom of choices: whether to be diffuse or centralized in its structure, to be predominantly college-based and undergraduate or postgraduate and advanced study in emphasis, to become more nationally and socially representative or more privately exclusive, to be a national or an international institution. These are matters which stretch far beyond Oxford. Yet whatever pattern eventually emerges from the mesh of these polarities is bound to have a knock-on effect on the city and its future growth.

'Go through Oxford streets and ponder what is left us there unscathed by the fury of the thriving shop and the progressive college ... Need I speak to you of the degradation that has so speedily befallen this city, still the most beautiful of them all, a city which with its surrounding world, if we had a grain of common sense, would have been treated like a perfect jewel, whose beauty was to be preserved at any cost.' These words, so applicable to the Oxford of today, were in fact spoken over a hundred years ago in a lecture given in the city by the artist and socialist, William Morris. They serve to remind us how little Oxford's underlying problems have changed.

It is all too easy to despair in the face of such pressures. But words such as William Morris's also demonstrate how deeply engrained is the Oxford habit of looking nostalgically backwards. Oxford was always a better place in the past. Somehow the city outlasts and surmounts its problems. It has an essential strength and resilience, a most tenacious *genius loci*. It is entirely fitting that the symbol of the city is the Ox as portrayed on its seal – a beast generally much burdened and goaded, but enduring in its slow-lidded patience, always managing, eventually, to cross its Ford.

Index